I0126276

JUNGIANEUM

An(n)uário / Yearbook / Jahrbuch / 年鉴 / Ежегодник

for Contemporary Analytical Psychology and neo-Jungian Studies

2022

Curated and edited by Stefano Carpani

Poetry Editor Roula-Maria Dib

PUBLISHED IN COLLABORATION WITH

CHIRON PUBLICATIONS
ASHEVILLE, NORTH CAROLINA

JUNGIANEUM
INITIATIVES FOR CONTEMPORARY ANALYTICAL
PSYCHOLOGY AND NEO - JUNGIAN STUDIES
CURATED BY STEFANO CARPANI

www.ChironPublications.com

Curator and Editor: Stefano Carpani
Poetry Editor: Roula-Maria Dib
Editorial Board: Stefano Carpani (Italy/Germany), Roula-Maria Dib (UAE/UK), Livia Di Stefano (Italy), Ludmilla Ostermann (Germany), Andrew Samuels (UK), Caterina Vezzoli (Italy)
Cover Illustration: Carla Indipendente
Cover Design: Niko Crnčević
Interior Design: Danijela Mijailovic

Printed primarily in the United States of America.

ISBN 978-1-68503-149-7 paperback
ISBN 978-1-68503-150-3 hardcover
ISBN 978-1-68503-151-0 electronic
ISBN 978-1-68503-152-7 limited edition paperback

Library of Congress Cataloging-in-Publication Data Pending

OPENING

What exactly is JUNGIANEUM/Yearbook? It is a yearbook, of course! Is it also a monograph, an almanac, a journal, and a poetry book? Indeed!

JUNGIANEUM/Yearbook expands our thinking with papers and poetry informed by analytical psychology and neo-Jungian studies. Its uniqueness and importance to the Jungian community lies in the work of the individuals contributing. JUNGIANEUM/Yearbook plays a role in expanding current discussions on Jung, post-Jungians, and contemporary analytical psychology studies. JUNGIANEUM/Yearbook consists of post-Jungians who shape analytical psychology and recognizes the third generation—the neo-Jungians—who are taking analytical psychology into the 21st century.

JUNGIANEUM/Yearbook is divided into three parts: papers, poetry, and a *Rite de sortie*.

How were contributors chosen? I contacted a diverse and international group of colleagues and asked them to provide a paper addressing 2022. Many accepted, but not all. This is the reason why this first issue is not as diverse and inclusive as I wished it to be. I asked Roula-Maria Dib to curate the poetical part. She contacted colleagues and poets and encouraged them to share their work. Lastly, I requested István Kupper-Meynen to take care of the last part: *Rite de sortie*. This part is intended— as it is typical for fairytales— to bring the *issue* to a conclusion. Each year this task will be commissioned to a different contributor, who will decide what to publish: a text, a painting, an image, a joke, etc.. He decided to publish poems he wrote back in 2006/7. Their continued relevance is astonishing!

Therefore, as usual for me, I did not choose what to publish. I chose who to publish. Each paper and poem— at some extent idiosyncratic— is published in English and in the original language it was written in. Papers are not peer reviewed, as I do not believe in such a top-down process. Each new issue will be edited by a different person.

Finally: the cover. I contacted Italian illustrator Carla Indipendente, asked her to think of 2022 and illustrate it. When I asked what her work is about, she wrote me that it "describes in abstract language the burden of 2022 or, in any case, events that we have experienced and are experiencing, such as the pandemic, climate crisis, wars, deprivation of rights, a burden that all spills over into our minds in the form of chaos and fears, also conditioning our vision of the future. The sign is chaotic, the colours are strong and strident to accentuate these concepts."

Many themes conveyed in the 2022's issue: the Russian invasion of Ukraine; the power of a cultural complex in Israel; the Shakespearean concept of "Time is out of joint" and Pasolini's Oedipus Re; AIDS, death and the analyst; transgender individuation; sufferings and individuation; personal memories of the Yom Kippur War; the patient/analyst confrontation in the analytical room and the problematic behavior of the analyst; mothers and fathers, leaving, returning, devotion, new birth, the wait and the end of certainties.

JUNGIANEUM/Yearbook is one of many initiatives by **Jungianeum: Contemporary Initiatives for Analytical Psychology and Neo-Jungian Studies**. Under this umbrella, since 2022, I am developing a series of initiatives called: JUNGIANEUM/books, JUNGIANEUM/talks, JUNGIANEUM/masterclasses, JUNGIANEUM/biennale and more. In summer 2022, in partnership with Chiron Publications, I launched a series called *JUNGIANEUM/books: Re-Covered Classics in Analytical Psychology*, aimed at (re)publishing masterpieces in analytical psychology that, for different reasons, are out of the market and find difficulty in getting (re)published. As of January 2023, PSYCHOSOCIAL WEDNESDAYS (an initiative started in 2020 by Bernhard von Guretsky, Paul Attinello, and me), were incorporated under the umbrella of *JUNGIANEUM/talks* and will be coordinated by Bernhard von Guretsky, Ludmilla Ostermann, and me. In September 2023, Pacifica Graduate Institute (CA/USA) and Jungianeum will release a PGI Graduate Certificate Course: *Contemporary Analytical Psychology and Neo-Jungian Studies: The Relevance of C.G. Jung to the Socio-Cultural Challenges of the 21st Century*.

As per my Youtube interviews, published books, and papers, I wish these initiatives will continue to help Jung's psychology become visible and audible, therefore, impactful for individuals and collectives, who benefit, respectively, from Jungian therapy and our knowledge in shaping policy and society.

I want to thank all contributors who generously accepted my invitation to join this first issue. My thanks goes to Roula-Maria Dib who brilliantly curated Part Two and to Carla Indipendente who portrayed 2022 so effectively on the cover. I am equally grateful to Chiron's Steve Buser who supported and made this new initiative possible. I hope this issue of JUNGIANEUM/Yearbook has many interested readers and that this can be the first of many other issues. I wish good luck to Caterina Vezzoli and Livia Di Stefano who will take the baton from me and edit the next issue.

Stefano Carpani, December 2022
Berlin (Germany)

TABLE OF CONTENTS

PART 1
PAPERS

A Russo-Ukrainian (Dis)Entanglement:
The "Brother Nation" Narrative as Legitimization for War

Ludmilla Ostermann and Julia Herzberg

Abstract

"Body and soul we give for our freedom, and we will show, brothers, that we are from the tribe of Cossacks!" This is the last line of the Ukrainian national anthem. It dates back to the 19th century and is an expression of Ukraine's centuries-long aspirations for independence. Historian Julia Herzberg is a professor of the history of East Central Europe and Russia in pre-modern times at Ludwig Maximilian University in Munich. In an interview with journalist and author Ludmilla Ostermann, explains that contrary to the Russian narrative of Ukrainians and Russians as "brother nations," the entangled Russian-Ukrainian history was marked by conflict long before the outbreak of Russia's war of aggression on Ukraine. An agreement between Cossacks and Russia in 1654 and the different interpretations of this event mark a central moment in the history of the two countries.

Ludmilla Ostermann: Until the beginning of the Russian invasion of Ukraine, the population of Western countries knew little about the country of Ukraine. Why is that so?

Julia Herzberg: Actually, Germans in particular should know Ukraine well, especially the older generation. Ukraine was one of the main theaters in World War II and the whole Ukraine was occupied by German and Romanian troops until November 1941 after the German invasion of the Soviet Union. But it is true, the history of Ukraine and the current situation is not clear in Germany. This is due to the fact that the Ukrainian territories had only short periods of sovereign statehood throughout their history; it belonged to fourteen different dominions such as the Kingdom of Poland-Lithuania, the Habsburg Monarchy, the Tsarist Empire, and the Soviet Union. Many people in Western Europe, for example, do not know about the 17th century Hetmanate, which many Ukrainians consider the precursor of a nation-state. Nor do many know that on January 12, 1918, the independence of the Ukrainian People's Republic was proclaimed in Kyiv, which lasted until 1920. However, the military, domestic, and foreign political situation of the Ukrainian People's Republic was fragile, and it did not succeed in building a nation-state.

Ludmilla Ostermann: What stood in the way of state formation?

Julia Herzberg: Devastatingly, the government of the Soviet Union did not recognize the independence of Ukraine. The Red Army emerged victorious from the civil war, occupying the central areas of Ukraine and reorganizing it as the Ukrainian Soviet Republic within the Soviet Union. Thus, unlike many other European peoples after World War I, Ukraine did not succeed in building and defending its own nation-state. In Germany and many other Western European countries, this leads to Ukraine often being perceived only in the context of Russia.

"The majority of Ukrainian territories belonged to Poland-Lithuania longer than it was part of the Tsarist Empire or the Soviet Union."

Ludmilla Ostermann: Has Ukraine ever *not* been connected with Russia in its history?

Julia Herzberg: Vladimir Putin and his ideologues like to claim that there is a continuity of Russian-Ukrainian relations since the Middle Ages. But the majority of Ukrainian territories belonged to Poland-Lithuania longer than they were part of the Tsarist Empire or the Soviet Union. There is no continuity of Russian-Ukrainian relations since the Christianization of the Kievan Rus in 988 until today. Only since the Pereyaslav Agreement in 1654 has the history of the two countries been more closely linked. However, this connection has never been without conflicts or alternatives as changing alliances with, for example, the Poles or the Swedes show, there have also been other possibilities for cooperation.

Ludmilla Ostermann: But why, then, do we often perceive the history of Ukraine as a history closely linked to the history of Russia?

Julia Herzberg: It is only since the middle of the 17th century that Russian and Ukrainian history have been closely connected. It is true that Russians and Ukrainians share the common heritage of Kievan Rus, a federation of various principalities between the Baltic Sea and the Black Sea. However, in the first half of the 13th century, the Mongols conquered the Rus' principalities and established a rule in the north and east that was to last two hundred years. While northeastern Rus was largely isolated from Europe by Mongol rule, the principalities on the territory of present-day Ukraine were only briefly under Mongol rule. Instead, they oriented themselves toward Western Europe. This change, of course, has significance up to the present day as the different historical experiences contributed to the formation of a Russian and Ukrainian nation. During the 14th century, the territory of present-day Ukraine came under the rule of Lithuania and the kings of Poland. With its incorporation into the Kingdom of Poland-Lithuania, Ukraine opened up even more to the West: cities such as Kyjiv and Lviv were even granted Magdeburg rights.

Ludmilla Ostermann: The Ukrainian lands were thus under Lithuanian, and Polish rule, respectively. But how did they come to Russia? After all, Putin always talks about Ukrainians sharing a common history, about them being "brother nations."

Julia Herzberg: To understand this, we need to look at the work of the Zaporozhian Cossacks. The term "Cossack" originally meant *a free warrior*. Cossack communities emerged in the 15th and 16th centuries in the south of Poland-Lithuania and the Moscow Empire, on the major rivers. Cossack formations had also emerged on the lower Dnipro and the steppe frontier. However, when Poland made attempts to bring the Cossacks under its control, uprisings broke out. Under the leadership of the Cossack Bohdan Khmelnytsky, a major uprising occurred, directed primarily against the Polish nobility, the Catholic clergy, and the Polish administration. Khmelnytsky acted extremely skillfully: He succeeded in creating the Hetmanate, an independent Cossack state, following the uprising. For many Ukrainians, the Hetmanate is the first Ukrainian nation-state and thus a precursor of today's independent Ukraine. But Poland did not want to simply accept Cossack separatism. Since the Cossacks could not do anything against the superiority of the Poles, they had to look for an ally: Khmelnytsky finally chose the Moscow Empire as a partner. But the tsar rebuffed the Cossacks. The ruler of the Moscow Empire did not want to stumble rashly into a conflict with Poland-Lithuania.

> *"From the tsar's perspective, the religious and ethnic similarities between the Ukrainians and the Russians were considered minor."*

Ludmilla Ostermann: So, for the tsar, an alliance with the Ukrainians was not a clear-cut matter?

Julia Herzberg: Precisely. His hesitation shows that from the tsar's perspective, the religious and ethnic commonalities between the Ukrainians and the Russians were considered minor. For Tsar Alexei Mikhailovich, it took strategic and military arguments to become a party to the conflict. Only in 1654, after a three-year period of hesitation, did the Moscow Empire agree to Khmelnytsky's request to become an ally of Cossack Ukraine. But it is very controversial what was actually decided in Pereyaslav. So is the interpretation of what happened: While Moscow diplomats recognized in the Cossacks' oath an act of submission, the Cossack elite saw their oath as "voluntary" and thus also dissolvable subordination. For the Cossacks, the Pereyaslav agreement established a form of protectorate, but not incorporation and integration into Muscovy. For Moscow, on the other hand, the act of Pereyaslav represented a first step towards the incorporation of Ukraine. Until the middle of the 18th century, the Hetmanate was only loosely dependent on Russia. It was Catherine the Great who put an end to the autonomy of the Hetmanate in 1764. The reason for this was not only Russian arrogance and fear of the Cossacks' love of freedom, but also economic and strategic consideration. The Ukrainian lands had gained importance with the appropriation of the steppe regions north of the Black Sea. By the end of the 18th century, the former peculiarity of the Hetmanate had disappeared except for a few remnants. The Pereyaslav Agreement was considered the beginning of voluntary subjugation.

Ludmilla Ostermann: However, the Ukrainian national movement flourished again and the idea came to life once more.

Julia Herzberg: In folk lore and Ukrainian society, the Cossack way of life with its ideas of freedom and equality remained alive as an ideal. The Ukrainian national movement since the 19th century drew on these ideas. This can be seen in the patriotic poem "Ukraine Has Not Yet Died" by the Ukrainian poet Pavlo Chubynsky, written in 1862. The poem, sung as Ukraine's anthem in 1917 and again in 2003, ends with a declaration of Cossackism: "Body and soul we give for our freedom, and we will show, brothers, that we are of the Cossack tribe!" This also meant that the Pereyaslav Agreement of 1654 was increasingly viewed critically by Ukrainians. Quite different from Russia.

Ludmilla Ostermann: How does the different view of the Pereyaslav Agreement manifest itself today?

Julia Herzberg: The Pereyaslav Agreement, like the Holodomor—the great famine of the 1930s— is one of those historical processes and events that are evaluated completely differently in Russia and Ukraine. This is still evident today in the hardships of everyday warfare: in Ukraine, many monuments have been toppled in recent months that focused on the supposed friendship between Russia and Ukraine. In April 2022, the Soviet Monument to Friendship with Russia was dismantled, a monument complex consisting of several parts. First, there is a huge rainbow under which two muscular workers hold up a common flag. They are supposed to symbolize the friendship between the Russian and Ukrainian people. One of the two workers was first beheaded before the entire statue was dismantled. On the initiative of the mayor of Kyiv, Vitali Klitschko, the Arch of Friendship between Peoples was renamed the "Arch of Freedom of the Ukrainian People." Klitschko justified the fact that the monument to the Rada of Pereyaslav, i.e. the Cossack Council of Pereyaslav, which is part of the complex, is still standing because it is simply too massive. It was covered with building slabs. It is very likely that this monument will soon be dismantled altogether. This has happened, for example, in Pereyaslav itself. At the beginning of the war, residents of the town had the monument, which originally bore the inscription "Together Forever," inscribed with the names of those places where Russian soldiers committed terrible war crimes against Ukrainians: Bucha, Hostomel, Irpin. In early July 2022, the monument was finally dismantled.

*"Opposing voices to the dictum of 'reunification' could appear
only in illegal self-publishing, in Samizdat."*

Ludmilla Ostermann: But it is not only a result of the attacks on Ukrainian territory since 2014 that the connection between Russia and Ukraine is viewed critically.

Julia Herzberg: Despite all the efforts of the governments in the Tsarist empire and the Soviet Union to evoke the common ground between the two supposedly "brother nations" through festivals, monuments and historical writings, the Pereyaslav agreement was usually viewed critically by Ukrainians. They regarded it, especially since the rise of the national movement in the 19th century, as the beginning of an unholy alliance that had prevented the formation of a separate nation-state. This attitude was in contrast to the Russian power elites, who referred to the Pereyaslav agreement to portray Russian rule over Ukraine as voluntary subordination. This was evident in 1954, for example, when the Central Committee of the Communist Party of the Soviet Union adopted a collection of "Theses on the Tercentenary of the Reunification of Ukraine with Russia." The interpretation of the Russian-Ukrainian relationship established in it played the central role until the collapse of the Soviet Union. These theses spoke only of "reunification," which had brought together two "blood-related brothers." Putin has not moved away from this to this day.

Ludmilla Ostermann: Were there ever critical voices against this Russian interpretation of history?

Julia Herzberg: Dissenting voices that opposed the dictum of "reunification" and held the view that they were two different peoples could only appear in illegal self-publishing, in Samizdat. It was not until the late 1980s, during the period of perestroika, that there was a more pluralistic debate, even in public, about the historical significance of the Pereyaslav Agreement. Now it was possible, even in public, to reject the reunification paradigm. Representatives of Ukrainian civil society in the late Soviet Union pointed out that the myth of "reunification" and the discourse of "brother nations" were intended to deny Ukrainians the right to an independent and separate state.

Ludmilla Ostermann: How was the memory of the Pereyaslav Agreement shaped after the collapse of the Soviet Union, after the Ukrainians had their own independent state?

Julia Herzberg: On June 21, 1992, 338 years after the Pereyaslav Agreement, Cossacks from all over Ukraine gathered in Pereyaslav, a small provincial town, to renounce the oath of loyalty they had taken to the tsar in 1654. Instead, they now wanted to swear loyalty to the Ukrainian people. In their declaration, they accused Moscow and the tsar of betraying them, destroying their language and customs, and usurping their territory. The term "reunification," permanently used in the Soviet Union, was completely rejected in independent Ukraine and disappeared from the media and the street scene. When Leonid Kuchma, one of Ukraine's pro-Russia presidents, tried to initiate a commemorative year in 2004— that is, on the 350th anniversary of Pereyaslav— he met with a wave of protest. With the exception of the government level, the celebrations were largely canceled. Vladimir Putin, who visited Ukraine in 2004, encountered neither decorated streets nor celebrating people. While he sat alongside the Ukrainian president at a gala concert dedicated to the Pereyaslav Agreement in January 2004, the people of Kyiv protested outside the door.

Ludmilla Ostermann: The events of 2004 also mark the beginning of a change of political course by Putin and his political elites toward Ukraine.

Julia Herzberg: Since the 2004 Orange Revolution in Ukraine, which prevented the election victory of Russia-friendly Viktor Yanukovych, Putin has shown a keen interest in Ukraine's history. Putin now increasingly assumed the role of an historical interpreter. In 2008, for example, he appeared for the first time at the NATO summit in Bucharest with the declaration that Ukraine was an artificially assembled state created only in Soviet times. He blanked out the Hetmanate, the Ukrainian People's Republic, as well as the conflict-ridden events of Russian-Ukrainian history, such as the Holodomor, in his historical remarks. In 2013, Putin claimed in an interview that Russians and Ukrainians were one people. His 2021 essay "On the Historical Unity of Russians and Ukrainians" repeated this thesis and can be seen as the prelude to the February 2022 war. It is therefore not surprising that this long essay became compulsory reading in Russian military schools. Three days before the invasion, Putin added to it. He claimed that Ukraine is an "integral part of our own history, our culture, our spiritual space" and emphasized "blood and family ties" that bind Ukrainians and Russians together.

Ludmilla Ostermann: So, history is being misused as a weapon here?

Julia Herzberg: The course of the war has clearly shown that the majority of Ukrainians want to live in a sovereign Ukraine. Even this could not shake Putin's view of history, which many Russians share. The exhibition "Ukraine: Seminal Tipping Points" conveys the image that Ukraine only has a future in union with Russia. The Kremlin purposefully uses its "historical" narratives to justify the Russian invasion of Ukraine. Discourses such as "brother nation" and "reunification" are a tool of imperial politics. They are used to obscure the conflictual events in the history of Russian-Ukrainian relations and to suppress the Ukrainian national movement. However, these discourses are also a means of eclipsing historical ties with Europe. It is no wonder that Ukrainians today see this historical image as a weapon directed against them like missiles and tanks. They counter these interpretations with monument demolitions. And we in the West are also called upon to critically question interpretations and discourses such as those of the "brother nations" when they are used to dispute the right of a sovereign state to exist and to justify a brutal, senseless war of aggression that is contrary to international law. When history is used to legitimize a war of aggression, it is misused.

Eine russisch-ukrainische Ver- und Entflechtung:
Das "Brudervolk"-Narrativ als Legitimation für Krieg

Ludmilla Ostermann and Julia Herzberg

Abstract

"Leib und Seele geben wir für unsere Freiheit hin, und wir werden zeigen, Brüder, dass wir vom Stamm der Kosaken sind!" So lautet die letzte Zeile der ukrainischen Nationalhymne. Sie stammt aus dem 19. Jahrhundert und ist Ausdruck der jahrhundertelangen Unabhängigkeitsbestrebungen der Ukraine. Die Historikerin Julia Herzberg ist Professorin für die Geschichte Ostmitteleuropas und Russlands in der Vormoderne an der Ludwig-Maximilians-Universität München und erklärt im Interview mit der Journalistin und Autorin Ludmilla Ostermann, dass entgegen des russischen Narrativs von den Ukrainern und Russen als „Brudervölker", die russisch-ukrainische Verflechtungsgeschichte schon weit vor dem Ausbruch des russischen Angriffskriegs auf die Ukraine von Konflikten geprägt war. Eine Vereinbarung zwischen Kosaken und dem Zarenreich aus dem Jahr 1654 und die unterschiedliche Deutung dieses Ereignisses markiert dabei einen zentralen Moment in der Geschichte der beiden Länder.

Ludmilla Ostermann: Bis zum Beginn der russischen Invasion in der Ukraine hat die Bevölkerung westlicher Länder wenig gewusst über das Land Ukraine. Warum ist das so?

Julia Herzberg: Eigentlich müssten vor allem die Deutschen die Ukraine gut kennen, besonders die ältere Generation. Schließlich war die Ukraine einer der Hauptschauplätze im Zweiten Weltkrieg. Die gesamte Ukraine wurde nach dem deutschen Überfall auf die Sowjetunion bis November 1941 von deutschen und rumänischen Truppen besetzt. Doch es stimmt schon, die Geschichte der Ukraine und die gegenwärtige Situation ist in Deutschland kaum bekannt. Das liegt daran, dass die ukrainischen Gebiete im Laufe ihrer Geschichte nur kurze Phasen einer souveränen Staatlichkeit hatten. Sie gehörte vierzehn verschiedenen Herrschaftsgebieten an, wie zum Beispiel dem Königreich Polen-Litauen, der Habsburger Monarchie, dem Zarenreich und der Sowjetunion. Viele Menschen in Westeuropa kennen beispielsweise nicht das Hetmanat des 17. Jahrhunderts, das vielen Ukrainer*innen als Vorläufer eines Nationalstaates gilt. Auch wissen viele nicht, dass am 12. Januar 1918 die Unabhängigkeit der Ukrainischen Volksrepublik in Kyjiv ausgerufen wurde, die bis 1920 bestand. Doch die militärische sowie innen- und außenpolitische Situation der Ukrainischen Volksrepublik war fragil, und es gelang nicht, einen Nationalstaat aufzubauen.

Ludmilla Ostermann: Was stand der Staatsbildung im Wege?

Julia Herzberg: Verheerend war, dass die Regierung der Sowjetunion die Unabhängigkeit der Ukraine nicht anerkannte. Aus dem sich nun entwickelten Bürger*innenkrieg ging die Rote Armee als Siegerin hervor, die die zentralen Gebiete der Ukraine besetzte und sie als Ukrainische Sowjetrepublik innerhalb der Sowjetunion neu organisierte. Anders als vielen anderen europäischen Völkern nach dem Ersten Weltkrieg gelang es der Ukraine also nicht, ihren eigenen Nationalstaat aufzubauen und zu verteidigen. In Deutschland und vielen anderen westeuropäischen Ländern führt dies dazu, dass die Ukraine häufig nur im Zusammenhang mit Russland wahrgenommen wird.

„Der Großteil der ukrainischen Gebiete gehörte länger zu Polen-Litauen, als dass er Bestandteil des Zarenreiches beziehungsweise der Sowjetunion gewesen ist."

Ludmilla Ostermann: Aber ist denn die Ukraine nicht auch einen Großteil ihrer Geschichte mit Russland verbunden gewesen?

Julia Herzberg: Von Wladmimir Putin und seinen Ideolog*innen wird gern behauptet, dass es eine Kontinuität russisch-ukrainischen Beziehungen seit dem Mittelalter gibt. Doch der Großteil der ukrainischen Gebiete gehörte länger zu Polen-Litauen, als dass er Bestandteil des Zarenreiches beziehungsweise der Sowjetunion gewesen ist. Es gibt keine durchlaufende Kontinuität der russisch-ukrainischen Beziehungen seit der Christianisierung der Rus im Jahr 988 bis heute. Erst seit der Vereinbarung von Perejaslav 1654 ist die Geschichte der beiden Länder wieder enger miteinander verbunden. Diese Verbindung war aber nie konfliktfrei beziehungsweise alternativlos, sondern es hat, wie wechselnde Allianzen zum Beispiel mit Polen oder Schweden zeigen, auch andere Möglichkeiten der Kooperation gegeben.

Ludmilla Ostermann: Aber warum nehmen wir dann die Geschichte der Ukraine häufig als eine Geschichte wahr, die eng mit der Geschichte Russlands verbunden ist?

Julia Herzberg: Erst seit der Mitte des 17. Jahrhunderts sind die russische und die ukrainische Geschichte eng miteinander verbunden. Russ*innen und Ukrainer*innen teilen zwar das gemeinsame Erbe der Kyjiver Rus', eines Verbandes von verschiedenen Fürstentümern zwischen der Ostsee und dem Schwarzen Meer. Doch in der ersten Hälfte des 13. Jahrhunderts eroberten Mongolen die Fürstentümer der Rus' und errichteten im Norden und Osten eine Herrschaft, die zweihundert Jahre dauern sollte. Während die nordöstliche Rus' durch die Mongolenherrschaft weitgehend von Europa isoliert war, standen die Fürstentümer auf dem Gebiet der heutigen

Ukraine nur kurz unter der Herrschaft der Mongolen. Sie orientierten sich stattdessen an Westeuropa. Diese Weichenstellung hat bis in die Gegenwart Bedeutung. Die nun einsetzenden unterschiedlichen historischen Erfahrungen trugen zur Bildung einer russischen und ukrainischen Nation bei. Im Laufe des 14. Jahrhundert kam das Gebiet der heutigen Ukraine unter die Herrschaft von Litauen und der Könige von Polen. Mit der Eingliederung in das Königreich Polen-Litauen öffnete sich die Ukraine noch mehr nach Westen: Städte wie Kyjiv und Lemberg erhielten sogar das Magdeburger Stadtrecht.

Ludmilla Ostermann: Die ukrainischen Länder standen also unter litauischer, beziehungsweise polnischer Herrschaft. Aber wie kamen sie nach Russland? Putin spricht doch immer davon, dass die Ukrainer eine gemeinsame Geschichte teilen, dass sie „Brudervölker" seien.

Julia Herzberg: Um das zu verstehen, müssen wir uns das Wirken der Zaporoher Kosaken anschauen. Der Begriff „Kosak" bezeichnet ursprünglich einen freien Krieger. Kosakische Gemeinschaften entstanden im 15. und 16. Jahrhundert im Süden Polen-Litauens und des Moskauer Reiches, an den großen Flüssen. Auch am unteren Dnipro und der Steppengrenze waren kosakische Verbände entstanden. Als aber Polen Versuche unternahm, die Kosaken unter seine Kontrolle zu bringen, brachen Aufstände aus. Unter der Führung des Kosaken Bohdan Chmelnyzkyj kam es zu einem großen Aufstand, der sich vor allem gegen den polnischen Adel, den katholischen Klerus und gegen die polnische Verwaltung richtete. Chmelnyzkyj handelte überaus geschickt: Ihm gelang es, im Anschluss an den Aufstand das Hetmanat zu schaffen, einen unabhängigen Herrschaftsverband. Für viele Ukrainer*innen ist das Hetmanat der erste ukrainische Nationalstaat und damit ein Vorläufer der heutigen unabhängigen Ukraine. Doch Polen wollte sich nicht einfach mit dem kosakischen Separatismus abfinden. Da die Kosaken gegen die Übermacht der Polen nichts ausrichten konnten, mussten sie sich einen Bundesgenossen suchen: Chmelnyzkyj wählte schließlich das Moskauer Reich zum Partner. Doch der Zar ließ den Kosaken abblitzen. In einen Konflikt mit Polen-Litauen wollte der Herrscher des Moskauer Reichs nicht unüberlegt hineinstolpern.

> *„Aus der Perspektive des Zaren wurden die religiösen und ethnischen Gemeinsamkeiten zwischen den Ukrainern und den Russen als gering angesehen."*

Ludmilla Ostermann: Für den Zaren war ein Bündnis mit den Ukrainern also keine klare Angelegenheit?

Julia Herzberg: Genau, an seinem Zögern zeigt sich, dass aus der Perspektive des Zaren die religiösen und ethnischen Gemeinsamkeiten zwischen den Ukrainer*innen und den Russ*innen als gering angesehen wurden. Für Zar Alexei Michailowitsch bedurfte es strategischer und militärischer Argumente, um Konfliktpartei zu werden. Erst 1654, nach einer dreijährigen Phase des Zögerns stimmte das Moskauer Reich dem Gesuch Chmelnyzkyjs zu, Bündnispartner der

Kosakenukraine zu werden. Doch es ist sehr umstritten, was eigentlich in Perejaslav beschlossen wurde. Ebenso die Deutung der Geschehnisse: Während die Moskauer Diplomaten in dem Eid der Kosaken einen Akt der Unterwerfung erkannten, sah die Kosakenelite ihren Eid als "freiwillige" und damit auch auflösbare Unterordnung an. Die Vereinbarung von Perejaslav begründete für die Kosaken eine Form des Protektorats, aber keine Aufnahme und Eingliederung in das Moskauer Reich. Für Moskau hingegen stellte der Akt von Perejaslav einen ersten Schritt zur Inkorporation der Ukraine dar. Bis Mitte des 18. Jahrhunderts stand das Hetmanat nur in loser Abhängigkeit von Russland. Es war Katharina die Große, die der Autonomie des Hetmanats 1764 ein Ende setzte. Grund dafür waren neben großrussischer Überheblichkeit und der Angst vor der Freiheitsliebe der Kosaken auch wirtschaftliche und strategische Überlegungen, denn mit der Aneignung der Steppengebiete nördlich des Schwarzen Meeres hatte die Ukraine an Bedeutung gewonnen. Am Ende des 18. Jahrhunderts war die vormalige Eigenheit des Hetmanats bis auf wenige Reste verschwunden. Die Vereinbarung von Perejaslav galt in Russland als der Beginn einer freiwilligen Unterwerfung.

Ludmilla Ostermann: Doch die ukrainische Nationalbewegung blühte wieder auf und die Idee wurde erneut lebendig.

Julia Herzberg: In der Volksüberlieferung und der ukrainischen Gesellschaft blieb die kosakische Lebensweise mit ihren Freiheits- und Gleichheitsvorstellungen als Ideal lebendig. Die ukrainische Nationalbewegung seit dem 19. Jahrhundert schloss an diese Vorstellungen an. Dies zeigt sich auch an dem 1862 verfassten patriotischen Gedicht „Noch ist die Ukraine nicht gestorben" des ukrainischen Dichters Pawlo Tschubynskyj. Das Gedicht, welches 1917 und erneut 2003 als Hymne der Ukraine gesungen wird, endet mit einem Bekenntnis zum Kosakentum: "Leib und Seele geben wir für unsere Freiheit hin, und wir werden zeigen, Brüder, dass wir vom Stamm der Kosaken sind!" Das bedeutete auch, dass die Vereinbarung von Perejaslav von 1654 von den Ukrainer*innen zunehmend kritisch bewertet wurde. Ganz anders als in Russland.

Ludmilla Ostermann: Wie äußert sich die unterschiedliche Sichtweise auf die Vereinbarung von Perejaslav heute?

Julia Herzberg: Die Vereinbarung von Perejaslav gehört wie der Holodomor, also die große Hungersnot in den 1930er Jahren, zu jenen historischen Prozessen und Ereignissen, die in Russland und der Ukraine vollkommen unterschiedlich bewertet werden. Diese zeigt sich noch heute in den Härten des Kriegsalltags: In der Ukraine wurden in den letzten Monaten viele Denkmäler gestürzt, die die angebliche Freundschaft zwischen Russland und der Ukraine in den Mittelpunkt gestellt haben. Im April 2022 wurde das sowjetische Denkmal der Völkerfreundschaft demontiert, ein Denkmalkomplex aus mehreren Teilen. Da ist zum einen ein riesiger Regenbogen, unter dem zwei muskulöse Arbeiter eine gemeinsame Flagge emporhalten. Sie sollen die Freundschaft zwischen dem russischen und dem ukrainischen Volk symbolisieren. Einer der beiden Arbeiter wurde zunächst enthauptet, bevor die gesamte Statue demontiert wurde. Auf Initiative des Bürgermeisters von Kyjiv, Vitali Klitschko, wurde der Bogen der Völkerfreundschaft in „Freiheitsbogen des ukrainischen Volkes" umbenannt. Dass das zum Komplex gehörende Denkmal für die Rada von Perejaslav, also dem Kosakenrat von Perejaslav, noch steht, begründete Klitschko damit, dass es schlichtweg zu massiv sei. Es wurde mit Bauplatten abgedeckt. Es ist sehr wahrscheinlich, dass dieses Denkmal bald gänzlich demontiert wird. Dies ist beispielsweise in Perejaslav selbst geschehen. Zu Beginn des Krieges haben Bewohner*innen der Stadt das Denkmal, das ursprünglich die Aufschrift „Für immer zusammen" trug, mit den Namen jener Orte versehen, in denen russische Soldaten schreckliche Kriegsverbrechen an Ukrainer*innen begangen haben: Butscha, Hostomel, Irpin. Anfang Juli 2022 wurde das Denkmal endgültig demontiert.

„Gegenstimmen zum Diktum der ‚Wiedervereinigung' konnten nur im illegalen Selbstverlag, im Samizdat, erscheinen."

Ludmilla Ostermann: Es ist aber nicht erst Folge der Angriffe auf ukrainisches Staatsgebiet seit 2014, dass die Verbindung zwischen Russland und der Ukraine kritisch gesehen wird?

Julia Herzberg: Trotz aller Bemühungen der Regierungen im Zarenreich und der Sowjetunion durch Feste, Denkmäler und historische Schriften die Gemeinsamkeit zwischen den beiden angeblichen „Brudervölkern" zu beschwören, wurde die Vereinbarung von Perejaslav von Ukrainer*innen meist kritisch bewertet. Sie galt ihnen – vor allem seit dem Aufkommen der Nationalbewegung im 19. Jahrhundert – als Beginn einer unheilvollen Allianz, die die Bildung eines eigenen Nationalstaates verhindert habe. Diese Einstellung stand im Gegensatz zu der der russischen Machteliten, die sich auf die Vereinbarung von Perejaslav bezogen, um die russische Herrschaft über die Ukraine als freiwillige Unterordnung darzustellen. Dies zeigte sich etwa 1954, als das Zentralkomitee der Kommunistischen Partei der Sowjetunion eine Sammlung von „Thesen zum dreihundertsten Jahrestag der Wiedervereinigung der Ukraine mit Russland" verabschiedete. Die darin festgelegte Interpretation der russisch-ukrainischen Beziehung spielte bis zum Zusammenbruch der Sowjetunion die zentrale Rolle. In diesen Thesen wurde nur noch von „Wiedervereinigung" gesprochen, die zwei „blutsverwandte Brüder" zusammengebracht habe. Putin hat sich bis heute nicht davon gelöst.

Ludmilla Ostermann: Gab es jemals kritische Stimmen gegen diese russische Interpretation der Geschichte?

Julia Herzberg: Gegenstimmen, die sich gegen das Diktum der „Wiedervereinigung" wehrten und die Ansicht vertraten, es handle sich um zwei verschiedene Völker, konnten nur im illegalen Selbstverlag, im Samizdat, erscheinen. Erst in den späten 1980er Jahren, in der Zeit der Perestrojka, gab es auch in der Öffentlichkeit eine vielstimmigere Debatte über die historische Bedeutung der Vereinbarung von Perejaslav. Nun war es möglich, auch in der Öffentlichkeit das Wiedervereinigungsparadigma abzulehnen. Vertreter*innen der ukrainischen Zivilgesellschaft wiesen in der späten Sowjetunion darauf hin, dass mit dem Mythos der „Wiedervereinigung" und dem Diskurs von den „Brudervölkern" den Ukrainer*innen das Recht auf einen unabhängigen und eigenen Staat abgesprochen werden sollte.

Ludmilla Ostermann: Wie gestaltete sich das Erinnern an die Vereinbarung von Perejaslav nach dem Zusammenbruch der Sowjetunion, nachdem die Ukrainer*innen einen eigenen unabhängigen Staat hatten?

Julia Herzberg: Dafür lohnt sich der Blick in das Jahr 1992 und die kleine Stadt Perejaslav: Am 21. Juni 1992, also 338 Jahre nach der Vereinbarung von Perejaslav, kamen Kosaken aus der ganzen Ukraine in der kleinen Provinzstadt zusammen, um den Treueeid aufzukündigen, den sie 1654 gegenüber dem Zaren geleistet hatten. Stattdessen wollten sie nun dem ukrainischen Volk die Treue schwören. In ihrer Erklärung beschuldigten sie Moskau und den Zaren, sie verraten, ihre Sprache und ihre Bräuche zerstört und sich ihr Territorium unter den Nagel gerissen zu haben. Der in der Sowjetunion permanent gebrauchte Terminus „Wiedervereinigung" wurde in der unabhängigen Ukraine vollkommen abgelehnt und verschwand aus den Medien und aus dem Straßenbild. Als Leonid Kutschma, einer der russlandfreundlichen ukrainischen Präsidenten, versuchte, 2004 – also zum 350. Jahrestag von Perejaslav – ein Gedenkjahr zu initiieren, stieß er auf eine Welle des Protests. Die Feierlichkeiten wurden – mit Ausnahme auf Regierungsebene – weitgehend abgesagt. Wladimir Putin, der die Ukraine 2004 besuchte, traf weder auf geschmückte Straßen, noch auf feiernde Menschen. Während er im Januar 2004 an der Seite des ukrainischen Präsidenten in einem Galakonzert saß, das der Vereinbarung von Perejaslav gewidmet war, protestierte vor der Tür die Kyjiver Bevölkerung.

Ludmilla Ostermann: Die Ereignisse aus dem Jahr 2004 markieren auch den Beginn eines politischen Kurswechsels von Putin und seinen Machteliten gegenüber der Ukraine.

Julia Herzberg: Seit der Orangenen Revolution 2004 in der Ukraine, die den Wahlsieg des russlandfreundlichen Viktor Janukowitsch' verhinderte, zeigt Putin ein großes Interesse an der Geschichte der Ukraine. Putin nahm nun immer häufiger die Rolle eines Geschichtsdeuters ein. So trat er 2008 auf dem Nato-Gipfel in Bukarest erstmalig mit der Erklärung auf, dass die Ukraine ein künstlich zusammengesetzter Staat sei, der erst zu Sowjetzeiten geschaffen worden ist. Das Hetmanat, die Ukrainischen Volksrepublik, aber auch die konfliktreichen Ereignisse der russisch-ukrainischen Geschichte, wie zum Beispiel den Holodomor, blendete er bei seinen historischen Ausführungen aus. 2013 behauptete Putin in einem Interview, dass Russ*innen und Ukrainer*innen ein Volk seien. Sein 2021 veröffentlichter Essay „Über die historische Einheit von Russen und Ukrainern" wiederholte diese These und kann als Auftakt der Kriegshandlungen im Februar 2022 angesehen werden. Es erstaunt daher nicht, dass dieser lange Essay zur Pflichtlektüre an russischen Militärschulen wurde. Drei Tage vor der Invasion hat Putin noch einmal nachgelegt. Er behauptete, dass die Ukraine ein „integraler Bestandteil unserer eigenen Geschichte, unserer Kultur, unseres geistigen Raums" sei und betonte „Bluts- und Familienbande", die die Ukrainer*innen und die Russ*innen miteinander verbinden.

Ludmilla Ostermann: Geschichte wird hier also als Waffe missbraucht?

Julia Herzberg: Der Kriegsverlauf hat deutlich gezeigt, dass die Mehrheit der Ukrainer*innen in einer souveränen Ukraine leben will. Selbst dies konnte Putins Geschichtsbild nicht erschüttern, das viele Russ*innen teilen. Die am 4. November 2022, dem Tag der Nationalen Einheit, im Zentrum von Moskau von Putin eröffnete Ausstellung "Ukraine. An den Wendepunkten einer Epoche" vermittelt das Bild, die Ukraine habe nur eine Zukunft im Zusammenschluss mit Russland. Der Kreml setzt seine „historischen" Narrative gezielt ein, um die russische Invasion der Ukraine zu rechtfertigen. Diskurse wie „Brudervolk" und „Wiedervereinigung" sind ein Mittel imperialer Politik. Sie werden genutzt, um die konfliktreichen Ereignisse in der russisch-ukrainischen Beziehungsgeschichte zu verschleiern und die ukrainische Nationalbewegung zu unterdrücken. Diese Diskurse sind aber auch ein Mittel, die historischen Verbindungen mit Europa in den Hintergrund zu stellen. Es ist kein Wunder, dass Ukrainer*innen heute in diesem Geschichtsbild eine Waffe sehen, die wie Raketen und Panzer gegen sie gerichtet ist. Sie treten diesen Deutungen mit Denkmalstürzen entgegen. Und auch wir im Westen sind angehalten, Interpretationen und Diskurse wie die der „Brüdervölker" kritisch zu hinterfragen, wenn mit ihnen das Existenzrecht eines souveränen Staates bestritten und ein brutaler, völkerrechtswidriger und sinnloser Angriffskrieg gerechtfertigt wird. Wenn Geschichte dazu benutzt wird, einen Angriffskrieg zu legitimieren, dann wird sie missbraucht.

When our Shadow Makes us Blind and Deaf to Suffering:
The power of a cultural complex in Israel

Elana Lakh

Abstract

When facing information about life under continuous trauma caused by humans, there is a part of the psyche that resists knowing. Various mechanisms of denial and disavowal are used in order to avoid knowing. Drawing on the concepts of collective shadow and cultural complex in the Israeli context, this paper examines the obstacles to seeing, hearing, and acknowledging the human experience of trauma suffered by Palestinian people. This paper offers a discussion of the threat that knowing presents to the conscious mind, and asks under which conditions will we be able to face this knowledge? How is it possible to agree to know, when the suffering is caused by our own group, and in our name? In light of Erich Neumann's idea of "New Ethics" based on taking responsibility for one's shadow, the paper looks at shadow projection processes that compromise the possibility of acknowledging the other's suffering. This paper describes the archetypal themes and historic processes that are at the basis of the Israeli cultural complexes of victimhood and power and tries to explain how the collective trauma of the past is used in the service of denying and justifying the suffering perpetrated in the present. It also offers a description of the effect that socio-political processes in contemporary Israel regarding the ongoing occupation of Palestinian lives have on the ability to take responsibility for our shadow and acknowledge the other's suffering.

In October 2015 I was asked by Amnesty International to comment on a documentary film screened in Jerusalem cinemas named "Shivering in Gaza" (2015). The film tells the story of a trauma treatment intervention conducted in Gaza by a Dutch therapist, Jan Andreae. The title, "Shivering in Gaza" elicited extreme reactions in the Israeli public screening the documentary and its screening had been banned in the south of Israel and was seriously threatened in Jerusalem.

I would like to consider the events surrounding this screening as examples of a collective psychological process of dealing with shadow contents in the Israeli context. I am writing as an Israeli analyst trying to understand collective psychological processes in the society that I am part of. I have no intention of analyzing Palestinian society, and I do not pretend to offer a balanced description of the two sides. I believe that one should look at one's own shadow.

C.G. Jung's concept of the shadow relates to a part of the psyche that consists of the tendencies the ego considers to be unwanted (Jung, CW 9.I,1959/1968, p. 284, para.513). These are the parts that we judge to be bad and shameful.

On a collective level, the culture's unwanted characteristics develop throughout the history of the group and are expressed in the values of the culture, as well as in cultural products such as myths, legends, and art (Neumann, 1990). The group's unwanted parts become the content of the shadow, projected in order to eliminate all that is bad and evil and maintain the goodness and cohesion of the group (Shalit, 2004).

The archetypal shadow is the dark side of culture and of human nature, repressed and rejected from the light of consciousness, and considered evil (Jung, CW 9I,1959/1968, para. 567, p. 322). This evil is what the ego experiences as harmful and damaging to its continuity and sense of safety. The ego, as the center of conscious personality, developed within the collective values that are transmitted through education, and identifies with those values, thus experiencing contradictions to them as threatening, and therefore evil (Neumann, 1990). Society, beginning in early infancy, teaches the growing child what is considered morally "good" and what is considered "bad" and inappropriate (Neumann, 1954; Neumann, 1990).

The shadow contents are alienated from consciousness because they form a threat to a person's or a group's self-perception of being good and living according to a moral code with high values, and so the shadow contents tend to be projected on the other, who is perceived as evil, and thus dangerous (Jung, CW 9II,1959, para. 15 p. 9; Neumann, 1990). These dynamics are characteristic of Neumann's "Old Ethics." In his "Depth Psychology and New Ethics" (1990), written in Tel-Aviv during WWII while the Holocaust was going on in Europe, Erich Neumann presents three forms of ethics, and their development in the individual psyche and the collective psyche, in regard to the collective. The first form is the collective group ethics, characteristic of a state of "primal unity" (Neumann, 1990, p. 59) of undifferentiated consciousness, in which the group and the individual are one. It is a state of unconscious existence, in which there is group responsibility, but no individual responsibility. The second form, evolving during history and representing the differentiation of the conscious from the unconscious, is the "Old Ethics." In this form there is a clear distinction between good and evil, defined by collective laws and values which informs individual moral judgements. Under this form of ethics, the differentiation of the conscious from the unconscious creates the distinction between good and bad, and elicits the need to deal with what is considered bad or evil. These mechanisms are suppression (Unterdrückung) in which the ego sacrifices personality characteristics and tendencies which are not in line with its moral values, judging them as bad and placing them outside, and repression (Verdrängun), in which these characteristics are alienated from the conscious ego but keep acting independently in the unconscious leading to shadow life, in a way that might be very dangerous, when this shadow is projected on the other. These collective values are the base of the conscience that dictates the individual's moral decisions. The third form is the "New Ethics," which involves acknowledgment of the shadow side and the evil within, and taking responsibility for the conscious parts of the psyche as well as for the unconscious shadow parts.

When confronted with our own shadow acts, various means are taken in order to avoid awareness of our shameful and hurtful deeds. These means will be discussed in the next pages, within the Israeli context.

In the spirit of these ideas, I will try to suggest an understanding of the reasons that make the screening of "Shivering in Gaza" and the human experience that it brings to our awareness, intolerable for the Israeli conscious.

The attempts to prevent the screening can be understood as an example of "actively wanting not to know" (Sharona Komem, personal communication, 2008). It is different from not wanting to know, which can be a rather passive process. Wanting not to know forces us to make an active effort not to let information reach our consciousness or deny information that evades this attempt at complete avoidance. This process lies within Neumann's (1990) explanation following Freud's term (Laplanche & Pontalis, 1973, p. 438) suppression.

In contemporary Israel, with all the available information about the atrocities of occupation, it becomes more and more difficult not to know, and requires stronger psychological measures of denial and disavowal of the Israeli acts, and of their effect on Palestinians lives.

In his book "States of Denial: Knowing about atrocities and suffering," the Israeli/British sociologist of South African origins Stanley Cohen (2001) asks what do we do with the notion of suffering of others and what does this knowledge do to us. In the case of Palestinian suffering and Israeli knowledge, the answer involves complex mechanisms. For Cohen, denial is the term describing people's way of not knowing what they know, or ignoring the implications of the facts, finding rationalizations. For Freud, denial or disavowal (verleugnung) is a defense mechanism that serves the refusal to recognize traumatic reality perception. This process lies in the basis of psychosis (Laplanche & Pontalis, 1973, p. 118-119). Cohen (2001) describes an array of denial responses to information that is threatening to individuals, societies, or organizations: repression, disavowal, ignoring, re-interpretation. If the information is registered, there is denial of its moral, emotional, or cognitive implications by neutralizing or normalizing. Cohen describes the reactions that reports about the torture of Palestinian detainees received in Israeli society: denying that the events happened, discrediting the reporting organizations, renaming the events as something other than torture, and justification on grounds of security. In other words, the information is well known.

In his comprehensive discussion of various forms of denial used by victims, perpetrators, and bystanders, Cohen (2001) elaborates on the feelings of shame, guilt, and loyalty experienced by the citizens of a perpetrator country. He mentions a global reason for denial: the inability to face unpleasant truths. When these truths have to do with deeds done by our own society, they involve complex feelings compromising the readiness to know. Jessica Benjamin (2015) writes that acknowledgment of the harm done to the other can pose a great threat to one's own identity and to the narrative of one's own suffering.

Back to "Shivering in Gaza" screening. On the way to the cinema, a taxi driver told me that the documentary must not be screened as it portrays Israel in a shameful way. When I said that the film is about trauma treatment in Gaza, he told me that Palestinians do not suffer from trauma because they are not human. His statement demonstrates the split that divides humans and non-humans, projecting the shadow onto the Palestinians. Neumann (1990) described the shadow as containing everything bad or sick, asocial, ugly, useless, sexual, animalistic, and infantile. Everything that is opposed to the self-perception of a civilized human. The taxi driver's statement can be viewed as a representation of this split, attributing the non-human parts of the self to the Palestinians. This statement holds a component of reality denial, and calls for understanding of the reason for this disavowal.

On the same day, a Jerusalem municipal council member tried to prevent the screening of the documentary in the Jerusalem cinema, and threatened to sanction it: "I will do anything in my power to prevent screening this false documentary about our soldiers!" (Anderman, October 17, 2015). It is obvious that there is something about the documentary that conscious cannot tolerate and therefore must be eliminated by any means. Her statement presents the group collective ethics, in Neumann's (1990) terms, any doubt or question about the goodness of the collective, the "we" notion, is experienced as dangerous and needs to be fought with all might.

The city council member also wrote: "These days, when Israeli security forces work day and night to defend our security, terrorism assisting organizations such as Amnesty are raising their heads again" (Anderman, October 17, 2015). In fact, the documentary does not mention Israeli soldiers, or Israel. But the council member does not know that, and the facts of reality do not matter to her. This can be seen as an example of the disavowal of reality, along the lines that Cohen (2001) proposes.

The council member's statement, and the taxi driver's words reflect the psychological processes of disavowal and projection of the shadow, characteristic of a state of mind that prevails in Israeli society. This state of mind is rooted in the cultural complexes of extinction versus redemption, as well as power and aggression as opposed to weakness and fear, described by the Israeli analyst Erel Shalit in "The Hero and his Shadow" (2004). Shalit presents the basic sources and myths determining Israeli society: disconnection from the land following 2000 years of exile led to the development of spiritual connectedness between the Jewish people, based on shared beliefs and religious practices, distinguishing them from the people among whom they lived. The loss of the connection to the land led to emphasis of the spiritual component and alienation of the physical component, resulting in weakness of the body and centuries of victimhood. Zionism was established as an actualization of the redemption motive, which was kept alive over the years in myths, longing and prayers. The Zionistic ethos that is influencing the Israeli society today, promotes physical actualization of the spiritual ideas, and emphasizes power as opposed to fear. Weakness and victimhood are of the past, and not to be experienced ever again: *We shall never again go like sheep to slaughter*, stresses the Israeli ethos. There is a split between power and weakness, aggression and victimhood. The weakness is despised and feared, and power is highly valued, and perceived as protection against annihilation. Aggression is justified as unavoidable and necessary for survival. Yet victimhood is used to cultivate a sense of constant fear of maintaining a threatened mode of existence. Shadow parts are split off from consciousness, generating a compensatory reaction. It is an interesting example of the dynamics of a cultural complex.

The concept of the cultural complex (Singer & Kimbles, 2004) tries to explain the group's psychic life. Within the individual realm of psychic life, the complex influences consciousness and prevents adjusting to inner and outer reality, impairs judgment, and compromises human contact (Jacobi, 1959). Similar to individual complexes, cultural complexes are autonomous and have a repetitive character. They have a hold over the individual psyche as well as of the group collective psyche, influencing imagination, behavior, and emotions, setting free powerful irrational forces which are rationalized by the complex. They are not accessible by consciousness, and they tend to accumulate experiences that justify them. They have a bi-polar nature: when a cultural complex is activated, the consciousness of the group identifies with one side of the complex, while the other, the denied shadow part, is projected onto another group. That can be very dangerous. Cultural complexes emerge through the group's experience, history, trauma and memory. They develop out of the interactions between the cultural unconscious and the archetypal psyche on one hand, and with the society's reality of the life of the group—communities, media, education, etc., on the other hand. Under the grip of the cultural complex, perception is distorted, the emotions are intense and the cultural identity is overtaken by the effect of the complex (Singer & Kimbles, 2004). In the case of Israeli society, it seems that the cultural complex of victimhood forms collective identity and defines reality perception, which is sometimes distorted.

Israeli society lives in an ongoing traumatic mode of experiencing reality. This mode has a dissociative nature. Donald Kalsched describes the dissociation as "a trick the psyche plays on itself" (1996, p. 13)— a trick that splits the unbearable experience, and makes part of it inaccessible to conscious, thus leaving elements of the traumatic experience in the unconscious where they become shadow parts. The traumatic events and relationship turn into an autonomous complex in the psyche, forcing itself on the conscious mind, as Jung described it (Jung, 1928, in Kalsched, 1996). Thus, trauma has a life of its own inside.

The cultural complex of the threat of annihilation of the Jewish people is based on a constitutional trauma of danger of extinction of the Jewish nation, since Biblical times, coming to a peak with the Holocaust. This constituting trauma that shapes the Israeli identity was already described by many writers (e.g., Gampel, 1992, 2020; Firestone, 2014; Ullman, 2011). The biblical myth of Amalek represents the archetypal aspect of this cultural complex. The bible describes Amalek as a tribe attacking the people of Israel on their way from Egypt in the desert, the first group to fight the Israelites (Exodus 17:8-15), threatening the existence of the newly emerged nation. Amalek has become a symbol of evil, which the Israelites are commended to annihilate: *"Now go, attack the Amalekites and totally destroy all that belongs to them. Do not spare them. Put to death men and women, children and infants, cattle and sheep, camels and donkeys,"* God orders King Saul (1 Samuel, 15:3).

In this myth, the threat to the Israelites exists alongside the command to annihilate Amalek; thus, the Israelites are both victims and aggressors. As happens in many myths of fighting groups throughout history, the evil is attributed to the other by the group that tells the story, projecting the shadow of archetypal evil. The history of the Jewish nation is pervaded by threats of extinction of Jewish lives, beliefs or practices, from the Babylonian exile in the 6th century BCE to the 20th century Holocaust, emphasizing the threat to survival. This constitutional traumatic mode is alive in the Israeli collective unconscious, and is sustained in the collective conscious public discourse by means of mass media, political agendas and the educational system beginning in kindergarten. For example, many high school children participate in journeys to concentration camps in Poland, journeys that are organized by the Israeli ministry of education, under the imperative to remember and not to forget, and the ethos of "Never again," which are widespread in Israeli society. At the same time, Arab school students in Israel do not learn about the "Nakba," the Palestinian disaster following 1948 war. The notion of the threat of annihilation and extinction of the Jewish people and the state of Israel is used to justify policies and acts. For example- the law of return (1950)[1] grants Israeli citizenship to any person who has a Jewish parent or grandparent, to their children and spouse, but not to other people who wish to become citizens. The Jewish immigration to Israel is called Aliya- ascent, presenting the symbolic value of the act, and the emphasis on the Jewish character of the nation state. In this line of action, Palestinians, who were born on the land which is now the state of Israel and were deported during the 1948 war, are denied the right to return to their homes.

The American-Israeli Jungian psychotherapist and a Jewish Rabbi Tirtza Firestone (2014) described very similar ideas about what she named the Jewish cultural complex, based on tribal survival trauma. Firestone (2014) describes the Jewish cultural complex as a primal sense of threat and fear for survival, combined with massive traumatic events leading to merging of lived reality with co-constructed mythology. This combination creates extreme defensiveness and a strong need to hold to the longed-for homeland as a sanctuary from the world. Firestone presents a profound discussion of the way in which the daimon of trauma (Kalsched, 1996) uses the Israeli power to protect the traumatized group psyche, and of the identification with the aggressor dynamics that lead to becoming perpetrators towards the Palestinians.

---

[1] https://www.nevo.co.il/law_html/law00/72231.htm, in Hebrew

In traumatic states, the conscious is possessed by the sense that one's life is threatened, and becomes entirely survival-oriented. Time, space, and context cease to exist and the person re-lives the traumatic events again and again. This state of mind prevails in Israeli society, leaving no space for complexity, and thinking processes are blurred. There is no distinction between kinds and levels of threat and danger. It does not allow any distinction between current events that are happening within a specific political context that has causes and possible solutions, and the constitutional Israeli trauma of victimhood and survival. It seems that under a symbolic equation (Segal, 1957), Palestinians and Nazis are the same, Amalekites. In situations dominated by the experience of a life threat there is an attack on thought processes and on linking (Bion,1959), and the notion of cause and context cannot be remembered. The Palestinian attacks are dissociated from the current context of decades of Israeli occupation of Palestinian lands and lives, and are thus experienced and presented as antisemitic, driven by hatred of Jews just for being Jewish. The current context is denied and forgotten, and only the belief in a threat to the Jews prevails, timeless and placeless. The perception of reality is taken over by the complex.

So why did the screening of a documentary about trauma treatment in Gaza in Jerusalem pose a threat the Israeli conscious? And what is the danger that Amnesty International presents that lead the Jerusalem municipality member to call it a "terrorism assisting organization?"

The danger is of connections and relatedness. Relatedness opens the way to complexity, and complexity compromises the clear distinction between good and bad, between ego and shadow and between "us" and "them." Thus, the active effort not to know is meant to protect the conscious against information that it cannot tolerate.

In such an ever-traumatic mode of thinking there is no place for two subjects, and it is impossible to see the suffering of the other. There is clear good and clear bad, victim and perpetrator. We can easily recognize them and distinguish them. In such a line of thinking, Amnesty International can be perceived as a terrorism assisting organization, because by screening "Shivering in Gaza," Amnesty is forcing the Israeli viewers to see the people in Gaza, the people who suffer trauma, and does not allow the active not knowing to go on. Firestone (2014) thinks the Israeli inability to see the suffering of the other involves a disturbed feeling function. The feeling function is impaired due to the activation of the dark side of the hero complex that cannot afford feelings, and needs to present power, after centuries of weakness and suffering. In such a situation, compassion is very compromised, and needs to be defended against.

Watching this documentary, seeing the faces of the Gazan people, their homes, their children and their pain, might compromise the dissociation that keeps the shadow away from the conscious. Seeing the humanity of the Gazan people makes it impossible to deny their suffering, and raises profound questions about Israeli responsibility for this suffering.

The Israeli cultural complex of victimhood makes it very difficult to acknowledge our perpetrator shadow part. Ullman (2011) also relates to this point from a relational psychoanalysis point of view, saying that Israeli mental health professional world is very developed in the treatment of suffering and trauma, but much less responsive as professionals witnessing the harm done by our group to the other. She cites the Jewish American psychoanalyst Sam Gerson who writes: "The imperative to bear witness and the seductions of blind denial are the everlasting legacies of the response to trauma" (2009, in Ullman, 2011). The effects of the cultural complex can be seen in Ullman's description of the Israeli oscillation between poles of denial and witnessing, in coexistence of denial and disavowal in certain areas, with profound professional occupation with trauma, trauma treatment, and the traumatic context (Ullman, 2011). The Israeli traumatic context in which the Palestinians are perceived as perpetrators.

The various mechanisms of denial that Cohen (2001) mentioned come to life in order to prevent the acknowledgment of the Palestinian suffering. The philosopher John Kekes defines evil as severe and unjustified suffering inflicted upon sentient beings (1998, p. 463). Acknowledgement of the Palestinian suffering might lead to recognition of evil within us, Israelis, and compromise our self-perception as victims. Acknowledgement makes things complicated.

As the Jerusalem city council member said: "The film stains our soldiers' morality" (Antman, October, 17, 2015), implying it is not the soldiers' acts that stain their (or our) morality, but the film. If the documentary is not screened, perhaps the clear-cut distinction between moral and immoral can be preserved.

According to this line of thinking, Breaking the Silence[2] activists are perceived as traitors, for confronting the Israeli public with details of the everyday suffering of Palestinians under occupation, and challenging the notion of goodness and justification of Israeli actions. By telling what they have done as soldiers sent by the state, Breaking the Silence activists are complicating the clear distinction between good us and evil them. Indeed, they betray the intact one-sided self-perception of the tribal collective, and compromise the projection of the shadow that permits this self-perception to prevail.

Suppression leads to suffering because the suppressing individual sacrificed parts of the shadow to the demands of the collective values, that cause shame and guilt (Neumann, 1990), but repression leads to projection of the shadow. The shadow is always visible when projected on the other (Jung, 1959, para. 16, p. 9), thus preserving self-perception, and the split between good and evil (Stein, 1995). In this way the Palestinians are perceived as violent, murderous, and immoral, keeping the Israeli self-perception of morality and goodness intact.

Encounter with our shadow parts is a painful one, since it forces us to see the dark and shameful parts in ourselves, and not in the other that we project upon. This is the danger that Israelis face

---

[2] Breaking the silence is an Israeli NGO of veterans who are committed to exposing the Israeli public to the reality of Palestinian life under Israeli occupation in the occupied territories. By testifying about what they have done as soldiers in the occupied territories, they try to elicit public debate. https://www.breakingthesilence.org.il/

watching "Shivering in Gaza." It is almost impossible for the collective Israeli conscious, based on a well-preserved narrative of victimhood, to acknowledge Palestinians as victims of trauma. To do so is dangerous because it means that we are the perpetrators causing their trauma and therefore acknowledging our own shadow, in our acts.

Jung stated in many of his writings that no one is free of evil within, and no one can be entirely good: *"None of us stands outside humanity's black shadow"* (Jung, CW 10, 1970, para. 572, p. 297). He thought that denying the shadow is dangerous, because *"negligence is the best means of making man the instrument of evil"* (ibid). Therefore, Jung considered the task of owning one's own shadow to be a crucial one: *"One does not become enlightened by imagining figures of light, but by making the darkness conscious. The latter procedure, however, is disagreeable and therefore not popular."* (Jung, CW 13, para. 335, pp. 265-266)

Jung called for self-knowledge, as the way for an individual to deal with the problem of evil. He related to this need for self-knowledge as a moral imperative, in response to cultural and mass processes of projecting evil on the other (Jung, CW 9II, 1959, para. 14, p. 8). This imperative is also valid on a collective level, as described by Erich Neumann in his "Depth Psychology and New Ethics" (1990), and forms the essence of the new ethics that stems out of acknowledgement of our own shadow.

Screening "Shivering in Gaza" in Jerusalem for an Israeli audience calls for acknowledgment and owning the shadow—but is very difficult to achieve, as the case of the reaction to the screening shows. Nevertheless, individuals and groups that insist on owning the shadow and bringing it into the collective's conscious, have a very important role to play in promoting moral responsibility and development of individual and collective conscious (Neumann, 1990), despite the attempts to silence them. Firestone (2014) thinks that the healing of the Jewish cultural complex will be possible with the restoration of the feeling function in the collective psyche by processes of grieving the trauma that might allow the empathy and justice to return. I believe that we need to take responsibility for our shadow acts by using the thinking function, but that encounters enormous forces of resistance. Perhaps the transcendent function can be of assistance here.

In the years that passed since the events described in this paper, aggression and racism within the Israeli collective have grown blunter. The cultural complex now takes an even stronger grip over the Israeli society. The inability to see Palestinian suffering and acknowledge Israeli responsibility for it becomes justified and prevails the public discourse, whether actively, by denying the suffering and justifying it in various ways, or passively, by ignoring the news about it out of indifference or out of helplessness and despair. Voices such as the taxi driver's voice, and similar ones, are now part of political agenda of parliament members who receive growing public support. Jung's and Neumann's calling for owning the shadow seems very far away.

References

Anderman, N. (2015, October, 17). The film 'Shivering in Gaza' will be screened in Jerusalem cinematheque today: City council member is acting to cancel it. *Haaretz Gallery*. https://www.haaretz.co.il/gallery/cinema/2015-10-17/ty-article/0000017f-e276-d75c-a7ff-feff69ba0000. (in Hebrew)

Benjamin, J. (2015). Acknowledging the Other's Suffering: A Psychoanalytic Approach to Trauma in Israel/Palestine. *Tikkun 30*(3) https://www.muse.jhu.edu/article/586868.

Bion, W.R. (1959). Attacks on Linking. *International Journal of Psycho-Analysis, 40*, 308-315.

Cohen, S. (2001). *States of Denial: Knowing about atrocities and suffering*. Polity press.

Firestone, T. (2014). The Jewish Cultural Complex. *Psychological Perspectives, 57:3, 278-290*. DOI: 10.1080/00332925.2014.936231

Gampel, Y. (1992). "I Was a Shoah Child." *British Journal of Psychotherapy, 8: 391-400*.

Gampel, Y. (2020). "The pain of the Social." *The International Journal of Psychoanalysis, 101:6, 1219-1235*.

Jacobi, J. (1959). *Complex, Archetype and Symbol*. Bollingen series, Princeton University Press.

Jung. C.G. (1959). *Aion*. (R.F.C Hull: Trans.) Routledge & Kegan Paul. CW 9II.

Jung. C.G. (1968). *The archetypes and the collective unconscious*. (R.F.C. Hull: Trans.). (2nd ed). Bollingen series XX, Princeton University Press. First published in 1959. CW 9I

Jung, C.G. (1970). *Civilization in transition*. (R.F.C Hull: Trans.). London: Routledge & Kegan Paul. First published in 1964. CW 10

Kalsched, D. (1996). *The Inner World of Trauma: Archetypal defenses of the personal spirit*. Routledge.

Kekes, J. (1998) Evil. *Routledge encyclopedia of philosophy. (vol 3, pp. 463-466)*. Routledge.

Laplanche, J., & Pontalis, J. B., (1973) *The Language of Psychoanalysis*. (D. Nicholson-Smith: Trans.) W.W. Norton & Company.

Neumann, E. (1954). *The Origins and History of Consciousness*. (Translator: R.F.C. Hull). Harper & Brothers. Vol. 1.

Neumann, E. (1990). *Depth Psychology and a New Ethics*. (E. Rolfe: Trans.) Boston & Shaftesbury: Shambala.

Segal, H. (1957). "Notes on Symbol Formation." *International Journal of Psychoanalysis. 38*, 391-397.

Shalit, E. (2004). *The Hero and his Shadow: Psycho-political aspects of myth and reality in Israel*. Fisher King Press.

Singer, T. & Kimbles, S.L., (2004). Introduction: Singer, T., & Kimbles, S.L. (Eds.). *The Cultural Complex: Contemporary jungian perspectives on psyche and society* (1st ed.). Routledge. (pp. 1-9). https://doi.org/10.4324/9780203536889

Stein, M. (Ed). (1995). *Jung on Evil*. Princeton University Press.

Ullman, C. (2011). "Between Denial and Witnessing: Psychoanalysis and clinical practice in the Israeli context." *Psychoanalytic Perspectives, 8:2, 179-200*. DOI: 10.1080/1551806X.2011.10486304

The Time is out of Joint: Pasolini's Oedipus Rex

Caterina Vezzoli and Livia Di Stefano

Abstract

The authors begin with the filmic reinterpretation of Sophocles' tragedy Oedipus Rex by Italian director and poet Pier Paolo Pasolini. The film inspired a deconstruction of the Sophoclean tragedy in order to clarify the effects of incest and the incestual dynamic in today's society, in individuals, and collective development. The Jungian conception of incest is symbolic and part of the individuation process and formation of a personality differentiated from parental complexes. They amplified the personal and collective history of incestual secrets with perpetuation of modalities replicating the old status quo with repercussions on the individual, culture, and society at large. Further deconstruction led the authors to consider the tragedy of Oedipus as an opportunity to question patriarchal values by confronting archaic aspects present in ourselves and the culture we live in. In this journey, the film and Pasolini's personality have been helpful in showing the need for a change of vision, well expressed by the famous verse in Hamlet "the time is out of joint," meaning the possibility of an interruption of thought in order to rework what has been oppressed historically and spiritually by the ruling class. The method employed by the authors is to use the film artwork to explore the creative rupture and let the possible meanings emerge in us to manifest transformative potential. Thus, the temporal fracture that Pasolini introduces in his narrative tells of our present in the light of the past so to not return to the blindness of the generations before us. For Pasolini, after two world wars, there was the transformation of Italian society from an agricultural to an industrial and consumer reality. For the authors, the reality of the pandemic and the outbreak of war in Ukraine. If the problem of Oedipus is the subject's path toward differentiation, the message that is captured in Pasolini's film and Jungian theory helps us clarify that unconscious forces require the redemption of archaic parts of our psyche. The elements that the collective consciousness tends to exclude are taboo because it is under the spell of the dominant collective power. In this paper the authors clarify how knowing Oedipus and how and why his differentiation failed is a task that never ends and concerns not only the individual but also a society that seeks blindness to pander to the illusion of richness.

Introduction

Pasolini, in his film *Edipo Re* (Oedipus Rex)[3] is rewriting the story of the Oedipus myth from his point of view as screen writer and director. In the late sixties Pasolini was aware that the Italian social landscape had changed from a traditionally agricultural country to an industrial consumeristic society. Pasolini's view of this transformation goes to the roots of the Italian political system and how the society at large is blind about the consequences of this disruption.

His film inspired our attempt to include a further deconstruction[4] of the narrative of Sophocles' tragedy *Oedipus Rex*. We tried to think 'beyond Oedipus' however when we use amplification from literature or art towards the clinical field, we must maintain a coherence with the clinical issues we want to investigate. In this case our aim is to clarify the effects of incest and the 'incestual' dynamic in society with regard to the development of individuals and the process of individuation.

To think of Oedipus is to think of incest, incestuous, and incestual as defined by Racamier: incestual is a neologism that describes a specific condition of psychic and relational life where, incest, unacted, hovers in the emotional atmosphere of a patient, family or groupwork, leaving its imprint. *Incestual is an atmosphere in which the wind of incest blows without there being incest. Wherever its gusts arrive, a desert is created, suspicion, silence and secrecy are instilled* (Racamier P. C., 2003, Italian version translated by the authors).

This point of view seems interesting to us in approaching the theories of modern, Jungian, and non-Jungian literature on the issues of separation from parental figures. Our assumption is to highlight how incestual nonseparation contaminates the lives not only of the individual but also of generations to come. In our amplification, we posit that the non-processing of personal and collective history of incestual secrets leads to the recurrence, pathological maintenance, replication of old status quo at the individual as well as collective level.

Jung on incest

We will begin by mentioning what incest is for Jung or rather what aspects of his definition we will consider. For Jung, incest is to be understood as a symbolic dimension of regression to the maternal and to the unconscious. As he stated in *Symbols of Transformation* (1967) when analyzing Miss Miller's material, regression is not necessarily pathological because one can regress to the maternal unconscious dimension in order to recover lost energy. In this

---

[3] Edipo Re, free version on YouTube: https://youtu.be/iT8xtiMQYy8

[4] We refer to *deconstructionism or deconstructivism* as a concept introduced into Western philosophy by Jacques Derrida. It can be described as close confrontation with texts and authors with the aim of exposing implicit assumptions, hidden biases, and latent contradictions in culture and language that, not too consciously, humans adopt. Ref. Wikipedia

sense, the return to the mother is a return to archetypal unconscious images from which to re-emerge with new energy and new responses *reculer pour mieux sauter*[5] (§483).

In Psychological Types (1974) Jung makes an explicit reference to Freud's Oedipus complex when he specifies on §201 that regression to 'parental imagoes' is a symbolization and *through acceptance of the "symbol" as a real symbol, the regression to the parents is instantly transformed into a progression, whereas it would remain a regression if the symbol were to be interpreted merely as a sign for the actual parents and thus robbed of its independent character*

In this sense, Jung does not exclude the incest as real but, as a symbol, is part of the process towards individuation. To separate from the real parents is necessary in order not to dissociate part of the psyche. Not all what constitute the complexes can be integrated as there are traumatic areas that, when constellated in the course of development had dissociated, becoming autonomous. They are the so-called splinter psyche that can turn into secondary personalities and development of false self instead of differentiation towards individuation.

This of course has repercussions on culture and society at large. We are assuming that transgression to the dominant culture is indeed a necessity if we have to separate from the parental vision of the world. To reconsider the Oedipus tragedy might be to return to the origins of patriarchal civilization, perhaps to question and confront archaic aspects present in ourselves, in society, and in the culture we live in.

From this point of view, dealing with the Oedipus complex would be an invitation to question the vaticinal of the oracle and turn it upside down, or we could say referring to the symbol as Jung understands it, would be to reactivate or rediscover the symbol or myth in a new form.

In *Psychological Types*, Jung writes "humanity came to its gods by accepting the reality of the symbol, that is, it came to the reality of thought, which has made man lord of the earth." (Jung 1974 §202)

The symbol thus is no longer *the synthetic resultant of all unconscious factors,* it is no longer *the living form,* it has lost its symbolic value and once reified loses its ability to transcend reality and it becomes a sign (Jung 1974 §202).

The loss of *unconscious factors* ignores traumas buried in the unconscious. To be more explicit, whatever remains unsolved or dissociated because it is unbearable at the individual or collective level will live in the unconscious. As Lanius (2010) says "ours is a traumatized society" then we cannot help but consider that in the transition from adolescence to adulthood, unresolved

---

[5] Trad. en: Stepping back to make the leap

traumas will reoccur and separation from deficient parental figures can be problematic and difficult to reach. What tools are we to use?

Pasolini's Oedipus rex

We had chosen for our amplification a work of art like Pasolini's film not to interpret but to allow other meanings to emerge and, in today frustrating reality when the *spirit of the time* is so discouraging, we are hoping that the *spirit of the depth* could guide us.

For his film's narrative, Pasolini chooses the Po Valley, the countryside around Lodi[6], as the birthplace of Oedipus; the landscapes of mythological Greece, on the other hand, are shot in Morocco mainly in desert areas and in nomads' camps. Immediately what emerges is the need to bring together the personal poet's existential geography combined with the collective archaisms of places that maintain archetypically grounded patterns in the present. The juxtaposition and enlargement of space-time becomes a mythical dimension; one in which present, past, and future are intertwined and reversed.

Our first notation concerns the transpositions between past and present, and we will start from the figure of Angelo the escort whom Pasolini places beside Oedipus in Bologna's Piazza Maggiore[7]. Angelo, made Benjamin's text Angelus Novo (2016) resonate. For Benjamin, materialistic historiography differs from historicism because it has at its basis a principle that is not the temporality of historicism:

> *The past carries with it a temporal index by which it is referred to as redemption. There is a secret agreement between past generations and the present one. Our coming was expected on earth. Like every generation that preceded us, we have been endowed with a weak Messianic power, a power to which the past has a claim. That claim cannot be settled cheaply. Historical materialists are aware of that*[8]

How to use the weak Messianic force? Benjamin (2016) says that for materialism, the revolutionary chance[9] is created when tensions of contrasting forces form a monad in which ideas become crystallized and create a halt in the repetition of the temporality of history. That is, the monad is an event that arrests dominant thinking: for example, the war in Ukraine interrupts the dominant idea that Russia has too many financial interests to wage war.

---

[6] These are the places where Pasolini spent part of his childhood
[7] Bologna is the city where Pasolini was born in 1922
[8] Walter Benjamin, *On the Concept of History*, on https://www.sfu.ca/~andrewf/CONCEPT2.html
[9] That's old-fashioned language... that we still like

Benjamin's reference to the weak messianic task of the generation has to do with the need for the new generation to face the rapture of the dominant assumption so that different answers might contrast the blind repetition of the dominant status quo.

The event, in Derridian terms, creates an interruption of thought and introduces the possibility of reworking the metaphor coined by Shakespeare's Hamlet *the time is out of joint*[10], and the specters can enter the world of the living. As mentioned earlier, we are referring not to constructivism but rather to the open field of the deconstruction of reality that allows the emergence of the new.

Here Angelo becomes the *terrifying angel* of Rilkean (2009)[11] memory, no longer a companion but a mediator between worlds who witnesses the emergence of another reality. Terrifying, therefore, because it brings the religious horror of beauty:

> *For beauty is nothing*
> *but the beginning of terror, which we still are just able to endure,*
> *and we are so awed because it serenely disdains*
> *to annihilate us. Every angel is terrifying.*[12]

It is thus a possibility for reflection, for a change of vision. Out of the temporal rift that has been created will emerge the implicit natures that have never been revealed before and that have been historically and spiritually oppressed by the ruling class. In this condition, the implicit could manifest transformative potential. Thus, a revolutionary chance is created in the struggle to redeem the oppressed past so conveyed by the class that writes history from the point of view of domination and wants to maintain the status quo and prevent history from being told from the point of view of subalterns.

Psychologically we cannot forget that any *daimonic*[13] potential can become demonic. Meaning, the *daimonic* can be transformed via possession by the dominant culture and become demonic. The dominant thought easily becomes demonic because it tends to use the spirit as the service of power thus preventing the development of the potential numinous charge of alternative thought. The process of thought degradation is unavoidable when we do not allow the unformulated unconscious contents, suspended in the psychoid unconscious, to emerge.

---

[10] Shakespeare, *Hamlet*, Act I Scene 5
[11] R.M. Rilke, I Elegy of *Duino Elegies*
[12] https://rilkepoetry.com/duino-elegies/first-duino-elegy/
[13] We refer to the philosophical term *daimon* and to Hillman theory.

Our transposition using Pasolini's film is to explore, through art, the creative rupture that can let new meaning emerge in the participative observer. The visionary function of the artwork[14] shapes the questions and mobilizes the search for answers that emerge from the unconscious psyche and are translated into visionary terms. Therefore, we do not interpret Pasolini's work, but try to give space and presence to the unconscious contents underlying the images, while at the same time revealing possible new understanding.

Thus, the temporal fracture that Pasolini introduces into his film's narrative is a revisitation of *Oedipus Rex* that recounts 'our present,' Pasolini's actual time as well as ours. The light of the past should illuminate us so that we don't return to the blindness of the generation that just preceded us. For Pasolini, the Italian society after the two World Wars and the transformation of the Italian Society of his time is for us the reality of the pandemic and the eruption of the war in Ukraine.

Who is Pasolini's Oedipus?

Pasolini's Oedipus, like the Oedipus of the tragedy, is born into a wealthy class. Thus, the starting image is the poplar trees of the plain, the green meadows, the infant lying on the blanket toddling happily in the sun, and the young women chasing each other.

The scene is so much reminiscent of the one Jung describes when in *Memories, Dreams, Reflections* (1989) he recalls being in a baby carriage and the pleasure of the warmth of the sun, the taste of milk and the young maid caring for him. Jung, at age 80, recounts the episode as his first self-awareness. A RIG[15] Stern would say, that will become a *now moment*[16].

For us, this beginning is both a personal association to Pasolini's biography he was born in Bologna, but also a reference to the narrative that the author will follow in the unfolding of the film: a memory that will be located within the maternal complex as an element that is not fully conscious in connection with the personal and collective unconscious. Oedipus/Pasolini is investigating the maternal complex and early memories.

Through dreams and archetypal images, the unconscious deconstructs for us emergence of early memories. The unconscious stories are the beginning from which we derive. In a sense, the unconscious, like the myths, posits the stories in an enigmatic way and asks us to

---

[14] We refer to Jung's theories on the *visionary function of imagination* in Jung, C.W., vol. 10

[15] RIG Stern (1985) means Representations of Interactions that have been Generalized, basic units, single experiences, which are then combined into networks concerning food, mother, trust. These early generalizations will develop over time into semantic memories that can be expressed verbally. Such representations, experiences, prototypes, and affective valences are consolidated into stable structures of self-regulation and relationship with reality.

[16] The *Now Moment* or *Present Moment* is according to Stern what is happening now in the relationship; it is the moment of creative change. "It is the moment of subjective affective experience in the act of its fulfillment, as it is experienced not afterwards when it is rephrased in words or rethought" (2004) Translation by the authors

deconstruct and make a personal story out of them. In the myth and in Pasolini's film, Oedipus tries to know his story and also to be the author of it, but there are too many secrets and lot of unresolved dilemmas on his way.

In the film, the baby Oedipus' relationship with his mother is all-encompassing but does not prepare him for the arrival of his father; living in a world of only women is idyllic. When his father arrives, he brings war. In the film his father arrives dressed as a World War I officer: the war of trenches, nervine gas, and millions of dead whose horrors have only recently been revealed. But even if it were World War II or the current invasion of Ukraine, it would be the same. The images of the war that show up on our television screens every night, are like the images of war films we are used to seeing, so there's a defense in us that looks at the devastations as in some other reality, not so near our homes.

If in the eyes of the mother Oedipus reads care and nurture, then what does he read in the eyes of the father? Distrust, competition, and rancor, likely. Is it what war accustoms the men who fight in it and is it what they bring home with them? So, traumas follow us and chase for generations to come.

Oedipus becomes the outcast, is left alone and he experiences the war his father carries within, he experiences it through the frightening noise of the fireworks. Was the mother no longer protecting him? Was he a narcissistic investment? Perhaps. But such an approach that interprets instead of amplifies is not ours.

The *son of fortune*, as he will be called in the film, survives and will find another father and mother but the dreams haunt him, and he want answers.

No matter that he finds in Polybus a playful and loving father, the stain of rejection, the trauma of rejection remains unresolved, the wound inflicted at his feet is unacceptable and there is no need to deny what everyone knows, he is the foundling son of fortune, he cannot hide, he is ashamed. He leaves his adoptive family in search of answers. The answer he finds pushes him toward despair and onto the road where he will meet the very fate he seeks to escape. The questions asked to the oracles and the Greek gods are many. Their truths are so cryptic however, they push toward catastrophe. They give no chance!

To paraphrase Benjamin (2019), the dominant power cannot be challenged, the tensions resulting from struggles against dominant thought do not create a constellation that destabilizes the immobility of historical time giving voice to the repressed. Only tragedies occur, and therefore art highlights the evil on which the power that traumatizes rests.

The murderous father whom Oedipus encounters on his way to Thebes has not changed; he is the pusillanimous murderer who sends others to their deaths. Oedipus, however, is a victim of the same dynamic and, instead of deconstructing within himself the parental imago, he kills the real parent and thus his trauma is not resolved, rather, it is aggravated. Oedipus acts out a drive, he cannot differentiate from his incestuous background buried in the deeper layer of his psyche, he is prey to an unconscious and archaic dynamic that is acted out but not recognized.

This is what often happens to adolescents who cannot separate themselves from the incestuous dynamics that hold them even though they have been taken away from their parents and adopted or partially protected. But in the journey towards the fulfillment of life, the encounters with change cannot be avoided, for better or worse.

Oedipus meets the Sphinx

In the film Pasolini inserts a novelty in the encounter with the Sphinx by omitting the classic exposition of the riddle to be solved. He moves to the real conflict by asking Oedipus to look in himself. It is the decisive moment when the Sphinx speaks with Oedipus's voice; it is Oedipus himself, that is, the voice of his own depths calling him back to the inner journey and not just the heroic one. The Sphinx lets him go through, and Oedipus deludes himself that he has finally found his place. But what Pasolini's sphinx foretold, *you cannot drive me back into the abyss, the abyss is within you* is presenting the bill.

The prize of marriage to the mother is regression to the mother-unconscious and, as we have seen, it could be part of a path that requires differentiation and sacrifice of omnipotence, but Oedipus is not ready.

Significantly for us is the dialogue in which Pasolini as actor asks Oedipus to liberate his people and free himself from the *oppression of thought that blindly repeats the already known* (Benjamin 2019) to find the answer to free Thebes from the plague. Pasolini as priest or representative of the citizens implores his king Oedipus:

> If we, these sons and I, are here praying to you before your hearth, it is certainly not because we judge you as a god. Was it not you as soon as you came to this city who delivered us from the nightmare of the sphinx? And thou didst this work not because thou knewest more than we, but as they all say, with the help of a God. And therefore, Oedipus our king, we all beseech you on our knees: find us a remedy, no matter what it is, whether a God or a man like us suggests it to you.

> You who are the best of us all, give us life once more. Let not the memory of your reign remain alive in us for first being lifted up and then falling back again (translation by the authors).

The Priest's plea appeals to Oedipus' humanity. Pasolini as film director incites his Oedipus to delve into his inner world, not to abandon himself to the plague but to seek the answer, and asks him to challenge the fate of the oppressed by affirming his thoughts, to eviscerate his knowledge as a suffering subject. He has killed to free himself from his murderous father, but then unwittingly takes his place. After killing his father, after freeing himself and us from the stereotypes of the oppressors he returns blind because he does not realize that he has betrayed himself for the possession of his father's trophy: the mother. Shame oppresses him for his desire for regression to an illusory and conflict-free world, and thus entangled in incestual desires Oedipus is called upon by his author Pasolini not to be blind, to differentiate himself.

The impossible differentiation

The tragedy returning to Piazza Maggiore in Bologna becomes a critique of the society that after coming out of World War II and defeating fascism finds itself with the industrial boom of the 1960s and 1970s sinking into the depths of what Pasolini will also call the "new capitalism." In his film it is represented by the final scene, where the couple Oedipus and Angelo return to the house where Oedipus saw the light: there is no longer a bicycle passing under the windows of the house in the square with the statue of the victorious soldier but the Fiat cars that mark the passage from peasant to industrial civilization and from there onward to the exclusive law of the market and finance that is our world today. The transition that even then Pasolini considered a political and personal failure.

A few months before he was assassinated, Pasolini published on the newspaper *Corriere della Sera* the article *La scomparsa delle lucciole. Il vuoto del potere in Italia*[17], in which he launched a very harsh polemical attack to the Christian Democrat Party, the undiscussed ruler of Italian political life at the time and for many years after his death. By using the metaphor of the death of fireflies, he accused the ruling class in power of having promoted a certain model of development, of having organized the life of the post-war generation with no memory of the past and of having polluted the countryside and cities. He criticized the corruption of political power and the tendency to favor the powerful lobbies instead of giving support to democratic intervention, to the life of villages and provinces that were brutally raped. He denounced the destruction of the fundamental values of equality and the possibilities for a real democracy that for him should give space to all cultures present in the country and not only to those of the dominant class.

In his films, he finds these values in the 'primitive' people or the poor and marginalized which are undermined by the capitalism; that is why his Oedipus becomes a beggar in Piazza Maggiore. Another interesting aspect that speaks to our ecological sensitiveness is the destruction of

---

[17] Trad eng. *The fireflies disappearance. The vacancy of power in Italy* This article reappeared in the book *Scritti corsari* (2011) with a title: L'articolo delle lucciole

the fireflies, that perished by the use of pesticides in agriculture that became intensive and chemically contaminated. Pasolini goes beyond the simple political criticism of the use of power just for power and speaks of the unawareness of the dominant political government, of the changes that were taking place, of the blindness and complete incomprehension of the country and society the Christian democrats were governing. He felt, as his primary moral, civil, and political duty, to call his contemporaries' attention to the 'blindness' of power that brings oppression of spirit and of the beauty of life and nature. Here we return to the theme of transgenerational blindness and trauma and the need for deep and profound personal and collective analysis.

Oedipus, blindness and transgenerational incestual oppression

From a more personal point of view, then, what is the significance of the backward journey of the Oedipus character? What is the new myth to be told...what is the new narrative? We have repeated several times the importance of differentiation for the growth and development of subjectivity. In our view, the priest Pasolini addressing his character Oedipus invites him to find the causes that led to the plague and does not ask him to consult the oracle but to look for the causes in the abyss *within him*. The Sphynx asks him to differentiate and thus deconstruct the events of his story by recognizing their transgenerational, and thus, incestual elements: his father Laius the pedophile-murderer and his mother Jocasta the victim and architect of the imprisonment of Oedipus' Soul.

Oedipus' problem is that he does not see the Shadow of his Soul and thus is imprisoned by it. In this sense the unconscious return to the mother is not the return to the unconscious to find the transformative energy (which would then be the answer) but is the fusion with the maternal Shadow and the imprisonment of the soul function.

Important in this regard is the figure of Tiresias who speaks of a different way of being blind: he urges Oedipus to leave the sight of sensible reality for the sight of intelligible reality that would serve awareness and differentiation. Here Tiresias plays an important role asking Oedipus to become aware of the two conditions of being blind. To distinguish by the blind that sees and the sighted that does not see.

Tiresias in the movie says:

> ...you hold my nature against me and reproach me, and you do not want to know the nature that is in you. The facts will speak even if I say nothing. Look at yourself! You are the murderer you are looking for...and you don't want to see the evil in you.... I don't depend on you but on God ....and I say to you: you look and you don't see all the shame and evil you are in. One day you will see only darkness, the day you will understand who you had been married to oh son of fortune.

Tiresias invites us to know one's own history in order to differentiate oneself from the incestual element, but Oedipus does not want to do so and so becomes blind. How can we not remember the blindness of Salome!

The Shadow of the Soul

The Shadow of the Soul is a concept Jung analyses in the *Black Books* (2021). The Soul speaks and on July 10, 1918 asks the question,

> My soul, what is happening? What sets me at odds with myself? What tears asunder?[18]

> Replies

> S. Poisoning by the earth spirits.[19]....

> S. The black one has an earth spirit with her, a spirit of the dead, who would like to live. He sucks force from you. He would like to come to life. She can't help it. She can do nothing about it, only you can. It is to be stood up to. You have still not tried everything, you have still not done everything.

> I....Does the black one have a spirit in her? Or is not rather something in me?

> S. Spirits are always between two people. They live from the relation of two people.... The spirits must be removed from a relation, so that they can die

> I. but how?...

> S. ...the how is not easy. It turns around and around and seeks an opening ... the spirit is this how. The spirit from the dead live from this how. Where there is a how, the unredeemed spirits gather....as long as men don't now the how, the spirits devour us.

> I. So help me...

> S. ... My other half, which is on the side of the earth, is another soul than I. She is between things and you. I am between the eternal image and you. I am mind, she is feeling. I am light, she is dark. The black one is her symbol. You have still not released Salome from her. She is the spirit of the earth that dances poisonous

---

[18] Black Books 7 p.185
[19] ibdm

dances. That bewitches and intoxicates, that drinks blood and causes magical sickness…. Why do you love the black one? Because she is the dancer?[20]

A noise at the door and the soul continues.

S. …she is a fire of voluptuousness and torment of voluptuousness. She is beautiful like hell. She gives pleasure and the craving for poison… she is hellish temptation. She is the compulsion of suffering. I am eternal contemplation. … she is the womb of the earth. Actual forms grow from her, but the eternal images grow from me[21].

I. Yet how can I release her.

S. How did you release me? Only differentiating me from reality. How will you release her? Only through differentiating her from reality. If you experience torment, then call her and ask her, as you call and ask me. What did I give you? I gave you the eternal images. She will also give it to you, if you differentiate her from reality and ask her and force her to speech and answer, as you forced me. I tormented you with impotent rage. She torments you with impotent pleasure and helpless longing. Call her and listen to what she says[22].

The emergence of the Soul and its Shadow leads us to reflect on how in the *Red Book* (2009) Salome is initially blind and is the Soul of I, Jung's avatar. It will take a long journey through the mysteries[23] and exploration of the demonic and finally numinous and diamonic components attached to her and Elijah's figure, before Salome regains sight and with it redeems or frees I's Soul from compulsion.

In our interpretation, the Soul Salome is the Shadow of the Soul that is to be recognized and redeemed, and, in particular, the two aspects of the soul, the spiritual function and the spirit of the dead, are to be recognized in their different aspects. In the *Black Books* the Soul dwells on how to redeem its form and how to unite contemplation, suffering, and pleasure. Moreover, the indication of how to redeem and integrate the aspects of the Soul and its Shadow are clearly stated in the clarification: *only by differentiating from reality, only by recognizing impotent anger and impotent pleasure-seeking and desire…call it and listen to what it tells you.* So, it is a process of differentiation that leads to the integration of both positive and negative aspects of different psychic functions. It is important to understand this dimension by approaching Psychological Types and, in particular, the construction of the 8/16 types or patterns of typological functions

---

[20] BB7 p. 186
[21] Ibdm
[22] Ibdm p. 187
[23] Jung C.G., *Misterium*, on The Red Book

that Beebe developed in his *Energy and Patterns in Psychological Type* (2016). According to Beebe, for each type there is an opposite personality, each type has its own shadow. But the 16 types are all present in each of us, so we cannot overlook the reverberation of the shadow aspects on the more conscious personality.

For example, the Soul as an inferior function stimulates the development and transformation of the personality: it is in this sense daimonic because it is in contact with numinous aspects. The unacknowledged Shadow of the Soul, is subtracting the transformative and creative energies, as said in the dialogue above: *"the black has with it a spirit of the earth, a spirit of the dead, which ...sucks the force from you."*

The imprisonment of the Soul in its Shadow brings us back to Oedipus' difficulty in differentiating the identification of the mother with the Soul and, consequently, the impossibility of breaking out of the yoke of repetition of something that has already been written by the psychological patterns inherited from both father and mother, which are also culturally determined.

This is the process of differentiation that take place in the course of adolescence towards adulthood: separation from the parental complexes, as we said, at the beginning or like in Pasolini film in becoming aware of the transformations taking place in our civilization. The implication being that the individual psyche has to break the incestual chains in which it is imprisoned in a repletion of schemata that want us to be subjected to the dominant collective stereotype. Paraphrasing Oedipus journey in the process towards differentiation, it is necessary to recover one's own history to get free from incestual ghosts and the spirit of the ancestors. Oedipus should be able to differentiate between the figures that are the source of the trauma and not idealize them, otherwise in doing so, the incestual transmission will continue.

Conclusion: what are the implications for Western society?

Pasolini asks, how can a society that has come out of two world wars, Nazism, and Fascism set out on a path where spiritual values, as recalled by Tiresias, can be denied in favor of an illusion that devalues human life and equality. Our society, like Oedipus, fails to differentiate between the development of an ethical and moral world and the illusion of material wealth. The unacknowledged Shadow of the Soul becomes the opposite personality where the daimon becomes demon and blindness reigns unchallenged.

Marx writes, *"Men make their own history, but they do not make it as they please; ... The tradition of all dead generations weighs like a nightmare on the brains of the living."* (1851, p. 102)

This observation concerning controlling minds obviously has many implications with respect to the influence of collective and personal history on the implicit patterns that control the collective, and it is what Benjamin and Derrida tried (in different ways) to analyze.

If the problem of Oedipus is the path of the subject toward differentiation, the message captured in Pasolini's film is this: unconscious forces demand the redemption of archaic parts of our psyche. Further, we require integration of elements that the collective consciousness tends to exclude because the primacy of the function exercised by the dominant collective power.

In our case, Pasolini's critique teaches that knowing Oedipus and how and why his differentiation failed is a task that never ends and concerns not only the individual, but also the society that seeks blindness indulging in the illusion of wealth.

Pasolini's Oedipus reads in the movie: *"O light I could no longer see, which before was somehow mine. Now enlighten me for the last time. I have come. Life ends where it begins"*

The process of integration and de-integration that begins at birth with the initial differentiations of the primary self continues with varying intensities throughout life. Just as the process of individuation is continuous, the differentiation of subjectivity is a path that also continues on. Questioning dominant thought, signified by Oedipus, both in the political and psychological sense, cannot be stopped on pain of becoming blind.

As Jung teaches us, the mythopoetic language of the unconscious urges us to find our own personal myth so as not to fall victim to the myths of others or imposed by collective thinking.

References

Beebe, J. (2016). *Energy and Patterns in Psychological Type: The reservoir of consciousness*, Routledge.

Benjamin, W. (2016). *On the Concept of History*. Createspace Independent Publishing Platform.

Benjamin, W. (2019). *Illuminations: Essays and reflections*. Mariners Book.

Lanius, R.; Vermetten, E.; Pain, C. (Eds.) (2010). *The Impact of Early Life Trauma on Health and Disease: The hidden epidemic*. Cambridge University Press.

Racamier P. C. (2003). *Incesto ed incestuale*. Franco Angeli, Milano.

Jung, C.G. (1967). *Symbols of Transformation*. C.W. Vol. 5, Princeton University Press.

Jung ,C.G. (1974). *Psychological Types*. C.W. Vol. 6, Princeton University Press.

Jung, C.G. (1989). *Memories Dreams Reflections*. Publisher Vintage.

Jung, C.G. (1970). *Civilization in Transition* (1930) in C.W. Vol 10, Princeton University Press.

Jung, C.G. (2009). *The Red Book: Liber novus*, W.W. Norton & Co.

Jung, C.G., (2020). *The Black Books:1913-1932*. W.W. Norton & Co.

Marx, C. (1994). *The Eighteenth Brumaire of Louis Bonaparte*. (Originally published 1851). International Publishers Co.

Rilke, R.M. (2009). *Duino Elegies and The Sonnets to Orpheus*. Stephen Mitchell.

Rilke, R.M. on https://rilkepoetry.com/duino-elegies/first-duino-elegy/

Pasolini, P.P., *Oedipus Rex*, Film in Blu -ray, Eureka, 2012

Pasolini, P.P. (2011). *Scritti corsari*. Garzanti, Milano.

Shakespeare. (1992). *Hamlet*. Simon & Schuster.

Stern D. (1985). *The Interpersonal World of the Infant. A view from psychoanalysis and developmental psychology*. Routledge.

Stern D. (2004). *The Present Moment in Psychotherapy and Everyday Life*, W.W. Norton & Company.

The time is out of Joint: Edipo Re di Pasolini

Caterina Vezzoli e Livia Di Stefano

Abstract

In questo lavoro siamo partite dalla rivisitazione filmica della tragedia di Sofocle Edipo Re da parte del regista e poeta italiano Pier Paolo Pasolini. Il film ha ispirato il nostro tentativo di effettuare una decostruzione della narrazione della tragedia sofoclea in modo da chiarire gli effetti dell'incesto e della dinamica incestuale nella società odierna e nello sviluppo individuale e collettivo. Partendo dalla concezione junghiana di incesto come dimensione simbolica e parte del processo individuativo verso la formazione di una personalità differenziata dai complessi parentali, abbiamo amplificato mettendo in relazione la non elaborazione della storia personale e collettiva dei segreti incestuali con la reiterazione del mantenimento patologico di modalità che replicano il vecchio status quo con ampie ripercussioni sull'individuo, sulla cultura e sulla società in generale. Un ulteriore decostruzione ci ha portato a considerare la tragedia di Edipo come possibilità di tornare alle origini e mettere in discussione la civiltà patriarcale confrontandoci con aspetti arcaici presenti in noi stessi, nella società e cultura che ci circonda. In questo percorso il film e la personalità di Pasolini ci sono stati di aiuto per mostrare la necessità di un cambio di visione, ben espressa dal celebre verso nell'Amleto the time is out of joint ad intendere la possibilità di un'interruzione del pensiero per rielaborare e far emergere gli impliciti mai svelati prima che sono stati oppressi storicamente e spiritualmente dalla classe dominante. La nostra trasposizione con il film consiste nell'utilizzare l'opera d'arte per esplorare la frattura creativa e lasciare che i possibili significati emergano in noi per manifestare un potenziale trasformativo. Così, la frattura temporale che Pasolini introduce nella sua narrazione racconta il nostro presente alla luce del passato che dovrebbe illuminarci per non tornare alla cecità della generazione che ci ha appena preceduto. Per Pasolini la società italiana dopo le due guerre mondiali e la trasformazione della società italiana da realtà agricola a realtà industriale e di consumo, per noi la realtà della pandemia e lo scoppio della guerra in Ucraina.

Se il problema di Edipo è il percorso del soggetto verso la differenziazione, il messaggio che si coglie nel film di Pasolini e che la teoria junghiana ci aiuta a chiarire è che le forze inconsce richiedono la redenzione di parti arcaiche della nostra psiche e di integrare gli elementi che la coscienza collettiva tende a escludere perché dominata da una funzione dominante collettiva di potere. In questo scritto chiariamo come conoscere Edipo e come e perché la sua differenziazione è fallita è un compito che non finisce mai e riguarda non solo l'individuo ma anche la società che cerca la cecità per assecondare l'illusione della ricchezza.

Introduzione

Nel suo film *Edipo Re*[24], Pasolini riscrive la storia del mito di Edipo dal suo punto di vista di sceneggiatore e regista. Alla fine degli anni Sessanta Pasolini era consapevole che il paesaggio sociale italiano era cambiato da un paese tradizionalmente agricolo a una società industriale consumistica. La visione di Pasolini di questa trasformazione va alle radici del sistema politico italiano e di come la società, in generale, sia cieca di fronte alle conseguenze di questo cambiamento epocale.

Il suo film ha ispirato il nostro tentativo di includere un'ulteriore decostruzione[25] della narrazione della tragedia Edipo Re di Sofocle. Abbiamo cercato di pensare "oltre l'Edipo", considerando però che quando utilizziamo un'amplificazione dalla letteratura o dall'arte verso il campo clinico, dobbiamo mantenere una coerenza con le questioni cliniche che vogliamo indagare. In questo caso, il nostro obiettivo è chiarire gli effetti dell'incesto e della dinamica *incestuale* nella società, nello sviluppo degli individui e nel processo di individuazione.

Pensare a Edipo significa pensare all'incesto, all'incestuoso e all'incestuale secondo la definizione di Racamier: *incestuale* è un neologismo che descrive una condizione specifica della vita psichica e relazionale in cui l'incesto, non agito, aleggia nell'atmosfera emotiva di un paziente, di una famiglia o di un gruppo di lavoro, lasciando la sua impronta. *L'incestuale è un'atmosfera in cui soffia il vento dell'incesto senza che vi sia incesto. Ovunque arrivino le sue raffiche, si crea un deserto, si instilla il sospetto, il silenzio e il segreto* (Racamier P. C., 2003).

Questo punto di vista ci sembra interessante per avvicinarci alle teorie della moderna letteratura, junghiana e non, sulla separazione dalle figure genitoriali che evidenziano come proprio la non separazione incestuale contamini la vita non solo dell'individuo ma anche delle generazioni a venire. Nella nostra amplificazione cercheremo di mettere in relazione il modo in cui la non elaborazione della storia personale e collettiva dei segreti incestuali porti alla reiterazione del mantenimento patologico di modalità che replicano il vecchio status quo sia a livello sia individuale che collettivo.

Jung e l'incesto

Cominciamo col dire che cos'è l'incesto per Jung o meglio quale aspetto prenderemo in considerazione.

Per Jung, l'incesto va inteso come una dimensione simbolica di regressione al materno e, a livello intrapsichico, all'inconscio. Come egli ha affermato in *Simboli della trasformazione* (1912)

---

[24] Edipo Re, versione gratuita su YouTube: https://youtu.be/iT8xtiMQYy8

[25] Ci si riferisce al *decostruzionismo o decostruttivismo* quale concetto introdotto nella filosofia occidentale da Jacques Derrida. Può essere descritto come confronto serrato con i testi e gli autori nell'intento di mettere in luce i presupposti impliciti, i pregiudizi nascosti, le contraddizioni latenti della cultura e del linguaggio che, non troppo consapevolmente, l'uomo adotta. Rif.Wikipedia

analizzando il materiale della signorina Miller, la regressione non è necessariamente patologica perché si può regredire alla dimensione inconscia materna per recuperare l'energia perduta. In questo senso, il ritorno alla madre è un ritorno alle immagini archetipiche inconsce da cui riemergere con nuova energia e nuove risposte: "reculer pour mieux sauter"[26] (ibidem pag. 349).

In Tipi psicologici (1921) Jung fa un esplicito riferimento al complesso di Edipo di Freud quando a pag. 132 specifica che la regressione alle "immagini genitoriali" è una simbolizzazione e *poichè la regressione, accettando il simbolo come simbolo reale, si tramuta tosto in progressione … sarebbe rimasta regressione se fosse stato …un segno per i genitori concreti e spogliato del suo carattere autonomo.*

In questo senso, Jung non esclude l'incesto come reale ma, inteso come simbolo, fa parte del percorso individuativo che richiede la separazione dai genitori reali altrimenti le parti dei complessi parentali che condizionano lo sviluppo dell'individuo porteranno alla dissociazione. La struttura dei complessi ha aree traumatiche non integrabili che, quando nel processo di sviluppo si costellano, possono portare alla dissociazione cosi ché le parti del complesso dissociate diventano autonome. Sono le *splinter psyche* che portano allo sviluppo di personalità secondarie e quindi non alla differenziazione verso l'individuazione ma alla creazione di un falso sé. A livello collettivo la non differenziazione ha delle ripercussioni sulla cultura e sulla società in generale, quindi la trasgressione alla cultura dominante diventa una necessità se dobbiamo separarci dalla visione genitoriale del mondo.

Riconsiderare la tragedia di Edipo potrebbe significare tornare alle origini e mettere in discussione la civiltà patriarcale confrontandoci con aspetti arcaici presenti in noi stessi, nella società e cultura che ci circonda.

Da questo punto di vista, affrontare il complesso di Edipo sarebbe un invito a mettere in discussione il vaticinio dell'oracolo e a capovolgerlo o, potremmo dire riferendoci al simbolo come lo intende Jung, sarebbe riattivare o riscoprire il simbolo o il mito in una nuova forma.

Ancora una volta, in Tipi psicologici Jung dice che

l'umanità, assumendo il simbolo come realtà… [crea] i suoi dei… e la concretezza del pensiero che ha reso l'uomo signore della terra.

Il simbolo quindi non è più *la risultante sintetica di tutti i fattori inconsci*, non è più la *forma vivente*, ha perso il suo valore simbolico e, reificato, perde la sua capacità di trascendere la realtà e diventa un segno (ibidem pag. 193).

---

[26] Trad. it. *Fare un passo indietro per fare il salto*

La perdita dei *fattori inconsci* è il mancato riconoscimento dei traumi sepolti nell'inconscio e, se come dice Lanius (2016) "la nostra è una società traumatizzata", allora non possiamo fare a meno di considerare che nel passaggio dall'adolescenza all'età adulta si ripresenteranno i traumi irrisolti e sarà problematica la separazione da figure genitoriali carenti. Quali strumenti utilizzare?

L'Edipo re di Pasolini

Abbiamo scelto per la nostra amplificazione un'opera d'arte come il film di Pasolini non per interpretare ma per provare a lasciar emergere altri significati e, nella frustrante realtà di oggi in cui lo *spirito del tempo* è così sconfortante, speriamo che lo *spirito del profondo* possa guidarci.

Per la sua narrazione filmica Pasolini sceglie, la Pianura Padana, la campagna lodigiana[27], come luogo di nascita di Edipo; i paesaggi della Grecia mitologica, invece, sono girati in Marocco principalmente in zone desertiche e in accampamenti di nomadi.

Emerge immediatamente la necessità di far incontrare il personale della geografia esistenziale del poeta con l'arcaicità collettiva di luoghi che mantengono, nel presente, schemi archetipicamente fondati. La giustapposizione e l'allargamento dello spazio-tempo diventa una dimensione mitica, in cui presente, passato e futuro si intrecciano e si invertono.

La nostra prima notazione riguarda le trasposizioni tra passato e presente e partiremo dalla figura di Angelo come accompagnatore che Pasolini colloca accanto al suo novello Edipo nella Piazza Maggiore di Bologna[28]. Angelo ha fatto risuonare in noi il testo di Benjamin *Angelus Novo* (2014). Per Benjamin, la storiografia materialista si differenzia dallo storicismo perché ha alla base un principio che non è la temporalità dello storicismo:

> *Il passato reca con sé un indice segreto che lo rinvia alla redenzione. Non sfiora forse anche noi un soffio dell'aria che spirava attorno a quelli prima di noi? Non c'è, nelle voci cui prestiamo ascolto, un'eco di voci ora mute? ... Se è così, allora esiste un appuntamento misterioso tra le generazioni che sono state e la nostra. Allora noi siamo stati attesi sulla terra. Allora a noi, come ad ogni generazione che fu prima di noi, è stata consegnata una debole forza messianica, a cui il passato ha diritto.* Questa esigenza non si lascia soddisfare facilmente. Il materialista storico lo sa. (Benjamin 2014 pag. 75-86).

Come usare la debole forza messianica per redimere il passato? Benjamin (1997) dice che per il materialismo la chance rivoluzionaria[29] si crea quando le tensioni di forze contrastanti formano una monade in cui le idee si cristallizzano e creano un arresto nella ripetizione della temporalità

---

[27] Sono questi luoghi dove Pasolini trascorse parte dell'infanzia
[28] Bologna è la città dove Pasolini nacque nel 1922
[29] è un linguaggio d'altri tempi... che ci piace ancora

della storia. La monade è, cioè, un evento che arresta il pensiero dominante: per esempio, l'evento della guerra in Ucraina interrompe l'idea dominante che la Russia abbia troppi interessi finanziari per fare la guerra.

Benjamin fa riferimento al debole compito messianico della generazione che deve affrontare il vuoto dell'assunto dominante per trovare una risposta diversa alla cieca ripetizione dello status quo che ancora domina le generazioni attuali.

Secondo l'evento, inteso in senso derridiano, si crea un'interruzione del pensiero e si introduce la possibilità di rielaborare come esplicita la metafora coniata dall'Amleto di Shakespeare: *the time is out of joint*[30] e gli spettri possono entrare nel mondo dei vivi. Come già accennato precedentemente, ci stiamo avvicinando ad un ambito che non è quello costruttivista ma piuttosto aperto al divenire e alla destrutturazione della realtà che permette l'emergere del nuovo.

Ecco che Angelo diviene qui *l'angelo tremendo* di rilkeana (2020)[31] memoria, non più un accompagnatore ma un mediatore tra mondi che è testimone dell'emergere di un'altra realtà. Tremendo quindi perché porta l'orrore religioso della bellezza:

Poiché il bello non è nulla,
null'altro che, del terribile, principio che noi appena sopportiamo ancora,
e tanto lo ammiriamo, perché esso disdegna, quieto,
di distruggerci. Ogni angelo è tremendo.

È quindi una possibilità di riflessione, di cambio di visione. Dalla frattura temporale che si è creata emergeranno gli impliciti mai svelati prima e che sono stati oppressi storicamente e spiritualmente dalla classe dominante. In questa condizione, l'implicito potrebbe manifestare un potenziale trasformativo. Si crea, quindi, una chance rivoluzionaria nella lotta per riscattare il passato oppresso così trasmesso dalla classe che scrive la storia dal punto di vista della dominazione e vuole mantenere lo status quo e impedire che la storia sia raccontata dal punto di vista dei subalterni.

Psicologicamente non possiamo dimenticare che ogni potenziale *daimonico*[32] può diventare demoniaco: il *daimonico* infatti, può essere trasformato in possessione e quindi diventare demoniaco. Questo intercalare serve a chiarire che il pensiero dominante diviene facilmente demoniaco perché finisce con l'intendere lo spirito come al servizio del potere impedendo così lo sviluppo della potenziale carica numinosa del pensiero alternativo. Il processo di degradazione del pensiero è costante se non lasciamo emergere i contenuti inconsci non ancora formulati sospesi nel regno dell'inconscio psicoide.

---

[30] Shakespeare, *Amleto*, atto I scena 5
[31] R.M., Rilke *Elegie Duinesi*. I Elegia
[32] Ci si riferisce al termine filosofico *daimon* e alla teoria hillmaniana in proposito

La nostra trasposizione con il film di Pasolini consiste nell'utilizzare l'opera d'arte per esplorare la frattura creativa e lasciare che i possibili significati emergano in noi come osservatori partecipanti. La funzione visionaria dell'opera d'arte[33] dà forma agli interrogativi e mobilita la ricerca di risposte che emergono dalla psiche inconscia e vengono tradotte in termini appunto visionari. Ecco perché, non interpretiamo l'opera di Pasolini, ma cerchiamo di dare spazio e presenza ai contenuti inconsci che sottendono alle immagini che racchiudono e, allo stesso tempo, di rivelare nuove possibili comprensioni.

Così, la frattura temporale che Pasolini introduce nella sua narrazione filmica è una rivisitazione dell'Edipo Re che racconta il "nostro presente", il tempo attuale di Pasolini come il nostro, alla luce del passato che dovrebbe illuminarci per non tornare alla cecità della generazione che ci ha appena preceduto. Per Pasolini la società italiana dopo le due guerre mondiali e la trasformazione della società italiana da realtà agricola a realtà industriale e di consumo, per noi la realtà della pandemia e lo scoppio della guerra in Ucraina.

Chi è l'Edipo di Pasolini?

L'Edipo di Pasolini, come quello della tragedia, nasce in una classe agiata. Così, l'immagine di partenza sono i pioppi della pianura, i prati verdi, il bambino sdraiato sulla coperta che sgambetta felice al sole e le giovani donne che si rincorrono.

La scena ricorda molto quella che Jung descrive quando, in *Memorie, sogni, riflessioni* (2012), ricorda di essere in una carrozzina per bambini e il piacere del calore del sole, del sapore del latte e della giovane cameriera che si prendeva cura di lui. Jung, all'età di 80 anni, racconta l'episodio come la sua prima consapevolezza di sé. Un RIG[34] direbbe Stern, che diventerà un *now moment*[35].

Per noi questo inizio è sia un'associazione personale alla biografia di Pasolini, che è nato a Bologna, sia alla narrazione che l'autore seguirà nello svolgimento del film: un ricordo che si collocherà all'interno del complesso materno come elemento non pienamente cosciente in connessione con l'inconscio personale e collettivo.

---

[33] Ci si riferisce alle teorie di Jung sulla funzione visionaria dell'immaginazione vedi Jung C.G., Opere vol X tomo I, 1985

[34] Per RIG Stern (1987) intende delle Rappresentazioni di Interazioni che sono state Generalizzate, unità di base, singole esperienze, che poi vengono combinate in *reti* riguardanti il cibo, la madre, la fiducia. Queste prime generalizzazioni si trasformeranno col tempo in ricordi semantici che potranno essere espressi verbalmente. Tali rappresentazioni, esperienze, prototipi e valenze affettive si consolidano in strutture stabili di autoregolazione e rapporto con la realtà.

[35] Il Now Moment o Present Moment è secondo Stern *ciò che sta accadendo ora nella relazione*, è il momento del cambiamento creativo. "*E' il momento di esperienza affettiva soggettiva nell'atto del suo compiersi, così come viene vissuta non dopo quando viene riformulata a parole o ripensata*" (2005)

È infatti con l'emergere di questi primi ricordi che l'inconscio decostruisce per noi, attraverso i sogni e le immagini archetipiche, le storie inconsce da cui deriviamo e che portiamo con noi fin dall'inizio. In un certo senso, l'inconscio, come i miti, pone le storie in modo enigmatico e ci chiede di decostruirle e di farne una storia personale. Nel mito e nel film di Pasolini, Edipo cerca di conoscere la sua storia e di esserne l'artefice, ma ci sono troppi segreti e molti dilemmi irrisolti che vengono disseminati sul suo cammino.

La relazione di Edipo con la madre è totalizzante ma non lo prepara all'arrivo del padre; vivere in un mondo di sole donne è idilliaco ma quando il padre arriva, porta con sé la guerra. Nel film egli arriva vestito da ufficiale della Prima Guerra Mondiale: la guerra delle trincee, del gas nervino e di milioni di morti i cui orrori sono stati rivelati solo di recente. Ma anche se si trattasse della Seconda Guerra Mondiale o dell'attuale invasione dell'Ucraina, sarebbe lo stesso. Le immagini della guerra che passano ogni sera sui nostri schermi televisivi sono come quelle dei film di guerra che siamo abituati a vedere, per cui attiviamo una difesa in noi che guarda alle devastazioni come a qualche altra realtà, non così vicina alle nostre case.

Se negli occhi della madre Edipo legge la cura e il nutrimento, negli occhi del padre cosa legge? Diffidenza, competizione, rancore, forse è questo a cui la guerra abitua gli uomini che la combattono e che portano a casa con sé? Così i traumi ci seguono e si rincorrono per generazioni.

Edipo diventa l'emarginato, viene lasciato solo e sperimenta la guerra che il padre si porta dentro, la vive attraverso il rumore per lui spaventoso dei fuochi d'artificio.

Il fatto che la madre non lo proteggesse più era perchè per lei era stato un investimento narcisistico? Forse. Ma un tale approccio che interpreta invece di amplificare non è il nostro.

Il *figlio della fortuna*, come verrà chiamato nel film, sopravvive e troverà un altro padre e un'altra madre, ma i sogni lo perseguitano e vogliono risposte.

Non importa che trovi in Polibo un padre giocoso e affettuoso, la macchia del rifiuto, il trauma del rifiuto rimane irrisolto, la ferita inferta ai suoi piedi è inaccettabile e non c'è bisogno di negarlo tutti sanno che è il figlio trovatello della fortuna, non può nascondersi, ha vergogna.

Lascia la sua famiglia adottiva in cerca di risposte. La risposta che trova lo spinge verso la disperazione e sulla strada che lo porterà a incontrare lo stesso destino a cui cerca di sfuggire.

Non sono poche le domande da porsi sugli oracoli e sugli dei greci, le verità che dicono sono così criptiche che spingono il malcapitato verso la catastrofe.

Non danno alcuna chance!

Parafrasando Benjamin (1997), il potere dominante non vuole essere messo in discussione, le tensioni derivanti dalle lotte contro il pensiero dominante possono non essere sufficienti a creare una costellazione che destabilizzi l'immobilità del tempo storico e dia voce al represso. La *debole forza messianica* può essere veicolata da un pensiero che emerge da quello insaturo delle tragedie, e quindi l'arte, può mettere in luce il male sul quale si regge il potere che traumatizza.

Il padre assassino che Edipo incontra sulla via di Tebe non è cambiato: è l'assassino pusillanime che manda altri a morire. Edipo, tuttavia, è vittima della stessa dinamica e, invece di decostruire dentro di sé l'imago parentale, uccide il genitore reale e così il suo trauma non si risolve, anzi si aggrava. Edipo agisce una pulsione, non riesce a differenziarsi dal suo background incestuoso sepolto nello strato più profondo della sua psiche, è preda di una dinamica inconscia ed arcaica che viene agita ma non riconosciuta.

Questo è ciò che spesso accade agli adolescenti che non riescono a separarsi dalle dinamiche incestuose che li trattengono anche se sono stati sottratti ai genitori e adottati o parzialmente protetti. Ma nel cammino di vita ci si imbatte sovente in ciò che permette il cambiamento nel bene o nel male....

Edipo incontra la Sfinge

Nel film Pasolini inserisce una novità nell'incontro, omettendo di ripercorrere la classica esposizione dell'enigma da risolvere per spaziare nella conflittualità del guardarsi dentro.

È il momento decisivo del film, la Sfinge parla con la voce di Edipo; è Edipo stesso, cioè la voce del suo profondo che lo richiama al viaggio interiore e non solo a quello eroico. La Sfinge lo lascia passare ed Edipo si illude di aver finalmente trovato il suo posto. Ma ciò che la Sfinge di Pasolini aveva predetto *non puoi ricacciarmi nell'abisso, l'abisso è dentro di te* sta presentando il conto.

Il premio del matrimonio con la madre è la regressione alla madre-inconscio e, come abbiamo visto, potrebbe essere parte di un percorso che però richiede differenziazione e sacrificio dell'onnipotenza ed Edipo non sembra pronto.

Significativo per noi è il dialogo in cui Pasolini attore chiede a Edipo, per liberare il suo popolo e liberarsi *dall'oppressione del pensiero che ripete ciecamente il già noto* (Benjamin 1997), di trovare la risposta per liberare Tebe dalla peste.

Pasolini come sacerdote o rappresentante dei cittadini implora il suo re Edipo:

Se noi, questi figlioli e Io, siamo qui a pregarti davanti al tuo focolare, non è certo perché ti giudichiamo come un Dio. Non sei stato tu appena giunto in questa città che ci hai liberato dall'incubo della sfinge? E tu quest'opera non l'hai compiuta perché sapessi più di noi ma come dicono tutti, con l'aiuto di un Dio.

E perciò Edipo nostro re, noi tutti ti scongiuriamo in ginocchio: trovaci un rimedio, non importa quale sia, che te lo suggerisca un Dio o un uomo come noi.

Tu che sei il migliore di tutti noi, ridacci un'altra volta la vita. Fa che non rimanga in noi vivo il ricordo del tuo regno per essere stati sollevati prima e poi di nuovo ricaduti.

La supplica del sacerdote fa appello all'umanità di Edipo. Pasolini incita il suo Edipo ad addentrarsi nel suo mondo interiore, a non abbandonarsi alla peste, a cercare la risposta; gli chiede di sfidare il destino dell'oppresso affermando il suo pensiero e di sviscerare il suo sapere di soggetto sofferente.

Egli ha ucciso per liberarsi dal padre assassino ma poi ne prende inconsapevolmente il posto. Dopo aver ucciso il padre, i padri, dopo aver liberato se stesso e noi dagli stereotipi degli oppressori, ritorna cieco perché non si rende conto di aver tradito se stesso per il possesso del trofeo paterno: la madre.

La vergogna lo opprime per il suo desiderio di regressione ad un mondo illusorio e senza conflitti e così, invischiato in desideri incestuali, Edipo viene richiamato dal suo autore Pasolini a non essere cieco, a differenziarsi.

Il mancato cammino verso la differenziazione

La tragedia ritornando in Piazza Maggiore a Bologna, diventa una critica alla società che dopo essere uscita dalla Seconda Guerra Mondiale, dopo aver sconfitto il fascismo si ritrova con il boom industriale degli anni '60 e '70 a sprofondare negli abissi di quello che anche Pasolini chiamerà "il nuovo capitalismo" e che nel suo film è rappresentato dalla scena finale. Qui ritorniamo alla casa dove Edipo vide la luce: non c'è più una bicicletta che passa sotto le finestre della casa nella piazza con la statua del soldato vittorioso, ma le auto Fiat che segnano il passaggio dalla civiltà contadina a quella industriale e da lì in poi alla legge esclusiva del mercato e della finanza che è il nostro mondo di oggi. Passaggio che già allora Pasolini considerava un fallimento politico e personale.

Pochi mesi prima di essere assassinato, Pasolini pubblicò sul Corriere della Sera l'articolo *La scomparsa delle lucciole. Il vuoto del potere in Italia*[36], in cui lanciava un durissimo attacco polemico alla Democrazia Cristiana, dominatrice indiscussa della vita politica italiana dell'epoca e ancora per molti anni dopo la sua morte. Utilizzando la metafora della morte delle lucciole, egli accusa la classe dirigente al potere di aver promosso un certo modello di sviluppo, di aver organizzato la vita della generazione postbellica senza memoria del passato e di aver inquinato le campagne e le città. Critica la corruzione del potere politico e la tendenza a favorire le lobby più potenti invece di sostenere l'intervento democratico, la vita dei villaggi e delle province brutalmente violentata.

---

[36] Questo articolo è stato inserito nel volume di Pasolini (2011), *Scritti corsari* con il diverso titolo di *L'articolo delle lucciole*

A livello più generale e profondo, si scaglia contro la distruzione dei valori fondamentali di uguaglianza e delle possibilità di una vera democrazia che dovrebbe dare spazio a tutte le culture presenti nel Paese e non solo a quelle della classe dominante.

Nei suoi film, egli ritrova questi valori nei popoli "primitivi" o nei poveri ed emarginati che sono minati dal capitalismo, motivo per cui il suo Edipo diventa un mendicante in Piazza Maggiore. Un altro aspetto interessante che parla alla nostra sensibilità ecologica è la distruzione delle lucciole, che muoiono a causa dell'uso di pesticidi nell'agricoltura che diventa intensiva e contaminata chimicamente.

Pasolini va oltre la semplice critica politica riferita al vuoto di potere per parlare della totale inconsapevolezza del regime politico dominante di tale cambiamento e quindi della cecità e della completa incomprensione del Paese e della società che pure governa. Egli sentiva come suo primario dovere morale, civile e politico quello di richiamare l'attenzione dei suoi contemporanei sulla cecità del potere che porta all'oppressione dello spirito, della bellezza della vita e della natura.

Torniamo qui al tema della cecità e del trauma transgenerazionale e alla necessità di un'analisi profonda e del profondo, personale e collettiva.

Edipo, cecità e transgenerazionale

Da un punto di vista più personale, qual è il significato del viaggio a ritroso del personaggio di Edipo? Qual è il nuovo mito da raccontare... qual'è la nuova narrazione?
Abbiamo ripetuto più volte l'importanza della differenziazione per la crescita e lo sviluppo della soggettività. A nostro avviso il sacerdote Pasolini rivolgendosi al suo personaggio Edipo lo invita a trovare le cause che hanno portato alla peste e non gli chiede di consultare l'oracolo ma di cercare le cause nell'abisso dentro di sé. Gli chiede di differenziare e quindi decostruire gli eventi della sua storia riconoscendone gli elementi transgenerazionali e anche incestuali: il padre Laio pedofilo-omicida e la madre Giocasta vittima ed artefice della prigionia dell'Anima di Edipo.

Il problema di Edipo è quindi che non vede l'Ombra della sua Anima e ne è imprigionato. In questo senso il ritorno inconscio alla madre non è un ritorno per trovare l'energia trasformativa (che poi sarebbe la risposta) bensì è la fusione con l'Ombra materna e l'imprigionamento della funzione animica nella madre.

Importante a questo proposito è la figura di Tiresia che parla di un modo diverso dell'essere ciechi: questi esorta Edipo a lasciare la vista della realtà sensibile per quella della realtà intelligibile che servirebbe all'elevazione della coscienza. Qui Tiresia svolge un ruolo importante nel meccanismo della presa di coscienza che contrappone il cieco vedente al vedente cieco.

Egli dice: *...tu mi rinfacci e mi rimproveri la mia natura e non vuoi conoscere la natura che è in te. I fatti parleranno anche se io non dirò niente. Guardati! Tu sei l'assassino che stai cercando...e non* *vuoi vedere il male che è in te…. io non dipendo da te ma da Dio….e ti dico: tu guardi e non vedi tutta la vergogna e il male in cui ti trovi. Un giorno vedrai solo oscurità, il giorno in cui capirai con chi ti sei sposato figlio della fortuna….*

Tiresia invita a conoscere la propria storia per differenziarsi dagli elementi incestuali, ma Edipo non vuole farlo e così ritorna cieco. Come non ricordare la cecità di Salomè!

L'Ombra dell'Anima

L'Ombra dell'Anima è un concetto che Jung cita nei *Libri neri* (2021).

Nei Libri Neri l'Anima interrogata parla a Io e il 10.VII.18 alla domanda

Anima mia, cosa sta succedendo? Cosa mi mette in contrasto con me stesso? Che cosa mi lacera?

My soul, what is happening? What sets me at odds with myself? What tears asunder?[37]

Risponde

A. Avvelenamento da parte degli spiriti della terra.

Poisoning by the earth spirits.[38]….

A. La nera ha con sé uno spirito della terra, uno spirito dei morti, che vorrebbe vivere. Succhia la forza da te. Vorrebbe tornare in vita. Lei non può evitarlo. Non può farci nulla, solo tu puoi. Bisogna affrontarlo. Non hai ancora provato tutto, non hai ancora fatto tutto.

The black one has an earth spirit with her, a spirit of the dead, who would like to live. He sucks force from you. He would like to come to life. She can't help it. She can do nothing about it, only you can. It is to be stood up to. You have still not tried everything, you have still not done everything

I….La nera ha uno spirito in sé? O non è piuttosto qualcosa in me?

I….*Does the black one have a spirit in her? Or is not rather something in me?*

A. Gli spiriti sono sempre tra due persone. Vivono della relazione tra due persone…. Gli spiriti devono essere rimossi da una relazione, in modo che possano morire.

---

[37] BB 7 p.185
[38] ibdm

S. *Spirits are always between two people. They live from the relation of two people…. The spirits must be removed from a relation, so that they can die*

I. ma come?
I. *but how?...*

A. ... il come non è facile. Gira e rigira e cerca un'apertura... lo spirito è questo come. Lo spirito dei morti vive di questo come. Dove c'è un come, si radunano gli spiriti non redenti.... finché gli uomini non conoscono il come, lo spirito ci divora.

S. *.. the how is not easy. It turns around and around and seeks an opening … the spirit is this how. The spirit from the dead live from this how. Where there is a how, the unredeemed spirits gather….as long as men don't now the how, the spirit devour us.*

I. Allora aiutami...
I. *So help me…*

A. ... L'altra mia metà, che è dalla parte della terra, è un'altra anima rispetto a me. Lei è tra le cose e te. Io sono tra l'immagine eterna e te. Io sono mente, lei è sentimento. Io sono la luce, lei è il buio. Il nero è il suo simbolo. Non hai ancora liberato Salomè da lei. È lo spirito della terra che danza danze velenose. Che ammalia e inebria, che beve sangue e provoca malattie magiche.... Perché ami quella nera? Perché è la danzatrice?

S. *… My other half, which is on the side of the earth, is another soul than I. She is between things and you. I am between the eternal image and you. I am mind, she is feeling. I am light, she is dark. The black one is her symbol. You have still not released Salome from her. She is the spirit of the earth that dances poisonous dances. That bewitches and intoxicates, that drinks blood and causes magical sickness…. Why do you love the black one? Because she is the dancer?*[39]

Un rumore alla porta e l'anima continua

A. ...è un fuoco di voluttà e un tormento di voluttà. È bella come l'inferno. Dà piacere e brama di veleno...è una tentazione infernale. È la costrizione della sofferenza. Io sono l'eterna contemplazione. ... Lei è il grembo della terra. Da lei nascono le forme reali, ma da me nascono le immagini eterne.....

S. *...she is a fire of voluptuousness and torment of voluptuousness. She is beautiful like hell. She gives pleasure and the craving for poison… she is hellish temptation. She is the compulsion of suffering. I am*

---

[39] BB7 p. 186

eternal contemplation. … she is the womb of the earth. Actual forms grow from her, but the eternal images grow from me[40]…..

I. Ma come posso liberarla?
I. *Yet how can I release her?*

A. Come mi ha liberato? Solo differenziandomi dalla realtà. Come la libererai? Solo differenziandola dalla realtà. Se provi tormento, allora chiamala e chiedile, come tu chiami e chiedi a me. Che cosa ti ho dato? Ti ho dato le immagini eterne. Anche lei te le darà, se la differenzierai dalla realtà e le chiederai e la costringerai a parlare e a rispondere, come hai fatto con me. Ti ho tormentato con una rabbia impotente. Lei ti tormenta con un piacere impotente e un desiderio impotente. Chiamala e ascolta quello che ti dice.

S.*How did you release me? Only differentiating me from reality. How will you release her? Only through differentiating her from reality. If you experience torment, then call her and ask her, as you call and ask me. What did I give you? I gave you the eternal images. She will also give you, if you differentiate her from reality and ask her and force her to speech and answer, as you forced me. I tormented you with impotent rage. She torments you with impotent pleasure and helpless longing. Call her and listen to what she says[41].*

L'emergere dell'Anima e della sua Ombra ci porta a riflettere su come nel *Libro Rosso* (2012) Salomè inizialmente è cieca ed è l'Anima di Io, l'avatar di Jung. Sarà necessario un lungo percorso attraverso i misteri e l'esplorazione delle componenti mortifere demoniache e infine numinose e daimoniche legate alla sua figura e a quella di Elia, prima che Salomè recuperi la vista e con essa redima o liberi l'Anima di Jung dalla compulsione.

Nella nostra interpretazione l'Anima Salomè è l'Ombra dell'Anima che va riconosciuta e redenta e, in particolare, i due aspetti dell'Anima la funzione spirituale e lo spirito dei morti vanno riconosciuti nei loro diversi aspetti. Nei *Libri neri* l'Anima si sofferma su come redimere la sua forma e come unire contemplazione, sofferenza e piacere. Peraltro l'indicazione del come redimere ed integrare gli aspetti dell'Anima e la sua Ombra sono chiaramente indicati nella precisazione: *solo differenziando dalla realtà, solo riconoscendo la rabbia impotente e la ricerca del piacere e desiderio impotente…chiamala e ascolta quello che ti dice.* Quindi, si tratta di un processo di differenziazione che porta all'integrazione degli aspetti sia positivi che negativi delle diverse funzioni psichiche. Per comprendere tale dimensione, è importante avvicinare i Tipi psicologici e, in particolare, la costruzione delle 8/16 tipologie o schemi di funzioni tipologiche che Beebe ha sviluppato nel suo *Energy and Patterns in Psychological Type* (2016). Secondo Beebe, per ogni tipologia esiste una personalità opposta, cioè ogni tipologia ha la sua ombra. Ma le 16 tipologie

---

[40] ibdm
[41] Ibdm p.187

sono tutte presenti in ognuno di noi e non possiamo quindi tralasciare la riverberazione degli aspetti d'Ombra sulla personalità più cosciente.

Così ad esempio, l'Anima come funzione inferiore permette di stimolare lo sviluppo e la trasformazione della personalità: è in questo senso daimonica perché in contatto con aspetti numinosi. L'Ombra dell'Anima non riconosciuta, come citato nel dialogo di cui sopra, spinge ad agire nella realtà risucchiando le energie trasformative e creative: *la nera ha con sé uno spirito della terra, uno spirito dei morti, che ...succhia la forza da te.*

L'imprigionamento dell'Anima nella sua Ombra ci riporta alla difficoltà di Edipo a differenziare l'identificazione della madre con l'Anima e, di conseguenza, all'impossibilità di uscire dal giogo della ripetizione di qualcosa che è già stato scritto dai modelli psicologici ereditati sia dal padre che dalla madre che sono anche culturalmente determinati.

Questo è il processo di differenziazione che avviene nel corso di tutta la vita e nel passaggio dall'adolescenza verso l'età adulta: la separazione dai complessi parentali, come abbiamo detto all'inizio o come nel film di Pasolini, consiste nel prendere coscienza delle trasformazioni in atto nella nostra civiltà. L'implicazione è che la psiche individuale deve rompere le catene incestuali in cui è imprigionata in un ripetersi di schemi che ci vogliono sottomessi allo stereotipo collettivo dominante. Parafrasando il viaggio di Edipo come processo di differenziazione, è necessario separarsi dalle figure genitoriali interiorizzate che non sono solo i genitori reali ma anche i genitori archetipici, recuperare la propria storia per liberarsi dai fantasmi incestuali e dallo spirito degli antenati. Edipo dovrebbe essere in grado di differenziare le figure che sono all'origine del trauma e non idealizzarle, perché altrimenti continua la trasmissione incestuale.

Conclusioni: quali implicazioni per la società occidentale?

Come già accennato, Pasolini si pone il problema di come una società uscita da due guerre mondiali, che ha conosciuto il nazismo e il fascismo, tragici esempi di incapacità di differenziazione, possa a soli 25 anni dalla fine dell'ultima guerra, incamminarsi su un percorso in cui i valori spirituali, richiamati da Tiresia, possano essere misconosciuti a favore di un'illusione che torna a svalutare la vita umana e l'uguaglianza verso valori effimeri legati alla parzialità del mercato e alla crescita continua ed illusoria dello stesso. La nostra società, così come Edipo, non riesce a distinguere tra lo sviluppo di un mondo eticamente e moralmente consapevole e la mortifera illusione della ricchezza materiale: l'Ombra dell'Anima non riconosciuta diventa la personalità opposta dove il *daimon* diventa demone e la cecità regna incontrastata.

L'autore Pasolini sembra conoscere le parole di Marx:

Gli uomini fanno la loro storia, ma non la fanno a loro piacimento... La tradizione di tutte le generazioni morte pesa come un incubo sul cervello dei vivi. (Marx 2015, 102)

Questa osservazione sulla possessione che controlla le menti ha ovviamente molte implicazioni rispetto all'influenza della storia collettiva e personale sugli impliciti che controllano la collettività, ed è ciò che Benjamin e dopo di lui Derrida cercano in modi diversi di analizzare.

Se il problema di Edipo è il percorso del soggetto verso la differenziazione, il messaggio che si coglie nel film di Pasolini è che le forze inconsce richiedono la redenzione di parti arcaiche della nostra psiche e di integrare gli elementi che la coscienza collettiva tende a escludere perché dominata da una funzione dominante collettiva di potere.

Nel nostro caso, la critica di Pasolini insegna che conoscere Edipo e come e perché la sua differenziazione è fallita è un compito che non finisce mai e riguarda non solo l'individuo ma anche la società che cerca la cecità per assecondare l'illusione del benessere.

L'Edipo di Pasolini recita infine:

O luce che non vedevo più, che prima era in qualche modo mia. Ora mi illumini per l'ultima volta. Sono giunto. La vita finisce dove comincia.

Come nel processo di integrazione e de-integrazione che inizia alla nascita con le differenziazioni iniziali del sé primario e continua con intensità variabile per tutta la vita. Così come il processo di individuazione è continuo, la differenziazione della soggettività è un percorso che continua. La messa in discussione del pensiero dominante, che Edipo rappresenta sia in senso politico che psicologico, non può fermarsi, pena il diventare ciechi.

Come ci insegna Jung, il linguaggio mitopoietico dell'inconscio ci spinge a trovare il nostro mito personale per non cadere vittima dei miti altrui o imposti dal pensiero collettivo.

Bibliografia

Beebe J., *Energy and Patterns in Psychological Type: The reservoir of consciousness*, Routledge, 2016

Benjamin W., *Angelus Novo. Saggi e frammenti*, Einaudi, Torino, 2014

Benjamin W., *Sul concetto di storia*, Einaudi, Torino, 1997

Lanius R., Vermetten E., Pain C., *L'impatto del trauma infantile sulla salute e sulla malattia. L'epidemia nascosta*, Giovanni Fioriti, Roma, 2016

Jung C.G., *Simboli della trasformazione* (1912-1952), in Opere vol.V, Bollati Boringhieri, Torino, 1992

Jung C.G., *Tipi psicologici* (1921), in Opere vol.VI, Bollati Boringhieri, Torino,1996

Jung C.G., *Ricordi, sogni riflessioni*, Rizzoli, Milano, 2012

Jung C.G., *Psicologia analitica e arte poetica* (1930) in Opere vol X tomo I, Boringhieri, Torino, 1985

Jung C.G., *Il libro rosso. Liber novus*, Bollati Boringhieri, Torino, 2012

Jung C.G., *The Black Books:1913-1932*. Notebooks of Transformation, W.W.Norton &Co. 2020

Lago P., *Lo spazio e il deserto nel cinema di Pasolini. Edipo Re, Teorema, Porcile, Medea*, Mimesi, Milano, 2020

Marx C.(1851), *Il 18 di brumaio di Luigi Bonaparte*, Editori Riuniti, Roma, 2015

Pasolini P.P.., *Scritti corsari*, Garzanti, Milano, 2011

Racamier P. C., *Incesto e incestuale*, Franco Angeli, Milano,2003

Rilke R.M., *Elegie Duinesi*, Einaudi, Torino, 2020

Shakespeare W., *Amleto*, Einaudi, Torino, 2019

Stern D. N., *Il momento presente. In psicoterapia e nella vita quotidiana*, Raffaello Cortina, Milano, 2005

Stern D. N., *Il mondo interpersonale del bambino,* Bollati Boringhieri, Torino, 1987

Death and the Analyst: Facing People with AIDS[42]

Paul Attinello

Abstract

In the darkest part of the HIV/AIDS crisis in the urban West, when its impact was clear, but no treatment was available, a number of analysts wrote about their analysands and their own countertransference. Even by the mid-90s, much of the literature focused on containing extreme anxiety, fear, despair – one is struck by their unprepared surprise, by their personal difficulty in engaging with illness and death. This paper focuses on Jungian analysts in the period 1956-99, considering their changing relationships to analysands and AIDS, and the powerful implications for how we relate to symbolic and real experiences. Seeing how the analyst faces suffering, death, or nonexistence has implications across several frames of reference. Not only during the COVID pandemic, or when we work with anyone in extremis or in circumstances that amplify projections of physical danger, but also in how we work with shared fear, and how a different understanding can offer other strategies, especially in relation to real or possible events, and as we relate to ourselves.

In the darkest years of the HIV/AIDS crisis in the urban West, when its impact was clear, but no treatment was available, a number of analysts wrote about analysands and countertransference linked to AIDS. Even in the mid-90s, much of this literature focused on containing extreme anxiety, fear, despair – one is struck by their unprepared surprise, by their personal difficulty in engaging with illness and death. A comparable difficulty has reappeared during the COVID crisis; it seems that many therapists and analysts are not as prepared to face illness and death as they could be.

It is worth noting that AIDS has been central to my own life for decades – I am probably infected in the winter of 1981-2, diagnosed in April 1987, and have lived, been treated, and participated in or managed support structures on four continents. Even now, after interesting shifts in my

---

[42] Earlier versions of this essay appear in: Attinello, P. (2019), *The Passionate Body: AIDS, Archetype, Cultural Complex* (C. G. Jung Institute Zürich, diplomate thesis); and the forthcoming *Proceedings* of the IAAP's XXII International Congress for Analytical Psychology (Buenos Aires, 2022).

later analysis and training, I expect it to remain the central locus of what I do as an analyst, as it is central to my understanding of meaning, time, and death. My view is unavoidably distorted by my subject position, but I urge you to consider that analysts should be deeply aware of illness and death – it should be part of everyone's training, and any analyst or therapist should at least have begun to explore that vast question: who are we, in relation to our deaths.

AIDS, and writing about it

It is worth recalling the basic timeline of the understanding of AIDS in culture, as it has caused many changes in psychological responses. Cases are first noted in the media in the summer of 1981; because the condition seemed both deadly and chaotically incomprehensible, it took on a huge symbolic charge between 1982 and 1985, generating anxiety and blame among populations, the expansion of infection images in the media, and the identification of a new kind of computer program as a 'virus.' The early days of rapid decline and death shifted around 1986-7 to something slower, though still inevitable and horrifying; a major change in cultural psychology comes in 1996 with the first effective medications, at which point the cultural and existential anxiety around the virus substantially decreased. Of course, AIDS remains vast and terrible – more than forty million dead in forty years, and another forty million living with the virus, makes it one of the largest pandemics in world history.

A great deal has been written about HIV/AIDS by psychologists – the American Psychological Association produced two substantial bibliographies before the introduction of protease inhibitors in 1996, with more than six thousand entries (APA 1991, 1995). Before 1996 most writings focused on serious health problems and the prospect of dying; since 1996 there is a shift towards taking care of one's physical health, maintaining emotional stability, and separating out associated stressors. This has become professionally familiar in most clinics and hospitals.

However, I am here interested in writers who take a specifically analytic, or psychoanalytic, depth psychology approach to the condition – especially those who offer insight into the peculiar intensity of the problems involved.

•••

On the subject of AIDS, most of the therapeutic literature, and much of the analytic and psychoanalytic literature, is oriented towards containing extreme anxiety, fear, despair – a broad-based approach to something defined as an *unusually* difficult situation. A number of publications take on the task of training people in basic medical information about HIV/AIDS, and how to communicate with patients. This is especially important not only because inexperienced professionals may say the wrong things – which is true with any condition – but because interpretations and advice become exceptionally charged for someone in a territory imbued with sexuality, morality, legality, and mortality.

Among decades of writings associated with AIDS, there are always stories of health care workers communicating with patients in ways that are seen as insensitive or brutal – members of my patient groups still, nearly forty years later, tell these stories frequently, with barely controlled rage and resentment:

> I decided to have a word with my GP… I remember this being an agonizing time… The consultant… told me he had little or no knowledge about the subject, no one did in those days…. He told me that I did not have syphilis or gonorrhea… 'but we have not got the HTLV-III result yet'. He picked up the phone and got in touch with the lab – gave my name and number to the technician and waited. 'He's positive. You sure?' Then to me, 'You're positive. Can you come back in another three weeks so I can see how you're doing?' Can you imagine the emotions that went through my head? I was going to die. How long would it take? Who should I tell? What to do about my son, my job, my house? I was also angry at the consultant, that he could give me this life-threatening result in a matter-of-fact way and not be able to do anything about it – no cure, no drugs, nothing… [Geoff, 1952, diagnosed May 1985] (Health First 1999, p. 11-12)

Analysts and psychoanalysts often frame their work with HIV-positive patients around one central concern: how can I contain this analysand's shock, confusion, grief? Many of the published case studies focus on this problem, as well as on strong countertransference issues – the analyst's difficulty in facing the illness, or the ways in which it might have been contracted, or the analyst's disorientation and depth of feeling in relation to a topic so close to death.

There are, however, more sophisticated and unexpected approaches – though I feel impelled to consider: when our theories become sophisticated, are we trying to bypass the intense realities of death? Are our most imaginative strategies and interpretations also intended to help us deal with existential situations that, ultimately, cannot be dealt with?

Bosnak and Christopher

Among writings by Jungians, Robert Bosnak's (Bosnak 1989, 1997) is the most substantial and best known. The only book-length narrative of an analytic relationship with a person with HIV/ AIDS, it was initially titled *Dreaming with an AIDS Patient;* when reprinted eight years later, with a new forward and accounts of later group therapy sessions, it was renamed *Christopher's Dreams: Dreaming and Living with AIDS.*

The "AIDS patient" is Christopher P., a young man who contacts Bosnak in 1984 and begins analysis with him in September 1985. The first sessions revolve around Christopher's anxieties about being gay, but he soon has a sudden health crisis, at which point he is diagnosed with AIDS. As Christopher dies in mid-March 1988, the entire relationship covers three and a half years across a time of intense change in the understanding of HIV/AIDS. Bosnak's main focus is on the dreams, which are at the center of the analysis.

Before his diagnosis, Christopher's initial presentation focuses on 'curing' his homosexuality – a plan Bosnak dislikes – and wrestling with his relationships to religion, vocation, and homophobia. So, when Christopher receives an AIDS diagnosis, there is a dramatic sense of betrayal, of a failure to act in time – the thing about which he is most anxious will now kill him, and suggestions of shadow and fate hang over the entire narrative. Christopher needs to work through a great deal of existential and sexual material, which appears throughout the dense and constantly developing dreamwork that makes up most of the book.

The close prospect of illness and death brings these concerns into sharper focus, but Christopher avoids engaging with it for nearly half the book, instead showing a great deal of resistance. His first real confrontation with dying seems to appear in Dream 24, a meditative dream of a large, deep body of water, which accelerates over a few weeks into a transformative vision that Christopher names "The Specter of Aids", drawing a strange figure to accompany it (Bosnak 1997, pp. 85, 93):

> [T]his is the Specter of Aids! I know that I've been trying not to relate to Aids at all. But now I must face Aids. I keep looking at him…. I'm terrified. I feel dark through and through. Dark and forsaken. Then I cried. When I stopped crying, he had gone. For several days it went like that… But it was different, because I invited him. Somehow that made me less scared of him. (Bosnak 1997, p. 91)

Christopher imagines an array of Christian figures that cross through light and dark, good and evil, and, abruptly and powerfully, he integrates them:

> I know that to really love God, I have to love Him when His face is averted. When He comes to me in apparent darkness…. With this insight, something has changed about the specter. I begin to see light… He is opening up his mantle, and I see eyes, thousands of eyes looking at me. I know that these are the eyes of Shekhina, the female aspect of God dwelling in the world. The light is magnificent, and I feel seen. I feel totally seen. And I feel love. (Bosnak 1997, p. 91)

This startling integration operates across several levels – male and female, good and evil, darkness and light – but, in the context of Christopher's narrative, it is unexpectedly forgiving: Christopher's anxieties and dislikes appear throughout his jokes and rationalizations and, though challenges arise frequently in dreams and in the external world, he resists acceptance of himself or others.

In contrast to his analysand, Bosnak engages deeply and honestly with the countertransference – including simultaneous disgust and attraction to homosexuality and, unexpectedly, AIDS. Around the time of the climactic point already mentioned (Bosnak 1997, pp. 92-4), Bosnak becomes aware of a desire to contract AIDS, but imagines it in a way that allows him to pass through the fantasy and recover.

When Bosnak discusses Christopher's individuation, he mentions images that are often tied to the most intense complexes around AIDS:

> Christopher's dying was paradoxical – that he had two ways of dying. One of the worst things he felt was that he was being cursed. If he hadn't had the work we did together, I think he wouldn't have had the experience of feeling that there was also blessing going on and that the curse had been lifted. He felt that his image was absorbed in the continuity of the Christian image, the Pietà, and thereby his soul could rest within that myth. So, there was a resting that took place on the one hand, but on the other there was the terrified animal, who felt only the horror of dying. Individuation is the coming into being – or the coming into consciousness – of the fundamental paradox. (Bosnak 1992, pp. 16-18)

These qualifications suggest patterns that seem common across the entire network of AIDS experiences – a person who is always-already damaged (because of being gay, sexual, using drugs, etc.) responds to an overwhelming concretization of damage (illness) with strategies that are both defensive and masochistic, followed by a decline that may galvanize the patient to move through individuation more quickly, ending with a frequently truncated or incomplete process. This pattern might be seen as a part of a larger pattern of transformation – if AIDS often involves more shame/guilt associated with one's image in the world, forcing the person with AIDS to take all of its meanings more seriously, an individuation process might be faster and more successful than one might expect..

Other Jungians on AIDS

There are a number of publications by Jungians in response to HIV/AIDS, including work by Beebe, Hopcke, Blechner, Frantz, Ruffino, and Dupont, among others. I want to look at a few whose work outlines not only at changes in the understanding of HIV but also shifts in Jungian engagement with the topic.

One of the earliest, and most powerful, of Jungian responses to AIDS is by Scott Wirth, a San Francisco analyst who spoke at a conference in September 1985 (Wirth 1986). Other papers in the same collection show intense engagement but great difficulty engaging with what was still a confusing situation – Sandner, for instance, writes about folk traditions around death and cancer patients, with no reference to the focus on AIDS. In contrast, Wirth is utterly direct:

> One of the worst feelings many of us have had about AIDS stems from our sense of its arbitrariness, its impenetrability, its cruelty, and its medical unyieldingness – no treatment, no medical cure, no end in sight to the epidemic. In a sense, the medical

intransigence of AIDS leaves us no choice but to work with the psyche – over that, at least, it seems we have some measure of influence. (Wirth 1986, p. 113)

Wirth pulls together extreme images – Pan, Artaud – as he looks for a place to stand in a chaotic professional and existential situation, noting that Pan is the only god to die during our historical time. He points to the state of San Francisco gay culture before AIDS – a combination of Dionysian freedom with the confusion of delayed adolescence, an unstable puer condition shared across an entire subculture. He articulates disaster, but also process:

AIDS, we might say, is the end of paradise. The bubble has popped. It is a shock, it is horrible, depressing, and disillusioning. But deep down inside no one is completely surprised. And in some sense, we feel relieved. It is time to change, to move on to a new stage…. [C]razily, AIDS first crushes us, then invites us and impels us to reintegrate, to make ourselves whole again in a new way. (Wirth 1986, p. 137-8)

Wirth suggests a pattern similar to the one I see in Bosnak's book – if gay men have been able to manage their dislocation from a developmental maturation process, they can keep their balance better than most when they are again dislocated, as they become virtually old and near to death. He links the difficult worlds of carer and patient in a way that recalls the deeply wounded 1980s San Francisco that I remember:

Anyone who comes close to AIDS can be emotionally overcome, inundated or inflated by the mystery and power of the pain beyond words, flooded with the enormity of it all, the ego overwhelmed by the contents of the collective unconscious. (Wirth 1986, p. 138)

Wirth then focuses on gay men with AIDS learning to imagine themselves as eternal, connected to others, and more deeply a part of the community than before the crisis. This seems both prescription and reassurance; one senses the chaotic forces, the helplessness, that surround his speech, but also an assertive assurance that meaning can and must be made of the whole.

•••

Sachiko Reece, a Los Angeles sandplay analyst, explains her sessions with an increasingly ill PWA beginning in 1990 (Reece 1998). Since Reece and the analysand were both Japanese-American, she focuses on cultural reflections; but an underlying story is about social and personal reserve blocking an engagement with difficult subjects, in a case where there is little time to spare.

The analysand presents as rather contained, nearly as anxious that people might discover he was HIV+ as he is about dying. Painfully difficult experiences with lesions, sicknesses, and medications (the main antiviral in 1990 was still AZT in high and so relatively toxic doses) generates fear, denial, and intellectualization; Reece explains a "loss of soul connection… a link between body and psyche was hindered. Therefore, the psyche's function for wholeness was lost" (Reece 1998, p. 42). At one point he asks when Reece will tell him to do some sandplay – she says, "When you feel like it", and he laughs at his polite reserve and says, "I've wasted my time."

I suggest that this is a serious concern in working with the ill or dying – the kind therapist who is concentrating on letting the patient move at their own speed ignores the unforgiving importance of time. A certain assertiveness is important here – if time may be short, there should be a willingness to push analysands as much as to accommodate them.

Reece's analysand makes twelve sandplay pictures over ten months, telling the story of a fairy-tale prince who is cursed with a short life. The central problem is not the fact that his life is itself short, but whether it is possible to come to terms with his life and death in that time. At one point he falls into despair, saying that "death is near" – Reece disagrees, defensively (Reece 1998, p. 52); again, this reflects the analyst's difficulty, which may get in the way of the process. Writing some years after her patient's death, Reece shows that she is painfully aware that she threw away valuable time because of her own resistance. When the analyst pushes back against reality, refusing to accept what is obvious to the analysand, there may be an opportunity for roles to be reversed, and the analysand to say: it is true, you must accept it.

The status of suffering

Jungian analysts have also responded to the most intensely physical aspects of illness and deterioration. However, an intermittent problem among Jungians is the tradition of focusing on symbolic meanings, with decades of images of sickness, rot and death used by analysts who may rarely experience such things in the real, physical world.

Before he wrote about AIDS, Sardello wrote of sickness as an aspect of the modern city, starting from the point of view of the unthreatened:

> We, the unhospitalized, relatively healthy, relate to disease as we do to death. It is someone that happens to someone else; or it is something reserved for the future. (Sardello 1983, p. 145)

He emphasizes illness as rooted in things that have been distanced from us, developing images of infection in terms of Philoctetes and his quarantine on an uninhabited island:

> Consider this possibility: the things of the technical manufactured world are killing us, and we do not feel it because the pain has been cast onto the island…. Sexuality is killing us because we experience only the pleasure of it and not the pain. That has been cast onto the island. (Sardello 1983, p. 148)

The final section of his article is about herpes, and he spins associational fantasies of viral contagion: herpes is the revenge of a sexuality that has been twisted away from its life and passion.

This discussion foreshadows what he will write later, and what will happen later. Sardello returns to the world of illness, this time including AIDS, in an article entitled 'The Illusion of Infection'. He first explains his own self-treatment for a pain condition:

> I believe there was importance in serving the disease as my teacher. Medical diagnosis has the effect of isolation, of restricting one's illness in such a fashion that it is quite impossible to fully experience an illness as soul-making. (Sardello 1988, p. 15)

Interpreting the incursion of an illness as an objective phenomenon that invades the body is, in his view, culturally sanctioned soul suppression. He creates a complex reading of AIDS as unavoidable and necessary, something that operates in the body and the world in the same way that shadow materials operate in the mind:

> … disease does not originate by infection, but by the medical procedure of hiding disease ever deeper and calling this suppression 'cure'…. AIDS can thus be imagined as a great liberator of the mechanical concept of disease, for it frees all disease that has been suppressed rather than allowed to be a guide to the soul of the body. (Sardello 1988, p. 20)

Sardello's reading is grounded not only in this shadow metaphor, but also on the medical ideas of Bechamp and others, who assert that infection does not work the way we think it does – which generates an argument against the 'materialism' of both allopathic and alternative medical systems. Though I am not unsympathetic to analyzing those ideologies, his argument devolves into aggressive fantasy when he links his ideas to those of Cantwell and other AIDS denialists, then spends some pages advertising the ability of alternative treatments to save people with AIDS. As someone who has used alternative treatments over the decades but has also seen them used as ideological weapons on those who are very ill or dying, I am skeptical of Sardello's motives – they suggest a desire to eliminate not only his own death anxiety, but the world's death anxiety, on rather paltry terms.

This is a serious problem at the core of the understanding of AIDS, and COVID, and other illnesse: must we accept some kind of complicity with the virus and condition, based on that which is repressed in our culture – and how is that different than blaming the 'mistakes' made by those who end up infected? Do the counterintuitive, anti-scientific paradoxes of such an analysis merely pull us back into an archaic world of vengeful guilt?

•••

In his late, dark *Archetype of the Apocalypse* (Edinger 1999), Edinger detours from a discussion of the angels pouring seven plagues onto the earth to make a point about the nature of AIDS. It is both insightful and offensive – Edinger's values are slightly more conservative than those of many writers on AIDS. He interprets the angels and their plagues as an overburdened unconscious dumping material back into the ego – material that had previously been dumped from the ego into the unconscious, so this is a version of the Freudian return of the repressed. A relatively simple process, but central to a great deal of thinking about HIV/AIDS: the sense that cultural, religious, and personal repressions of sexuality and pleasure were being turned back on us is not unfamiliar, though it raises cultural and political questions about how that understanding can be used..

Edinger points out that AIDS and its relation to the immune system is a problem in border protection, and he views promiscuous sex as a disastrous offense against such borders.

> There is a profound symbolism involved in the phenomenology of the AIDS virus. And I suggest that the mistake which causes AIDS – speaking on the symbolic level – is a failure to 'guard the borders' of one's individual identity. AIDS first appeared in what are euphemistically called 'sexually active' male homosexuals. Some of these individuals are almost unbelievably promiscuous…. these individuals feel so profoundly empty within themselves, that there arises a compulsion to be filled with some kind of intimate contact…. Consider now the symbolism of the AIDS virus…. Whenever matter enters the blood stream, it is the immune system that asks: 'Is this I or not-I?'… But the AIDS virus attacks this protective agent by sneaking into its cells and directing the cells to make more of the virus – destroying the immune system cells from within. I think it is clear that the physiological operation of the virus is a picture of the psychological mistake that opened the door to the virus in the first place. (Edinger 1999, 128-9)

There is a confusion of levels here – symbolic, personal, cultural, medical: for Edinger this is not a major concern, because he is distant from the people he is speaking about. He seems to find it easy to interpret them symbolically, as well as embedding them in a relatively traditional system of individual identity and controlled social interaction. For instance, I strongly, and obviously, dislike generalizing male homosexuals as "profoundly empty" – there are clear and relatively common wounds in our population, especially older generations, but profound emptiness is not a realistic characterization, and as a description it is unempathetically, unanalytically, and unprofessionally brutal.

Edinger follows this general overview with a more personal dream, and a more personal analysis: the image of a gay Catholic priest dying of AIDS in the hospital, whose mouth and nose are rotten – symptoms of tertiary syphilis, rather than AIDS. The dream progresses through ecological disaster, Florence falling to pieces, and an escape to higher ground (Edinger 1999, 129). Edinger's interpretation focuses on collapsing boundaries, a sense of danger and invasion – I would also point out the clear disgust at the immanent sickness of the body.

I suggest a different approach to his entire approach: what if these 'borders' are those between our desires and our control of them, between eros/pleasure/joy and civilized post-Enlightenment

Western behavior? Or, more radically – and in line with current biomedical thinking about the relationship between what we regard as the 'body', and the microorganisms that make up so much of its crucial functions – what about Deleuze and Guattari's idea that bodily boundaries are created by a paranoid-fascist society, and there might be a freedom in a schizoid-leftist approach that create breaks and detours in those boundaries, allowing for a less controlled and more *lively* freedom for the body?...

•••

Monick took a more physicalized, more sympathetic approach to suffering and illness, rooted in a radical Christianity. The point of origin is his own (possibly mistaken) understanding of a theology lecture, which he linked to what appears to have been a deep commitment to finding existential meaning in Christ:

> Mollegen said that Grünewald painted Jesus in the Crucifixion panel of the Isenheim altarpiece as having syphilis, the scourge of human sexuality. I was dumbstruck. A sexual Jesus? The thought had never seriously entered my mind. A Jesus dead from his love certainly had, but his being dead from his sexual love was exhilaratingly iconoclastic. (Monick 1993, p. 3)

Miller's foreword to the book points out that Jung saw Christianity as also monstrous (Monick 1993, xii-xiii), something that causes us to experience its shadow in aggressive and painful ways. Monick connects this with AIDS, which takes so many Christian tropes – chastity, purity, restriction of pleasure, control of the body – and shows us their brutal shadows. Monick wants to engage with evil, not fight it – a symbolically homeopathic rather than allopathic approach. For him, contact with the sensual in both its positive and negative aspects is transformative – is it possible for individuals, and even more for culture, to be transformed in this way?

Monick's discussion of AIDS follows a discussion of syphilis in natural progression from the historical to the contemporary – a progression similarly implied by Edinger; but Monick works more slowly, with more personalized awareness. He moves from amplification to association: AIDS is *not* directly connected to the Grünewald, but it is a valuable association.

> In our day [1993], AIDS is a parallel to the ravage Grünewald painted in his Isenheim Christ. AIDS can have a sexual point of contagion similar to syphilis. Both may be incurable. Both have moral overtones – they are transmitted by disreputable behavior. Both cause uninfected people to shrink away, afraid to touch, afraid to associate. Both ostracize. Both conditions existed before anyone knew what they were or how they were spread. Both hide and gestate in the body long before they are discovered.... The common thread that binds advanced syphilis and AIDS is twofold: a mortality

flashed on the screen of one's awareness, coupled with a common point of contagion – the victim's supposedly unclean life. (Monick 1993, pp. 102-3)

This view of the situation as it stood when Monick wrote his book, after the nature of AIDS and its impact were abundantly clear but before the appearance of effective medications, still hangs behind the condition today – not only because its mythology remains powerful (as it is embedded in the archetypal and cultural complexes, as well as left over from our denied histories), but also because a substantial part of the world with poor access to medications still experiences the condition in this way:

Once one becomes HIV-positive, there is little one can do to prevent… the collapse of the immune system. Malevolence has fixed its hold, disfiguring the life that remains. One is caught in a trajectory with but one outcome. (Monick 1993, p. 103)

There are of course endogenous and exogenous origins for illness – with AIDS, the virus is understood to come from outside. For Monick, this is important: evil exists, but when we view it as an invasion from outside, we blame, defend, resent, etc. AIDS is often interpreted as coming from outside, from another location or culture or race or sexual group, and that has resulted in some fantastic plans and policies – exiling American PWAs to Utah, or British ones to the Isle of Wight. Connecting this problem with his central assertion, the quasi-Buddhist statement, "Suffering is a condition of life" (Monick 1993, p. 105), is a demanding project: in many ways liberal policies that do *not* exclude people or populations are doing what Monick demands, though their cultural and political justifications speak to different levels.

Monick's interconnection of disease and sexuality, evil and innocence, does involve a quasi-Christian anti-sexuality, but it resonates deeply from an analytical point of view:

Disease becomes, literally for some, metaphorically for everyone, sexual wound. There is no escape from its potential once one moves beyond innocence. (Monick 1993, p. 135)

This powerful but painful statement is expanded into a discussion that seems, to me, easier to accept than that of Edinger – perhaps because of its larger frame and its integration of light and darkness into one symbol:

Sex has become a symbol for death…. Now, even when safe, it is tinged with terror. Since the advent of AIDS, one can see clearly that sex was never just fun…. Because sexuality is sacred power – where animal and symbol coalesce – it always has been a source of human distress as well as gratification… a brush with the divine. (Monick 1993, pp. 135-6))

"Sex was never just fun:" one can go off in a number of directions from this statement, but in at least one of those directions one finds the painful realization that the sexual revolution, women's liberation and gay liberation, the pleasures and projections of the modern sexualized world, are all not only admittedly risky – as they are seen to be by conservative politicians, by the most anxious and controlling parts of society – they also involve deep power: a return to Dionysus is not something we can do casually, with no consequences, but its nature also suggests its deep necessity.

Monick responds directly to Sardello, outlining some of the ideas he finds more useful, but critiquing the desire for a 'magical' cure:

> While [Sardello] holds that disease is a natural process, he seems to suggest that health – as the absence of illness – is attainable, if humanity were to listen to disease and learn from it…. If Sardello envisions psychotherapy as cure, in the sense that cure eliminates disease, he appears to be caught in the conventional paradigm himself. The Isenheim Crucifixion suggests, on the other hand, that healing is not cure, that there is no way to live desire and not also and thereby encounter illness. (Monick 1993, pp. 138-9)

That final sentence has massive, but for me deeply sane, power: it parallels Edinger's approach, but empathy and ruthlessness are distributed quite differently here – those who have AIDS are not cordoned off as sacrifices to the body and to illness, as we are all already embedded in the patterns of good and evil that are created by sexuality. It also clarifies that all the stigma, rejection, and paranoia aimed at people with AIDS by the 'worried well' can be seen as the predictable rejection of one's own shadow.

•••

For me at least, questions remain. It is plausible that we would not want to accept the link between sex and death out of our own childishness; but such an interpretation takes on a very different slant in the madness of the monastery or the convent, or the whorehouse or the bathhouse – pro- and anti-sexual ideologies remain powerful in Western culture and must be taken into account, even in the consulting room and in each analysis. The substantial long-term splitting that these ideologies exhibit has been catastrophically exposed in the age of AIDS, but our culture still has not developed much skill at holding the tensions between them.

Perhaps Monick's analysis seems the most complete, and the most empathetic, not merely because he spends more care and energy on it, but because his core image is a suffering body, one that should be loved and held. That is very different than focusing on illness and cure, or on AIDS as apocalyptic disaster – and it may bring us closer to people who have a deadly condition now, rather than in some distant country or century.

References

APA (American Psychological Association) (1991). *AIDS: Abstracts of the Psychological and Behavioral Literature, 1983-91*, third edition. Washington, DC: APA.

APA (American Psychological Association) (1996). *AIDS: Abstracts of the Psychological and Behavioral Literature, vol. 2, 1991-1995*. Washington, DC: APA.

Bosnak, R. (1989). *Dreaming with an AIDS Patient*. Boston: Shambhala.

Bosnak, R. (1992) & Michael Adams, Image, Active Imagination and the Imaginal Level: A *Quadrant* Interview. *Quadrant* 25/2, 9-29.

Bosnak, R. (1997). *Christopher's Dreams: Dreaming and Living with AIDS* (includes 1989 text). New York: Dell/Delta.

Edinger, E. (1999). *Archetype of the Apocalypse: Divine Vengeance, Terrorism and the End of the World*. Chicago: Open Court.

Health First (1999). *In a Positive Light, vol. 1: Stories by gay men about their experiences of living with HIV*. London: Health First.

Monick, E. (1993). *Evil, Sexuality, and Disease in Grünewald's Body of Christ*. Dallas: Spring.

Reece, S. T. (1998). Jungian Approach to AIDS Counseling: Preparation for death expressed in sand play. In: *Seeing in the Dark: Current Questions in Analytical Psychology, Proceedings of the 1998 California Spring Conference of Jungian Analysts and Control Stage Candidates*, La Jolla, CA, 40-64.

Sardello, R. (1983). The Suffering Body of the City: Cancer, Heart Attack and Herpes. *Spring*, 145-64.

Sardello, R. (1988). The Illusion of Infection: a Cultural Psychology of AIDS. *Spring*, 15-26.

Wirth, S. (1986). Reflections on Archetypal Aspects of AIDS and a Psychology of Gay Men. In: Leon McCusick, editor, *What to Do about AIDS: Physicians and Mental Health Professionals Discuss the Issues*. Berkeley: U. of California.

Transgender Individuation:
An ethical and non-pathologizing reflection

Giulia Pepe

Abstract

Transgender people often find themselves in the position of having to negotiate one's identity in a society that sees gender essentially as binary and determined by biological sex. For these people, identification represents a particularly complex challenge, since to become themselves in the most authentic way, they must defy the pressure of social norms, internalized prejudices, family expectations, and social stigma. Since contemporary culture does not yet offer a space of recognition for the trans experience, perhaps we need to ask ourselves whether the suffering of these people derives from a closure of imaginal horizons on a collective level rather than by any personal factor. Even the analytic setting risks becoming a place of non-reflection, of failure empathic and retraumatization, if lacking a clear and problematized vision of change of gender paradigm that has been going on for several years now and without a profound knowledge of the instances of identities that fall under the trans definition. Starting from the recent contributions of contemporary authors of the post-Jungian and psychoanalytic vein we will try to outline an analytic way of treating these patients by encouraging unfolding of their personal process of individuation, without renouncing an analytical way of thinking about question, but having the courage to open up to an ethical and non-pathologizing reflection.

Introduction

The gender variance is a phenomenon that has not had as much attention from science, the media, or politics as it is attracting recently. Even still, it does not represent something new to deal with. The gender variance, even the transition, has been present for centuries, perhaps even millennia, in human history through mythology and lived life[43].

---

[43] Marsman, 2017.

Transgender is an umbrella term referring to those whose gender identity does not correspond with the sex assigned at birth. The identities that fall under the vast transgender domain challenge the fixity of gender and impose a revision of the way we look at masculine and feminine, no longer as two opposite poles, but as a spectrum in which individuals can place themselves, in a fluid sense in the position that best coincides with their own feeling.

The great activation around this issue seems to suggest a shift in the way we experience and understand gender identity, even at a collective level. Our current society seems to be traversed by an archetypal androgynous energy, represented by Dionysus in the pantheon of Greek deities. For Jung, the androgyne represents the Original Man, preceding Adam and Eve, male and female together[44]. The Original Man is subsequently divided into the opposite terms of masculine and feminine, from One to Two, making consciousness possible. An erosion of the stereotypical patterns of masculine and feminine and the rise of gender fluidity is taking place now. Perhaps we are witnessing, through some emerging identities, an archetypal shift in our society under the sign of the Androgyne, a creative and fluid overcoming of principles that are no longer relevant and have also been used as instruments of oppression by patriarchy[45].

The time of change is always turbulent, capable of moving deep emotional waves denoted by fear, confusion, and radicalization of thinking. Current cultural forms now prove to be crumbling, inadequate to encompass the reality that is taking shape. The challenge of individuation that is experienced by gender nonconforming people is paralleled on a collective level. These individuals can be seen as prophets, bearers of the new, knocking at the door of humanity, forcing it to question itself.

It is necessary to mobilize new energies to embrace change, develop ethical and creative thinking, and not to invest in painful resistance that insists on oudated planes of reality, even on the analytical level.

The need for the development of analytical thinking is getting stronger, but there is often a polarization of rigid positions around this issue including prejudice, alarmism, and reference to theories that are no longer adequate in an attempt to understand what is happening.

When reflection becomes radicalized and takes on the confrontational tone, it is not useful for either psychoanalysis or the transgender population[46].

If the analyst has not adequately worked on his or her own personal beliefs, as well as political and religious views, these can become a source of problems in the treatment of transgender people, resulting in an interruption of the analytic work. The setting risks becoming a place of

---

[44] Jung, 1951.
[45] Gosling, 2018.
[46] Saketopoulou, 2020.

failed mirroring and empathy, as well as retraumatization, echoing the negative experiences of denigration and rejection that that patient has already repeatedly experienced in the outer world.

Jung and Gender

The legacy left us by Jung on the topic of gender is nothing short of difficult to discern because some of his ideas sound far removed from today's Zeitgeist; they are steeped in a patriarchal and occasionally sexist view. However, at the same time, other insights of his on gender can still be considered relevant today and useful in thinking about the topic. It will be necessary to start with the contra-sexual archetypes of Animus and Anima.

Although these concepts are often useful in analysis in helping patients to work out an idea of themselves free of preconceptions, in practice, the definitions Jung used as to what is feminine and what is masculine originated from the gender stereotypes of his time[47].

James Hillman also found some aspects of Jung's Anima concept problematic. Hillman states that the Anima is always observed as part of a fantasy of opposites, in which it is always given the task of compensating for an opposite pole: the Persona or masculine Shadow. Jung's description of the feminine as the inferior side of man is anachronistic for Hillman, as well as derived from a rigidly patriarchal, puritanically defensive stubborn historical period[48]. The notion of Anima appears deeply dependent on the idea of femininity and masculinity as represented in their own cultural and historical actualizations.

However, the most controversial aspect for Hillman remains the contra-sexual one. The psychoanalyst argues that precisely as an archetype, Anima cannot be placed in the psyche of one sex and excluded from that of the other. Although Jung states that it is not possible to find this image in the imaginal heritage of the female unconscious[49], on the contrary, it is evident that images and motifs that have been connected to Anima archetype frequently appear in the phenomenology of the female psyche. Pursuing the logic of the contra-sexuality of the archetype is equivalent to considering the same inner image as noble in case it is perceived in male psychology and as Shadow in the case of female psychology[50].

Jungian analyst Gary Toub (2013) has more recently developed an interesting reflection on Jung's thinking about gender, weighing its critical issues and strengths. First, Toub points out how many Jungian definitions of masculine and feminine are narrow-minded, if not cloaked in misogyny. Masculine energy is described as penetrating and creative, related to rational thinking,

---

[47] Kast, 2006.
[48] Hillman, 1985.
[49] Jung, 1938/1940.
[50] Hillman, 1985.

while feminine energy is depicted as receptive, characterized by irrationality and passivity. It emerges that many of the qualities that the Jungian thought identifies as feminine are related to inferiority, at least from the Western culture's perspective. Furthermore, Toub points out how the use of these definitions that belong to classical Jungian theorizing can have negative effects on analytic work, because they carry with them the risk of perpetuating gender myths and prejudices that are harmful. As mentioned above, the view of male and female as complementary opposites raises issues. Such a postulate closely recalls a binary view of gender, nowadays largely outdated in favour of a perspective in which they are seen as situated along a continuum. Consequently, a dichotomic view may prove fallacious, or even discriminatory, when dealing with transgender or intersex patients.

Going further, thinking of men and women as opposites puts the focus on the differences between them and not on the psychological similarities they share. To categorize human qualities as prerogative of males or females does not serve the purpose of pursuing individuation, a process that places all human beings at the same essential and deep level, in the desire to actualize the uniqueness of everyone.

In a reversal of perspective, Toub (2013) posits which of Jung's ideas about the masculine and the feminine are still valid and current for the analytical work. The process of integrating the instances represented by Anima and Animus can help patients recognize in their psyche traditionally feminine or masculine qualities, helping them expand their identities and go beyond male-female polarization. Moreover, by recognizing a feminine inner image in men and a masculine inner image in women, it is possible to withdraw the projections on the opposite sex and take responsibility for those qualities that are denied in one's person and attributed to the outside.

Lastly, Susan McKenzie (2006) has taken into consideration the theorizing of contra-sexual archetypes precisely in relation to the new instances that trans identities are bringing to light. She states:

> Jung's anima/animus (A/A) thinking leads us into a trap of linear orderliness, fixed identities, androgynous symmetries, and archetypes that are differentially inherited, based on sexual anatomy, a breach in the universality of the collective unconscious. [...] Jung's A/A is a terrible fit for our time. We live in an era of emergent, not fixed realities, and are beginning to value the overt display of masculinity and femininity in both sexes (p. 407).

As shown by the fervent work of theoretical reflection and analytical practice that American Jungian authors have done and are continuing to perform around the theme and with trans patients, we can say that Jung has left a fertile legacy to reflect on this topic.

Psychotherapy with Transgender Patients

Psychotherapy with transgender patients involves matters that affect the life of any other person. Like everyone else, in fact, they deal with problems related to their own internal world or with issues that concern the negotiation of their own identity in the external reality. However, in the gender nonconforming person, these instances can be complicated by an unease inherent in a fracture between mind and body called gender dysphoria, today replaced by the WHO in the latest version of the ICD of 2019 with the less stigmatizing definition of "Gender Incongruence."

In the psychodynamic field, Lin Fraser (2009), an analyst from San Francisco and Past President of WPATH, has developed a model for a deep work with transgender patients. In a Jungian perspective, the profound meaning of any path is to foster the patient's individuation. It has been defined by Jung as "an expression of that biological process…by which every living thing becomes what it was destined to become from the beginning" (Jung, 1938/1940). For gender nonconforming people, the individuation represents a particularly complex challenge because to become who they are in the most authentic way they must defy the pressure of social norms, internalized prejudices, family members' expectations and what others would like them to be. Often the initial question is about the possibility of embracing the emergence of transgender feelings and the search for that position along the gender spectrum in which to place oneself or the uncertainty about the possibility of going through a complete transition (Fraser, 2009). The therapist must be able to keep within himself all future developments and all possible outcomes.

Fraser's approach builds on attachment theory[51], according to which one of the fundamental developmental challenges is to develop a separate sense of self along with basic trust and attachment. To develop a coherent sense of self, it is crucial to receive adequate mirroring. The gender identity, an identity aspect that is constructed from the earliest years of life, is one of the cornerstones of a sense of self. The experience of the gender-variant child is almost always not properly reflected by significant others, mainly because it is not always visible from the outside. According to Fraser's hypothesis (2009), due to the lack of mirroring the child would resort to a double strategy: to keep secret this authentic aspect of the sense of self and to develop a false self, which is reflected and validated by the outside world. The consequences of a lack of mirroring in this area of self can cause distortions in the development of the ability to relate and develop a basic sense of trust. For these reasons, the essential tasks of a psychotherapeutic treatment with transgender patients concern seeing and mirroring (perhaps for the first time) the person in the experienced gender and help them progressively relate to their gender identity. In the early stages of therapy, it will be appropriate to work with the processes of separation and identification, with the aim of promoting the development of a coherent sense of self. The emerging self is a very fragile material to handle with care. Feelings of shame, guilt, and distrust are often very much alive. Except for some peculiar aspects, working with transgender patients

---

[51] See: Bowlby, 1969, 1973; Ainsworth, 1979.

is not so different from a depth psychology course with any other person. It is very important to pay attention to inner images, for example those produced through dreams, in order to help the person navigate the options of gender identity and expression, since the outer images they may often refer to are few or distorted by social representations.

After the transition (for those who choose to undergo gender affirmation surgery), the identification continues with the consolidation of the sense of self. The fracture between the psyche and the soma can gradually heal, as they are confronted with mourning the reality and the initial fantasies of sex change. In Jungian terms, during this phase, there is an expansion of the Self and an enhancement of the archetypal models not developed in the new gender role. Another complex challenge will then be the relationship with one's past: each person will have to evaluate how much and how to negotiate his own authenticity, to reveal his own story or hide it from others to live fully in the gender experienced and to avoid coping once again with the social stigma. For the transgender person, the task of all life becomes to come to terms with the external reality and to welcome their own inner truth as they advance along their process of identification. This includes looking for a unique meaning in their own path and celebrating their own journey[52].

In the psychoanalytic field, the transgender person (especially those who wish to face gender affirmation surgeries) is often attributed a deficient symbolization ability and a failure of imaginative processes, which would then be shifted to a concrete dimension, particularly on the body. Marsman (2017) points out how contemporary culture still does not offer a space of recognition for the trans experience, and he raises the question that perhaps these people are suffering not because of a lack of imagination on their part, rather because of a closure of imaginal horizons on a collective level. The psychological suffering of trans people could then stem from the lack of psychic space that society fails to contemplate for their existences. A deep understanding of these lives should begin with an admission of societal unawareness, by questioning the limits of the individual and collective imaginary and excluding the preconceptions through which we demarcate the boundaries between the symbolic and the concrete.

Saketopoulou (2014) developed the concept of massive gender trauma to describe the effects impacting the transgender person's well-being starting with the intersection between the painful experience of the body and the suffering caused by the external world. The first of these elements is characterized by gender dysphoria, the profound suffering that results from the mismatch between the physicality of one's body and the experienced gender identity. The second has to do with the experience of misgendering, namely the failure to recognize and misrepresent one's gender identity by the outside world and by primary objects. Facing this developmental challenge can often result in the development of personality disorders, difficulties in emotional regulation and an altered reality-testing.

---

[52] Fraser, 2009.

The traumatic gap between the psychic reality and the external world is the cause of psychic suffering in this population, not the other way around, as is often claimed. The main task of the analyst is to help the patient abandon a rigid connection between the materiality of the body and the experience of gender and to create psychic spaces of symbolization. This is not to say that a process of this kind will have the result of avoiding a medical and surgical path of gender affirmation, but it has the objective of allowing the patient a mentalization of his own body, regardless of what outcome the gender affirmation process will have.

As has been shown, the experience of being constantly unrecognized belongs to the everyday experience of gender-nonconforming people and it has an extremely harmful impact on their mental health and greatly increases their risk of suicide compared with that of the general cisgender population[53]. For this reason, it is fundamental that the analytical work with these people is carried out with an adequate knowledge of the subject, in compliance with the guidelines and that it can represent a safe place of personal care and exploration. The impact of stigma and lack of recognition in places of care leaves these patients with a deep and durable wound, which could also discourage a new request for psychological and medical assistance[54].

Transference and Counter-Transference Phenomena

In therapeutic work with transgender people, it is crucial that the therapist is as free as possible from preconceived ideas. It is important that he has confronted himself with his own beliefs about gender variance and sexual orientation and that he is able to maintain an open attitude and ready to question once again his ideas when he encounters the world of the patient[55]. Moreover, in order not to repeat the stigma already present in society, it is very important that he knows how to use an adequate and inclusive language.

Countertransference is a fundamental tool underlying analytical practice. A reflection on it leads the analyst to ask himself how his unconscious experiences can guide his clinical practice. Countertransference can be a very important tool to draw a map about the course of treatment, but it also introduces an element of responsibility for the analyst, who must constantly monitor his reactions in response to the patient's content[56].

A countertransference trap might involve igniting the analyst's fantasies of omnipotence, which take the form of the belief that they know what the "true gender" of their patient is, that they can predict if and when the patient will regret the changes made to their body, or the fear of becoming the patient's accomplice with respect to their decisions about medical transition.

[53] Marshall, Claes, Bouman, Witcomb, & Arcelus, 2016.
[54] Donal, Strauss, Winter, & Lin, 2020.
[55] Fraser, 2009.
[56] Porchat & Santos, 2021.

These attitudes of the analyst may betray a failure to process their own fears about confronting the patient and the uncertainties that the therapeutic journey brings[57].

Especially in cases where the analyst is cisgender, one of the most intense countertransference experiences that might take shape is the fear of experiencing—or worse, externalizing—transphobic reactions. Griffin Hansbury (2017), a transgender analyst, traces transphobic countertransference reactions to the activation of "unthinkable anxieties." These anxieties are in the deepest recesses of the psyche and may be related to distressing childhood fantasies.

For example, they could lead the analyst who meets the trans patient to experience a rupture of the continuity of his own sense of self, of his adherence to reality and of the sense of incarnation in his own body. He may experience the sensation of slipping out of his body and his own identification of gender. He may feel a terrifying anguish about the possibility that his body may break up or may be afraid of going crazy[58]. In some cases, the cisgender analyst might be led to idealize the transgender condition, through the fantasy that these people experience being able to adhere to any gender and experience fluidity, to "be able to be everything," a possibility denied to those who identify as cisgender. Such a counter-transference configuration is not free from feelings of envy that the analyst might experience towards his patient[59]. In fact, the fantasy described above is not present in a ubiquitous way in people gender non-conforming, who often oscillate between the need to experience a multiplicity of gender and the desire to find a stable position within the gender spectrum.

Another possible scenario is the concern to be a "safe analyst" and the attempt to avoid interpretations that might sound to the ear of the patient as transphobic. The cisgender analyst, especially when confronted with stories of discrimination and violence perpetrated against his patient, may feel that he has no right to speak from the top of his privileged position in a heteronormative society. These fantasies at the head of the analytic process could cause a slowdown, if not a halt, in the progress of the analysis and they could leave unexplored various areas of shadow, preventing the analyst's unconscious from listening and expressing itself (2021).

The desire for one's analysis room to be a safe place for one's patients hides quite a few traps in the transference field. In view of the traumatizing impact that society often has on outsiders of the binary gender paradigm, patient and analyst may lock themselves into a reassuring defensive dual arrangement that can be described by the expression "us versus everyone"; or the analyst may harbour maternal fantasies of nurturing towards the patient, in an attempt to compensate for the patient's affective shortcomings and experiences of rejection that the latter may have experienced in his or her past. Such a desire for containment, aroused by a fear and a desire for

---

[57] Saketopoulou, 2020.
[58] Hansbury, 2017.
[59] Porchat & Santos, 2021.

reparation towards the patient can become blind spots and give the therapeutic relationship a devouring, centripetal character[60].

The counter-transference question, on closer inspection, cannot be read only as an internal disagreement with the analyst's opinions about the transition. To complete the picture, we must also consider the cultural pressures that, today more than ever, those who work with this type of user can sense during the analysis.

Susan McKenzie (2015) has commented on the topic. The author states that psychopathology might hypothetically be present in the transgender patient, but it certainly resides in the collective cultural unconscious, which assumes that a person's feelings correspond to his or her sexual anatomy. She performs a reversal of perspective and asks herself why the therapist should be so anxious about the medical transition if the patient is not. Culturally, we accept surgery for aesthetic purposes without much resistance and therefore perhaps this aspect it is not what causes dismay, but rather that application of surgery that disrupts those cultural assumptions that the appearance of bodies and gender identity should always correspond in a normative gender logic. The author continues that we should abandon the psychoanalytic pathologizing assumptions on the patient but begin to reflect on what happens in the analyst, both on an individual and cultural level. The disturbing feelings aroused by the deviance that the trans patient may arouse are evidence of the effects of a complex in action.

No analyst can completely prevent the effect of complexes. However, he can attempt to be at least aware of them. The author sees gender affirmation surgery as a form of art, an individuative work of sculpting one's body so that it can express who one really is. Taking up the Jungian conception of the "subtle body," McKenzie (2006) defines gender as an expression of that dance that perpetually takes place between body and mind and that derives from an emerging process, and it is not rigidly fixed to some biological imposition.

Still, McKenzie (2010) argues that the gendered feelings we experience in our bodies and which our culture calls masculinity and femininity are located in the realm of embodied imagination. They are an intermediate experience between the physical and the imaginary, driven by the actions of the mind embedded in the body and the body embedded in the cultures of family, society, space, and time. It is not important how the eternal images of masculine and feminine combine in the psyche but rather it is the ability to be able to distinguish between one's personal experience with one's feelings related to gender and sexuality and society's culturally oriented need to find symbolic expression and containment for such powerful aspects of human experience.

---

[60] Boland, 2017.

For Boland (2017), the inspiring god of an adequate analytical attitude in the relationship with transgender patients may lie behind the polyvalent Trickster archetype. The Trickster is a transformist and as such he shows the world different perspectives to look at things differently. He is a boundary crosser, a promoter of psychic reorganization. He is the living symbol of the need to transgress, to go beyond the pre-established limits when preparing for important identifying junctions. The Trickster is a deceiver in nature, he is not interested in conflict between two contrasting realities, but he invents a third way. "The trickster is neither the god of the door leading in nor the god of the door leading out. He resides within the hinge" (Boland, 2017, p. 68).

For the analyst who welcomes gender nonconforming patients to his or her practice, a not simple challenge is prepared: it will be necessary to move away from the certainties of what is conventional and generally accepted, to delve into shame, humiliation, and loneliness, to go through a metamorphosis with an uncertain outcome in order to re-emerge together with the patient bringing to light new resources.

Transgender patients are outlaws. They walk together with their analysts an unusual path far from the beaten track, toward awareness, guided by images, and Hermes prepares the way for them, moved by necessity. The lack of boundaries, of course, can be a frightening and confusing experience at times, but there will be the God of the Hinge to illuminate the path and mark new ways so that what is to come can be allowed to emerge[61].

Conclusions: Going back to look forward

In the work of post-Jungian authors who have written on the topic, it is impressive that sometimes the treatment includes resonances about the authors' own experience of having felt like outsiders of gender norms or an open declaration of their membership in the LGBTQI+ community[62]. This perhaps might indicate that once again we need to refer to the tutelary archetypal image of analytic work, the Wounded Healer.

This is not meant to argue that one person must be necessarily queer in order to empathize with the feelings of a transgender person, but it is meant to argue exactly the opposite. A society that remains stubbornly anchored to its gender stereotypes, to unjust divisions of roles and privileges, to cultural customs that no longer keep pace with a changing humanity, hurts even those who, by choice or by chance, adapt well to a binary view of gender.

It is precisely the healer's wound that is the gateway to his therapeutic power towards the patient and the society[63]. The power is a dimension that is present in every therapeutic relationship, but it is constellated with its own precipitous figure in the case of pathways with transgender patients.

---

[61] Boland, 2017.
[62] McKenzie, 2006; Solem, 2017; Literski, 2018.
[63] Guggenbühl-Craig, 1971.

The fact that the mental health professional is called upon to certify the gender dysphoria and that this act can allow or deny the medical stages of gender affirmation to proceed places the therapist (and the psychiatrist) in a very uncomfortable position. A dark shadow looms on the practice of the profession. The therapist is invested by society with an enormous power in relation to the future of his patient. And the use he will make of this power does not depend merely on his assessments about his patient's health, but also on his own personal variables, both conscious and unconscious. At this point, it seems to be precious that the therapist may be able to remember his own wound and to keep clear before him the awareness that in treating those who sit before him, he also heals himself and perhaps also soothes the wounds of society. The therapist faces the danger of removing the two poles of the archetypal image of the wounded healer to the point of causing a dramatic split. In this way, the malaise will be projected onto the patient, who will be reduced to such an impairment that his own account of himself cannot be reputed to be true, while the sapiential endowment will illusorily reside entirely in the therapist, capable of mastering the others' pain and anguish without feeling touched in his own soul. If the therapist unilaterally identifies with the role of the healer, there could be a risk of inflectional acting out, which could lead the therapist to be possessed by the Shadow of the omnipotent healer. The archetype would thus encounter a split: the sense of omnipotence that invests the therapist plunges him or her into Shadow identifications, for which the interests of the healer prevail over the dimension of care toward his patients, enslaved to his power.

One of the dark sides that can replace the therapeutic function of the healer is represented by the image of the charlatan: when this image is constellated horizons of healing are promised, drawing even on pseudo-scientific methods. The ethics of care fades, by giving way to the logic of interests and dreams of glory[64].

The anti-therapeutic attitude embodied by the charlatan recalls, when examined with respect to work with transgender patients, those "reparative" approaches, the so-called conversion therapies aimed at returning the patient to a heterosexual orientation or gender identity that conforms to the sex assigned at birth. Therapists using these methods, often belonging to radical religious communities, by relying on quasi-scientific practices condemned by law and professional societies in many countries, promise they can heal from an existential condition that is not pathological per se. These practices lead often to nefarious results[65].

The other Shadow figure that personifies the possible drifts of an unethical attitude to treatment is that of the false prophet. Just as it may be important for a man of faith never to show his worshippers he has any doubt with respect to his faith, similarly, the false prophet embodies the attitude of those therapists who cannot tolerate the uncertainty surrounding their mysterious

---

[64] Guggenbühl-Craig, 1971.
[65] Jenkins & Johnston, 2004.

work and tend to adhere uncritically to the precepts of their own training schools or to empirical evidence of treatment efficacy[66].

There are a variety of mental health professionals who, after only one or two clinical interviews, agree to certify the applicants' gender dysphoria and then give their approval to proceed with the administration of hormone therapy and then gender affirming surgeries. This unconditional adherence to such a treatment model is not free from pitfalls. This way of operating resembles a renunciation by the analyst of the ethical responsibility of which he is invested, leaving the patient alone to decide his own fate, carrying the full weight of the consequences on his shoulders. This position seems to set the therapeutic work on the sole register of consciousness, of what is explicitly stated, forgetting the unconscious dynamics that operate below the threshold.

On the contrary, the true healer is the one who knows how to live the archetype's wounded pole, by remaining mindful of his own wounded parts and the one who knows how to accompany the patient in the discovery of the other pole, by awakening the healer inherent in him.

A Jungian analyst can never forget the goal of his work: to guide the patient towards identification. This is a staple to always keep even with gender nonconforming patients.

After having pointed out all the specifics of working with this type of patient, it is worth returning to the focal point of any analytic journey, that human factor that ultimately clears the field of power dynamics, countertransference traps, and presumptions of knowledge: these people must be accompanied along the path of their individuation, like any other.

Gender nonconforming individuals challenge cultural limits in the pursuit of their own self-realization, this is a source of great creative potential. They are bearers of the possibility of an expansion of consciousness about gender at the personal level, but also at the collective level[67].

There is a need to mobilize new energies to embrace the change above, to field ethical and creative thinking and not to invest in painful resistance that insists on obsolete planes of reality.

It seems necessary, in this perspective, to abandon the rhetoric that imposes the vision of transgender people as subjects "born in the wrong body" but to operate a reversal of perspective.

What if society is inadequate?

The individuation process moves in the direction of development of a higher ethics. In these people's path towards their Self, there is a potential richness also for the collective: the possibility

---

[66] Guggenbühl-Craig, 1971.
[67] McKenzie, 2010.

that society wonders about its own fixities and the wounds that a rigid system causes to some of its components.

There cannot be individuation that does not involve society, in that case it would be equivalent to falling into a mere individualism. In the individuation there are the seeds of a new community[68], the possibility of the creation of a new human consciousness based on the consciousness of the collective unconscious, common to all human beings[69].

In conclusion, it is a fact that every person who wishes to walk the impervious path of self-realization of the Self must be able to tolerate the strident dissonance of opposites, the view of his own Shadow and the comparison with the archetypal figures that inhabit the psyche. At the same time, we must not forget the society surrounding to which we must offer an equivalent, a contribution to the expansion of the collective consciousness. It is equally crucial that society can imagine an individuation for all its members, since the gift of closure and repression of nascent identities is very high not only for the recipients of such treatment, but also for the whole world.

---

[68] Shamdasani, 2003.
[69] Jung, 1916.

References

Ainsworth, M.D. (1979). Infant-mother attachment. *American Psychologist*, 34(10), 932–937.

Boland, A. (2017). God of the hinge: treating LGBTQIA patients. *Journal of Analytical Psychology*, *62*(5), 688-700.

Bowlby, J. (1969). *Attachment and loss. Vol. I: Attachment*. Basic Books.

Bowlby, J. (1973). *Attachment and loss. Vol. II: Separation, anxiety & anger*. Basic Books.

Dolan, I. J., Strauss, P., Winter, S., & Lin, A. (2020). Misgendering and experiences of stigma in health care settings for transgender people. *Medical Journal of Australia, 212*(4), 150-151.

Fraser, L. (2009). "Depth psychotherapy with transgender people." *Sexual and Relationship Therapy, 24 (2)*, 126-142.

Gosling, J. (2018). "Gender fluidity reflected in contemporary society." *Jung Journal, 12*(3), 75-79.

Guggenbühl-Craig, A. (1971). *Power in the helping professions*. Spring Publications.

Hansbury, G. (2017). Unthinkable Anxieties: Reading Transphobic Countertransferences in a century of Psychoanalytic writing. *TSQ: Transgender Studies Quarterly*, 4(3-4), 384-404.

Hillman, J. (1985). *Anima: An Anatomy of a Personified Notion*. Spring Publications.

Jenkins, D., & Johnston, L. B. (2004). "Unethical treatment of gay and lesbian people with conversion therapy." *Families in Society*, 85(4), 557-561.

Jung C. G. (1916). The relation between the Ego and the unconscious. *The Collected Works of C. G. Jung, vol.7*. (originally published 1966). Princeton University Press.

Jung C. G. (1938/1940). Psychology and Religion. *The Collected Works of C. G. Jung, vol.11*. (originally published 1969). Princeton University Press.

Jung, C. G. (1951). Aion: Researches into the Phenomenology of the Self. *The Collected Works of C. G. Jung, vol. 9, pt 2*. (originally published 1968). Princeton University Press.

Kast, V. (2006). Anima/Animus. In Renos K. Papadopoulos (ed.), *The Handbook of Jungian Psychology: Theory, Practice and Applications*. London and New York: Routledge.

Literski, N. S. (2018). "Dionysus reviled: Transgender visibility and the Pentheus Complex." *Immanence Journal, 2* (2), 54-66.

Marshall, E., Claes, L., Bouman, W. P., Witcomb, G. L., & Arcelus, J. (2016). "Non-suicidal self-injury and suicidality in trans people: A systematic review of the literature." *International review of psychiatry, 28*(1), 58-69.

Marsman, M. A. (2017). "Transgenderism and transformation: An attempt at a Jungian understanding." *Journal of Analytical Psychology, 62*(5), 678-687.

McKenzie, S. (2006). "Queering gender: anima/animus and the paradigm of emergence." *Journal of Analytical Psychology, 51*, 401–421.

McKenzie, S. (2010). "Genders and sexualities in individuation: theoretical and clinical explorations." *Journal of Analytical Psychology, 55*, 91-111.

McKenzie, S. (2015). "A response to Robert Withers." *Journal of Analytical Psychology*, 60(3), 413-418.

Porchat, P., & Santos, B. (2021). "Are We Safe Analysts?" Cisgender Countertransferential Fantasies in the Treatment of Transgender Patients. *The Psychoanalytic Review, 108*(4), 411-431.

Saketopoulou, A. (2014). "Mourning the body as bedrock: Developmental considerations in treating transsexual patients analytically." *Journal of the American Psychoanalytic Association, 62*(5), 773-806.

Saketopoulou, A. (2020). "Thinking psychoanalytically, thinking better: Reflections on transgender." *The International Journal of Psychoanalysis, 101*(5), 1019-1030.

Shamdasani, S. (2003*). Jung and the making of modern psychology: The dream of a science.* University Press.

Solem, D. (2017). "Genders as Theater: The Dionysian dismemberment of the culturally normative narrative in service to the Self." *Psychological Perspectives, 60,* 333–344.

Toub, G. (2013). Jung and gender: Masculine and feminine revisited. *C. G. Jung Institute of Colorado.* Retrieved September 20, 2022 from: http://jungpage.org/learn/articles/analytical-psychology/147-jung-and-gender-masculine-and-feminine-revisited

Individuazione transgender
Una riflessione etica e non patologizzante

Giulia Pepe

Abstract

Le persone *transgender* si ritrovano spesso nella condizione di dover negoziare la propria identità in una società che vede il genere essenzialmente come binario e determinato dal sesso biologico.

Per queste persone l'individuazione rappresenta una sfida particolarmente complessa, poiché per diventare se stessi nella maniera più autentica, devono sfidare la pressione delle norme sociali, i pregiudizi interiorizzati, le aspettative dei familiari, lo stigma sociale.

Dal momento che la cultura contemporanea non offre ancora uno spazio di riconoscimento per l'esperienza *trans,* forse bisogna domandarsi se la sofferenza di queste persone derivi da una chiusura degli orizzonti immaginali ad un livello collettivo piuttosto che da qualche fattore personale.

Anche il setting analitico rischia di divenire un luogo di mancato rispecchiamento, di fallimento empatico e di ritraumatizzazione, se privo di una visione chiara e problematizzata del cambiamento di paradigma di genere in corso ormai da diversi anni e senza una conoscenza profonda delle istanze delle identità che rientrano sotto la definizione *trans*.

Partendo dai recenti contributi di autori contemporanei del filone post-junghiano e psicoanalitico si cercherà di delineare una modalità analitica di trattare questi pazienti incoraggiando il dispiegarsi del loro personale processo di individuazione, non rinunciando ad un modo di pensare analitico sulla questione, ma avendo il coraggio di aprirsi ad una riflessione etica e non patologizzante.

Introduzione

La varianza di genere è un fenomeno che non ha mai avuto un'attenzione scientifica, mediatica, politica pari a quella che sta calamitando in questi anni. Essa, tuttavia, non rappresenta una novità con cui confrontarsi. La varianza di genere, perfino la transizione, sono state presenti per secoli, forse anche per millenni, nella storia dell'umanità attraverso la mitologia e la vita vissuta (Marsman, 2017).

Transgender è un termine ombrello con cui si indicano in maniera generale coloro la cui identità di genere non corrisponde con il sesso assegnato alla nascita.

Le identità che ricadono sotto il vasto repertorio *transgender* sfidano la fissità del genere e impongono una revisione del modo in cui guardiamo al maschile e al femminile, non più come due poli opposti, ma come uno spettro rispetto al quale ogni individuo può collocarsi -in maniera più o meno transitoria- nella posizione che meglio coincide con il proprio sentire.

La grande attivazione attorno a questo tema sembra suggerire che stia prendendo forma, anche ad un livello collettivo, un cambiamento riguardo al modo in cui facciamo esperienza ed interpretiamo l'identità di genere.

La nostra attuale società sembra percorsa da un'energia archetipica androgina, che nel *pantheon* delle divinità greche è rappresentata da Dioniso. Per Jung, l'androgino rappresenta l'Uomo Originario, precedente ad Adamo ed Eva, maschio e femmina insieme (Jung, 1951). L'Uomo Originario viene successivamente diviso nei termini opposti di maschile e femminile, dall'Uno al Due, rendendo possibile la coscienza. Adesso sta avendo luogo un'erosione dei modelli stereotipati di maschile e femminile e il sorgere della fluidità di genere. Forse stiamo assistendo, per mezzo di alcune identità emergenti, ad un passaggio archetipico della nostra società sotto il segno dell'Androgino, un superamento creativo e fluido di principi che non stanno più in piedi e che sono stati anche strumenti di oppressione da parte del patriarcato (Gosling, 2018).

Il tempo del cambiamento è sempre turbolento, capace di muovere profonde ondate emotive, denotate da paura del nuovo, confusione e radicalizzazione del pensiero. Le forme culturali attuali si rivelano ormai fatiscenti, inadeguate a contenere la realtà che si sta concretizzando. La sfida individuativa che viene vissuta dalle persone *gender non conforming* viene riproposta parallelamente su un piano collettivo. Questi individui possono essere visti come dei profeti, portatori di un nuovo, che bussano alla porta dell'umanità, costringendola ad interrogarsi.

È necessario mobilitare nuove energie per accogliere il cambiamento che sopravanza, mettere in campo un pensiero etico e creativo e non investire in resistenze penose che insistono su piani di realtà obsoleti, anche sul piano analitico.

La necessità dello sviluppo di un pensiero analitico è sempre più forte, ma attorno a questo tema si assiste spesso ad una polarizzazione di posizioni rigide, di pregiudizi, allarmismo e al riferimento a teorie che non sono più adeguate a contribuire ad una comprensione di quanto sta avvenendo. Quando la riflessione si radicalizza ed assume il tono di un conflitto non è utile né per la psicoanalisi né per la popolazione transgender (Saketopoulou, 2020).

Se l'analista non ha lavorato adeguatamente sulle proprie convinzioni personali -oltre che sulle proprie idee politiche e religiose- esse possono divenire fonte di problemi nel trattamento delle persone *transgender*, causando l'interruzione del lavoro analitico. Il setting rischia di divenire un luogo di mancato rispecchiamento, di fallimento empatico e di ritraumatizzazione, facendo eco alle esperienze negative di denigrazione e rifiuto che quel paziente ha già ripetutamente sperimentato nel mondo esterno.

Jung e il genere

L'eredità lasciataci da Jung sul tema del genere è a dir poco ardua da raccogliere, perché alcune delle sue idee possono suonare lontane dall'attuale *Zeitgeist*, perché intrise di una visione patriarcale e a tratti sessista. Allo stesso tempo però, altre sue intuizioni sul genere possono essere considerate ancora oggi attuali e utili nella riflessione sul tema.

Bisognerà partire dagli archetipi controsessuali di Animus e Anima.

Sebbene questi concetti siano in analisi spesso congeniali nell'aiutare i pazienti ad elaborare un'idea di sé libera da preconcetti, di fatto per definire ciò che è femminile e ciò che è maschile Jung ha utilizzato come base proprio gli stereotipi di genere dei suoi tempi (Kast, 2012).

Nell'elaborazione del concetto di Anima, sembra trasparire un'idealizzazione dell'immagine eterna della donna che l'uomo porta in sé, una natura femminile ancora più ispiratrice e creativa di quanto non possa mai essere una donna in carne e ossa. Inoltre, particolarmente critica è l'identificazione operata da Jung tra l'Anima e il principio di Eros e l'Animus e il principio di Logos; se come scrive Jung (1954/1968), l'Animus corrisponde alla coscienza maschile e l'Anima alla coscienza femminile, ne risulta che uomini e donne vengono percepiti come opposti per natura, nonché portatori di qualità fisse, corrispondenti ai ruoli sessuali tradizionali (Kast, 2012).

Anche James Hillman ha trovato problematici alcuni aspetti della nozione di Anima così come sono stati formulati nell'opus junghiano. Hillman afferma che l'Anima è sempre osservata come parte di una fantasia degli opposti, in cui le viene sempre dato il compito di contrapporsi e compensare un polo ad essa antitetico: la Persona o l'Ombra maschile. La sua descrizione sul piano sociale come lato femmineo ed inferiore dell'uomo, risulta anacronistica per Hillman, nonché figlia di «*un periodo storico rigidamente patriarcale, puritanamente difensivo, estroversamente caparbio e privo di senso d'anima*» (Hillman, 2002, p. 29). La nozione di Anima appare profondamente dipendente dall'idea di femminilità e mascolinità così come sono rappresentati nelle loro attualizzazioni culturali e storiche.

Tuttavia, l'aspetto più controverso rimane per Hillman quello controsessuale. Argomenta lo psicoanalista che proprio in quanto archetipo, Anima non può essere collocata nella psiche di un sesso ed esclusa da quella dell'altro.

Nonostante Jung affermi che «*non si trova questa immagine nel patrimonio di immagini dell'inconscio femminile*» (Jung, 1938/1940, p.40), al contrario è evidente che nella fenomenologia della psiche femminile compaiono di frequente le immagini e i motivi che sono stati connessi all'archetipo dell'Anima. Perseguire la logica della controsessualità dell'archetipo equivale a considerare la medesima immagine interiore come nobile nel caso in cui venga ravvisata nella psicologia maschile e come Ombra nel caso della psicologia femminile (Hillman, 2002).

L'analista junghiano statunitense Gary Toub (2013) ha più di recente elaborato un'interessante riflessione sul pensiero di Jung riguardo al genere, soppesandone le criticità e i punti di forza. Per prima cosa, anche questo autore sottolinea come molte definizioni junghiane di maschile e femminile siano di vedute ristrette, se non addirittura ammantate di misoginia. L'energia maschile è descritta come penetrante e creativa, legata al pensiero razionale, mentre l'energia femminile è rappresentata come ricettiva, caratterizzata da irrazionalità e passività. Ne emerge che molte delle qualità che il pensiero junghiano identifica come femminili sono legate all'inferiorità, almeno dal punto di vista della cultura occidentale. Inoltre, l'autore sottolinea come l'uso di queste definizioni che appartengono alla teorizzazione junghiana classica possa avere effetti negativi sul lavoro analitico, perché portano con sé il rischio di perpetuare miti e pregiudizi di genere che sono controproducenti e dannosi. Come si accennava sopra, la visione di maschile e femminile come opposti complementari solleva delle problematiche. Innanzitutto, tale postulato ricorda molto da vicino una visione binaria dei generi, oggi ampiamente superata a favore di una prospettiva in cui essi sono visti come situati lungo un continuum; conseguentemente una visione dicotomica può rivelarsi fallace, se non discriminatoria, quando si ha a che fare con pazienti *transgender* o intersessuali. Andando oltre, il pensare a uomini e donne come opposti pone il focus dell'attenzione sulle differenze tra essi e non sulle similitudini psicologiche che li accomunano. Categorizzare delle qualità umane come appannaggio dei maschi o delle femmine non è funzionale ai fini del perseguimento dell'individuazione, processo che pone tutti gli esseri umani ad un profondo ed essenziale medesimo livello, nell'anelito verso l'attualizzazione dell'unicità di ogni individuo.

Operando un capovolgimento di prospettiva, Toub riporta quali delle idee di Jung intorno al maschile e al femminile egli ritiene ancora oggi valide ed attuali per il lavoro analitico. Il processo di integrazione delle istanze rappresentate da Anima ed Animus può aiutare i pazienti e le pazienti a riconoscere nella propria psiche qualità tradizionalmente femminili o maschili, aiutandoli ad espandere le loro identità ed andare oltre la polarizzazione maschio-femmina. Inoltre, riconoscendo un'immagine interiore femminile negli uomini e un'immagine interiore maschile nelle donne, è possibile ritirare le proiezioni sul sesso opposto ed assumersi la responsabilità di quelle qualità che vengono rinnegate nella propria persona ed attribuite all'esterno (*ibidem*).

Susan McKenzie (2006), infine, ha preso in considerazione la teorizzazione degli archetipi controsessuali proprio in relazione alle nuove istanze che le identità *trans* stanno portando alla luce; afferma: «*Il pensiero anima/animus (A/A) di Jung ci conduce in una trappola di ordine lineare, identità fisse, simmetrie androgine, e archetipi che sono ereditati in maniera diversa, in base all'anatomia sessuale, una breccia nell'universalità dell'inconscio collettivo [...] è terribilmente inadatto al nostro tempo. Viviamo in un'epoca di realtà emergenti, non fisse, e stiamo cominciando a dare valore alla palese evidenza di mascolinità e femminilità in entrambi i sessi»* (McKenzie, 2006, p. 7).

Come dimostra il fervente lavoro di riflessione teorica e di pratica analitica che autori junghiani statunitensi hanno svolto e stanno continuando a svolgere intorno al tema e con pazienti *trans* (che verrà presentato nelle pagine a venire), possiamo affermare che lo psichiatra svizzero abbia lasciato una fertile eredità per poter riflettere anche su questo argomento.

La psicoterapia con i pazienti *transgender*

La psicoterapia con persone *transgender* coinvolge questioni che ineriscono alla vita di qualsiasi altra persona. Come chiunque altro, infatti, esse si confrontano con problemi legati al proprio mondo interno o con tematiche che riguardano la negoziazione della propria identità nella realtà esterna. Nella persona *gender non conforming*, tuttavia, queste istanze possono essere complicate da un disagio che inerisce ad una frattura tra mente e corpo, la disforia di genere, oggi sostituita dall'OMS nell'ultima versione dell'ICD del 2019 con la definizione meno stigmatizzante di "Incongruenza di genere".

In ambito psicodinamico, Lin Fraser (2009), analista di San Francisco e *Past President* del WPATH, ha elaborato un modello per un lavoro del profondo con pazienti *transgender*.

In una prospettiva junghiana, il senso profondo di ogni percorso è quello di favorire l'individuazione del paziente. Essa è stata definita da Jung come *«quel processo biologico [...] attraverso il quale ogni essere vivente diventa quello che è destinato a diventare fin dal principio»* (1938/1940, p. 294). Per le persone *gender non conforming* l'individuazione rappresenta una sfida particolarmente complessa, poiché per diventare ciò che essi sono nella maniera più autentica, devono sfidare la pressione delle norme sociali, i pregiudizi interiorizzati, le aspettative dei familiari e quello che gli altri vorrebbero che fossero. Spesso la domanda iniziale riguarda la possibilità di accogliere l'emergenza dei sentimenti *transgender* in modo autentico e la ricerca di quella posizione lungo lo spettro di genere in cui collocarsi o l'incertezza circa l'eventualità di attraversare una transizione completa (Fraser, 2009). Il terapeuta deve essere capace di tenere dentro di sé tutte gli sviluppi futuri e tutti gli esiti possibili.

L'approccio di Fraser (*ibidem*) prende le mosse dalla teoria dell'attaccamento (Bowlby, 1969, 1973; Ainsworth, 1979), secondo cui una delle fondamentali sfide evolutive consiste nello sviluppare un senso di sé separato insieme ad una fiducia di base e alla capacità di attaccamento. Ai fini dello sviluppo di un coerente senso di sé, è fondamentale ricevere un adeguato rispecchiamento. L'identità di genere, aspetto identitario che si costruisce fin dai primissimi anni di vita, è uno dei capisaldi del senso di sé. L'esperienza del bambino *gender-variant* quasi sempre non viene correttamente rispecchiata dagli altri significativi, soprattutto perché non sempre è visibile dall'esterno. A causa della mancanza di rispecchiamento, il bambino ricorrerebbe, secondo l'ipotesi di Fraser (2009) ad una doppia strategia: tenere segreto questo aspetto autentico del senso di sé e sviluppare di rimando un falso sé, che viene rispecchiato e validato dal mondo esterno. Le conseguenze di un mancato rispecchiamento in questa area del sé possono causare delle distorsioni nello sviluppo della capacità di entrare in relazione e sviluppare un senso di fiducia di base. Per queste ragioni, compiti irrinunciabili di un percorso di psicoterapia con pazienti *transgender* riguardano il vedere e rispecchiare (forse per la prima volta nella sua vita) la persona nel suo genere esperito ed aiutarla progressivamente a relazionarsi con la propria identità di genere. Nelle prime fasi della terapia, sarà opportuno lavorare con i processi di separazione e individuazione, con l'obiettivo di promuovere lo sviluppo di un senso di sé coerente. Il sé emergente è un materiale molto fragile da maneggiare con cura, spesso sono molto vivi i sentimenti di vergogna, il senso di colpa e la diffidenza.

Fatta eccezione per alcuni aspetti peculiari, il lavoro con pazienti *transgender* non è tanto diverso da un percorso di psicologia del profondo con qualsiasi altra persona. È molto importante prestare attenzione alle immagini interiori, per esempio a quelle prodotte per mezzo dei sogni, per aiutare la persona ad orientarsi tra le opzioni di identità ed espressione di genere, poiché spesso le immagini esteriori cui possono far riferimento sono poche o distorte dalle rappresentazioni sociali.

Dopo la transizione (per coloro che scelgono di sottoporsi all'intervento chirurgico di affermazione di genere), l'individuazione prosegue con il consolidamento del senso di sé. La frattura tra psiche e soma può progressivamente rimarginarsi, mentre devono confrontarsi con un'elaborazione del lutto circa la realtà e le fantasie iniziali di cambio di sesso. In questa fase, in termini junghiani, si assiste ad una espansione del Sé e ad un potenziamento dei modelli archetipici non sviluppati nel nuovo ruolo di genere. Un'altra complessa sfida riguarderà poi il rapporto con il proprio passato: ogni persona dovrà valutare quanto e come negoziare la propria autenticità, ovvero il rivelare la propria storia o il nasconderla agli altri per vivere appieno nel genere esperito ed evitare di far fronte ancora una volta allo stigma sociale. Per la persona *transgender*, il compito di tutta la vita diventa quello di venire a patti con la realtà esterna ed accogliere la propria verità interna mentre avanza lungo il suo processo di individuazione. Questo include il cercare un significato unico nel proprio percorso e di celebrare il proprio viaggio (*ibidem*).

Spesso in ambito psicoanalitico, alla persona *transgender* -soprattutto a coloro che desiderano affrontare gli interventi chirurgici di affermazione di genere- viene attribuita una carente capacità di simbolizzazione e un fallimento dei processi immaginativi, che verrebbero quindi spostati su una dimensione concreta, in particolare sul corpo. Marsman (2017) sottolinea come la cultura contemporanea non offra ancora uno spazio di riconoscimento per l'esperienza *trans* e pone l'interrogativo che forse queste persone stiano soffrendo non per una loro mancanza di immaginazione, quanto invece per una chiusura degli orizzonti immaginali ad un livello collettivo. La sofferenza psicologica delle persone *trans* potrebbe allora derivare dalla mancanza di spazio psichico che la società non riesce a contemplare per le loro esistenze. La comprensione profonda di queste vite dovrebbe iniziare con un'ammissione di non conoscenza da parte della società, mettendo in discussione i limiti dell'immaginario individuale e collettivo e ponendo tra parentesi i preconcetti attraverso cui delimitiamo i confini tra simbolico e concreto.

Saketopoulou (2014) ha elaborato il concetto di trauma di genere massivo per descrivere gli effetti traumatici che impattano sul benessere della persona transgender a partire dall'intersezione tra la dolorosa esperienza del corpo e la sofferenza provocata dal mondo esterno. Il primo di questi elementi è caratterizzato dalla disforia di genere, la profonda sofferenza che deriva dalla mancata coincidenza tra la fisicità del proprio corpo e l'identità di genere esperita. Il secondo, ha a che fare con l'esperienza del *misgendering*, ovvero dal mancato riconoscimento e travisamento della propria identità di genere da parte del mondo esterno ed in particolare dagli oggetti primari.

Spesso, il confrontarsi con questa sfida evolutiva può esitare nello sviluppo di disturbi di personalità, difficoltà nella regolazione emotiva e un danneggiamento dell'esame di realtà.

La frattura traumatica tra la realtà psichica e il mondo esterno è la causa da cui scaturisce la sofferenza psichica di cui spesso questa popolazione è portatrice e non il contrario, come spesso viene affermato.

Il principale compito dell'analista è quello di aiutare il paziente ad abbandonare una rigida connessione tra la materialità del corpo e l'esperienza del genere e di creare spazi psichici di simbolizzazione. Con ciò non si vuole affermare che un processo di questo tipo avrà il risultato di evitare un percorso medico e chirurgico di affermazione di genere, ma ha l'obiettivo di consentire al paziente una mentalizzazione del proprio corpo, a prescindere da quale esito avrà il processo di affermazione di genere.

Come si è mostrato, l'esperienza di essere costantemente non riconosciuti appartiene all'esperienza quotidiana delle persone *gender-non-conforming* e ha un impatto estremamente dannoso sulla propria salute mentale, incrementando notevolmente il rischio di suicidio, a confronto con quello della popolazione generale cisgender (Marshall, Claes, Bouman, Witcomb, & Arcelus, 2016). Per questa ragione, è di fondamentale importanza che il lavoro analitico con queste persone sia svolto con una adeguata conoscenza dell'argomento, nel rispetto delle linee-guida e possa rappresentare un luogo sicuro di cura ed esplorazione personale. L'impatto dello stigma e del mancato riconoscimento nei luoghi di cura lascia su questi pazienti una ferita profonda e resistente nel tempo, che potrebbe inoltre scoraggiare una nuova richiesta di assistenza psicologica e medica (Donal, Strauss, Winter, & Lin, 2020).

Fenomeni transferali e controtransferali

Nel lavoro terapeutico con persone *transgender* è fondamentale che il terapeuta sia il più possibile libero da idee preconcette. È importante che egli si sia confrontato con le proprie convinzioni circa la varianza di genere e l'orientamento sessuale, nonché che egli sia in grado di mantenere un atteggiamento aperto e pronto a mettere in discussione ancora una volta le proprie idee quando entra a contatto con il mondo del paziente (Fraser, 2009). Inoltre, ai fini di non reiterare lo stigma già presente nella società, è molto importante che sappia padroneggiare un linguaggio adeguato e inclusivo.

Il controtransfert è uno strumento fondamentale sotteso alla pratica analitica. Una riflessione su esso porta l'analista a domandarsi come i propri vissuti inconsci possano orientare la propria pratica clinica. Il controtransfert può essere uno strumento importantissimo per tracciare una mappa circa l'andamento del trattamento, ma introduce anche un elemento di responsabilità per l'analista, che deve monitorare costantemente le proprie reazioni in risposta ai contenuti portati dal paziente (Porchat & Santos, 2021).

Una prima trappola controtransferale potrebbe riguardare l'accendersi nell'analista di fantasie di onnipotenza, che si concretizzano nella convinzione di conoscere quale sia il "vero genere" del proprio paziente, di poter prevedere se e quando il paziente si pentirà dei cambiamenti apportati al proprio corpo o nel timore di divenire complice del paziente rispetto alle sue decisioni in merito alla transizione medica. Questi atteggiamenti dell'analista possono tradire una mancata elaborazione delle proprie paure circa il confronto con il paziente e con le incognite che il percorso terapeutico porta con sè (Saketopoulou, 2020).

Soprattutto nei casi in cui l'analista sia *cisgender*, uno dei più intensi vissuti controtransferali che potrebbe prendere forma è la paura di provare -o peggio esternare- delle reazioni transfobiche. Griffin Hansbury (2017), un analista *transgender*, riconduce le reazioni controtransferali transfobiche all'attivarsi di "ansie non pensabili". Queste ansie sono situate nei recessi più profondi della psiche e possono essere legate ad angoscianti fantasie infantili.

Per esempio, potrebbero portare l'analista che incontra il paziente *trans* a sperimentare una rottura della continuità del proprio senso di sé, della propria aderenza alla realtà e del senso di incarnazione nel proprio corpo. Questi potrebbe sperimentare la sensazione di scivolare fuori dal proprio corpo e dalla propria identificazione di genere; provare una terrificante angoscia circa la possibilità che il proprio corpo possa andare in pezzi o temere di impazzire (*ibidem*). In alcuni casi, l'analista *cisgender* potrebbe essere portato ad idealizzare la condizione *transgender*, attraverso la fantasia che queste persone vivono l'esperienza di poter aderire a qualsiasi genere e sperimentare la fluidità, di "poter essere tutto", una possibilità negata a chi si identifica come *cisgender*. Tale configurazione controtransferale non è scevra da sentimenti di invidia che l'analista potrebbe sperimentare nei confronti del proprio paziente (Porchat & Santos, 2021). In realtà, la fantasia sopradescritta non è presente in modo ubiquitario nelle persone *gender non conforming*, che spesso oscillano tra il bisogno di sperimentare in sé una molteplicità rispetto al genere e il desiderio di trovare una posizione stabile all'interno dello spettro del genere.

Un altro scenario possibile è rappresentato dalla preoccupazione di essere "un analista sicuro" e dal tentativo di evitare a tutti i costi interpretazioni che potrebbero suonare all'orecchio del paziente come transfobiche. L'analista *cisgender*, soprattutto se posto di fronte a storie di discriminazione e violenze perpetrate ai danni del proprio paziente, potrebbe sentire di non aver diritto di parlare dall'alto della propria posizione di privilegiato in una società eteronormativa. Queste fantasie alla guida del processo analitico potrebbero comportare un rallentamento, se non un arresto, nel progredire dell'analisi e lasciare inesplorate varie zone d'ombra, impedendo all'inconscio dell'analista di ascoltare ed esprimersi (*ibidem*).

Il desiderio che la propria stanza d'analisi sia un luogo sicuro per i propri pazienti nasconde non poche trappole nel campo transferale. Paziente e analista, in considerazione dell'impatto traumatizzante che spesso la società ha sugli *outsider* del paradigma binario del genere, possono chiudersi in un rassicurante assetto duale difensivo che può essere descritto dall'espressione "noi contro tutti"; oppure l'analista potrebbe nutrire fantasie materne di accudimento verso il paziente, nel tentativo di compensare alle mancanze affettive e alle esperienze di rifiuto che quest'ultimo può avere sperimentato nel suo passato. Un simile desiderio di contenimento, suscitato dalla paura e dal desiderio di riparazione verso il paziente possono diventare punti ciechi e dare alla relazione terapeutica un carattere divorante e centripeto (Boland, 2017).

La questione controtransferale, a ben vedere, non può essere unicamente letta come un dissidio interno alle opinioni dell'analista circa la transizione; a completare il quadro vanno tenute in considerazione anche le pressioni che culturalmente, oggi che più mai, chi lavora con questo tipo di utenza può avvertire nel corso dell'analisi.

Susan McKenzie (2015) si è espressa sull'argomento. La psicopatologia, afferma l'autrice, potrebbe ipoteticamente essere presente nel paziente *transgender*, ma risiede certamente nell'inconscio culturale collettivo, che presume che il sentire di una persona corrisponda alla sua anatomia sessuale. Ella opera un capovolgimento di prospettiva e si chiede come mai il terapeuta debba essere così ansioso circa la transizione medica se il paziente non lo è affatto. Culturalmente accettiamo senza grandi resistenze la chirurgia per fini estetici; quindi, forse non è questo aspetto a suscitare sgomento, quanto piuttosto quella particolare applicazione della chirurgia che stravolge quei presupposti culturali per cui l'apparenza dei corpi e l'identità di genere debbano sempre corrispondere in una logica normativa di genere. Continua l'autrice, che bisognerebbe abbandonare le premesse psicoanalitiche patologizzanti a carico del paziente e iniziare a riflettere anche su ciò che accade nell'analista, sia ad un livello individuale che culturale. I sentimenti disturbanti suscitati dalla devianza che il paziente *trans* può suscitare sono prove degli effetti di un complesso in azione. Nessun analista può annullare del tutto l'effetto dei propri complessi, però può tentare di esserne quantomeno consapevole. L'autrice vede la chirurgia di affermazione di genere come una forma d'arte, un lavoro individuativo di scultura del proprio corpo affinché essa possa esprimere chi uno è veramente. Riprendendo la concezione junghiana di "corpo sottile", McKenzie (2006) definisce il genere come un'espressione di quella danza che perpetuamente si compie tra corpo e mente e che deriva da un processo emergente e non è rigidamente fissato ad alcune imposizione biologica. Ancora McKenzie (2010) sostiene che i sentimenti di genere che sperimentiamo nel nostro corpo e che la nostra cultura chiama mascolinità e femminilità siano situati nel regno dell'immaginazione incarnata. Sono un'esperienza intermedia tra il fisico e l'immaginario, guidata dalle azioni della mente incorporata nel corpo e del corpo incorporato nelle culture della famiglia, della società, di spazio e tempo. Non è importante come le immagini eterne di maschile e femminile si combinano nella psiche, quanto la capacità di saper distinguere la personale esperienza di ognuno con il proprio sentire relativo al genere e alla sessualità e il bisogno culturalmente orientato della società di trovare un'espressione simbolica e un contenimento per aspetti così potenti dell'esperienza umana.

Per Boland (2017), il nume ispiratore di un adeguato atteggiamento analitico nella relazione con pazienti transgender potrebbe celarsi dietro il polivalente archetipo del Trickster.

Il Trickster è un trasformista e come tale mostra al mondo diverse prospettive per guardare alle cose in modo diverso; è un valicatore di confini, un promotore della riorganizzazione psichica. È il simbolo vivente della necessità di trasgredire, di andare oltre i limiti precostituiti quando ci si prepara ad importanti snodi individuativi. Il Trickster ha la natura di ingannatore, egli non è interessato ad entrare in conflitto tra due realtà contrastanti, ma inventa una terza via. «Non è né il dio della porta che conduce dentro né il dio della porta che conduce fuori. Risiede all'interno della cerniera» (Boland, 2017, p. 689).

Per l'analista che accoglie presso il proprio studio pazienti *gender non conforming*, si prepara una sfida non semplice: bisognerà allontanarsi dalle certezze di ciò che è convenzionale e generalmente accettato, addentrarsi nella vergogna, nell'umiliazione e nella solitudine, attraversare una metamorfosi dall'esito incerto per riemergere insieme al paziente portando alla luce nuove risorse.

I pazienti transgender sono dei fuorilegge, essi percorrono insieme ai loro analisti, guidati dalle immagini, un sentiero insolito, lontano dalle strade battute, verso la consapevolezza e Hermes prepara per loro il tragitto, mosso dalla necessità. La mancanza di confini, naturalmente, può essere un'esperienza spaventosa e confusiva talvolta, ma ci sarà il Dio della Cerniera ad illuminare il percorso e segnare nuove vie per poter lasciare emergere quel che ha da venire (*ibidem*).

Conclusioni: Tornare indietro per guardare avanti

Nei lavori degli autori post-junghiani che hanno scritto sull'argomento, colpisce il fatto che talvolta la trattazione include delle risonanze circa i vissuti degli autori stessi riguardo all'esperienza di essersi sentiti degli *outsider* delle norme di genere o una aperta dichiarazione della propria appartenenza alla comunità LGBTQI+ (McKenzie, 2006; Solem, 2017; Literski, 2018).

Forse questo potrebbe indicare che ancora una volta bisogna far riferimento all'immagine archetipica tutelare del lavoro analitico, quella del Guaritore ferito.

Con questo non si intende affermare che bisogna necessariamente essere *queer* per poter empatizzare con i sentimenti di una persona *transgender*, si vuole sostenere esattamente il contrario. Una società che rimane strenuamente ancorata ai propri stereotipi di genere, a delle ingiuste divisioni di ruoli e privilegi, a dei costumi culturali che non tengono più il passo di un'umanità che cambia, fa del male anche a chi, per scelta o per caso, ben si adegua ad una visione binaria dei generi.

È proprio la ferita del guaritore che è la via d'accesso al suo potere terapeutico, verso il paziente e verso la società (Guggenbühl-Craig, 1971). Il potere è una dimensione presente in ogni relazione terapeutica, ma nel caso dei percorsi con pazienti *transgender* esso si costella con una sua cifra precipua. Il fatto che il professionista della salute mentale sia chiamato a certificare la disforia di genere e che tale atto possa consentire o negare il procedere delle fasi mediche di affermazione di genere pone il terapeuta (e lo psichiatra) in una condizione assai scomoda. Sull'esercizio della professione si allunga un'ombra non indifferente. Il terapeuta è investito dalla società di un potere enorme in relazione al futuro del proprio paziente. E l'uso che farà di questo potere non dipende meramente dalle sue valutazioni circa la salute del proprio paziente, ma anche da proprie variabili personali, consce ed inconsce. A questo punto, appare prezioso il fatto che il terapeuta possa essere in grado di ricordarsi della propria ferita e di tenere chiara davanti a sé la consapevolezza che nel curare chi gli siede di fronte, egli cura anche se stesso e forse nel suo piccolo lenisce anche delle ferite della società. Il pericolo cui va incontro il terapeuta è quello di allontanare, fino a provocare una drammatica scissione, i due poli dell'immagine archetipica del Guaritore ferito. In questo modo, tutto il malessere verrà proiettato sul paziente, ridotto ad una compromissione tale che il proprio racconto su di sé non potrà esser reputato veritiero, mentre la dote sapienziale risiederà illusoriamente tutta nel terapeuta, capace di padroneggiare il dolore e l'angoscia altrui senza sentirsi sfiorato nel proprio animo. Qualora il terapeuta si identifichi unilateralmente con il ruolo del guaritore, si potrebbe presentare il rischio di un agito inflattivo, che potrebbe portare il terapeuta ad essere posseduto dall'Ombra del guaritore onnipotente. L'archetipo andrebbe così incontro ad una scissione: il senso di onnipotenza che investe il terapeuta lo sprofonda in identificazioni d'Ombra, per le quali gli interessi del curante prevalgono sulla dimensione della cura verso i propri assistiti, asserviti al suo potere.

Uno dei volti oscuri che può sostituirsi alla funzione terapeutica del curante è rappresentato dall'immagine del ciarlatano: quando questa immagine si costella vengono promessi orizzonti di guarigione, anche attingendo a metodi pseudo-scientifici. L'etica della cura sfuma lasciando il posto a logiche di interessi e sogni di gloria (*ibidem*). L'atteggiamento anti-terapeutico incarnato dal ciarlatano, se preso in esame rispetto al lavoro con pazienti *transgender*, fa pensare a quegli approcci "riparativi", le cosiddette terapie di conversione volte a riportare il paziente verso un orientamento eterosessuale o un'identità di genere conforme al sesso assegnato alla nascita. I terapeuti che si servono di questi metodi, spesso appartenenti a comunità religiose radicali, basandosi su pratiche para-scientifiche e condannate dalla legge e dalle società professionali di molti Paesi, promettono di poter guarire da una condizione esistenziale che non è patologica di per sé. I risultati di queste pratiche sono spesso nefasti (Jenkins & Johnston, 2004).

L'altra figura d'Ombra che personifica le possibili derive di un atteggiamento non etico alla cura è quella del falso profeta. Così come può essere importante per un uomo di fede non mostrare mai di fronte ai propri fedeli di aver alcun dubbio rispetto alla propria fede, allo stesso modo, il falso profeta incarna l'atteggiamento di quei terapeuti che non riescono a tollerare l'incertezza che circonda il loro misterioso lavoro e tendono ad aderire acriticamente ai precetti delle proprie scuole di formazione o a prove empiriche di efficacia dei trattamenti (Guggenbühl-Craig, 1971).

Esistono svariati professionisti della salute mentale, che dopo solo uno o due colloqui di consulenza accettano di certificare la disforia di genere dei richiedenti e danno quindi il loro benestare per procedere con la somministrazione della terapia ormonale e successivamente con gli interventi chirurgici di affermazione di genere. Questa adesione incondizionata a tale modello di trattamento non è libera da insidie. Questo modo di operare assomiglia ad una rinuncia dell'analista della responsabilità etica di cui è investito, lasciando da solo il paziente a decidere del proprio destino, portando sulle proprie spalle tutto il peso delle conseguenze. Questa posizione sembra settare il lavoro terapeutico sul solo registro della coscienza, di ciò che viene esplicitamente dichiarato, dimenticandosi delle dinamiche inconsce che operano sotto la soglia.

Al contrario, il vero curante è colui che sa vivere il polo ferito dell'archetipo, rimanendo memore delle proprie parti ferite, e sa accompagnare il paziente nella scoperta dell'altro polo, risvegliando il guaritore insito in lui.

Un analista junghiano non può mai dimenticare il fine ultimo del proprio lavoro, quello di guidare il paziente verso l'individuazione. Questo è un punto fermo da tenere, naturalmente, anche con i pazienti *gender non conforming*.

Dopo aver sottolineato tutte le specificità del lavoro con questa tipologia di pazienti, vale la pena tornare al punto focale di ogni percorso analitico, quel fattore umano che alla fine sgombera il campo da dinamiche di potere, trappole controtransferali, presunzioni di conoscenza: queste persone vanno accompagnate lungo il sentiero della loro individuazione, come ogni altro.

Le persone *transgender* in analisi necessitano di poter guardare alle proprie immagini interiori, raccontare i propri sogni, integrare quei frammenti di inconscio che si avvicinano all'Io, esattamente come ogni altra persona.

I soggetti *gender non conforming* sfidano i limiti culturali nel perseguire la propria autorealizzazione, ciò è fonte di un potenziale creativo non indifferente, essi sono portatori della possibilità di un'espansione della coscienza sul genere a livello personale, ma anche collettivo (McKenzie, 2010).

È necessario mobilitare nuove energie per accogliere il cambiamento che sopravanza, mettere in campo un pensiero etico e creativo e non investire in resistenze penose che insistono su piani di realtà obsoleti.

Appare necessario, in questa ottica, abbandonare la retorica che impone la visione delle persone transgender come soggetti "nati nel corpo sbagliato" e operare un capovolgimento di prospettiva.

E se fosse la società ad essere inadeguata?

Il processo di individuazione muove nella direzione dello sviluppo di un'etica superiore. Nel percorso di queste persone verso il proprio Sé, vi è una ricchezza potenziale anche per il collettivo: la possibilità che la società si interroghi circa le proprie fissità e le ferite che un sistema rigido provoca ad alcuni suoi componenti.

Non può esistere un'individuazione che non coinvolga la società, in quel caso equivarrebbe allo scadere in un mero individualismo. Nell'individuazione esistono i semi di una nuova collettività (Shamdasani, 2007), la possibilità della creazione di una nuova coscienza umana, che si fonda sulla coscienza dell'inconscio collettivo, comune a tutti gli uomini (Jung, 1916).

In conclusione, è un dato di fatto che ogni persona che voglia percorrere l'impervio cammino dell'autorealizzazione del Sé deve essere capace di tollerare la stridente dissonanza degli opposti, la vista della propria Ombra e il confronto con le figure archetipiche che abitano la psiche e al contempo non deve essere dimentico della società circostante, cui dovrà offrire in dono un equivalente, un contributo all'ampliamento della coscienza collettiva. Tuttavia, è altrettanto vero che è fondamentale che la società possa prevedere un'individuazione per tutti i suoi membri, poiché il prezzo della chiusura e della repressione delle identità nascenti è molto alto non solo per i destinatari di tale trattamento, ma anche per il mondo intero.

Bibliographia

Ainsworth, M.D. (1979). Infant-mother attachment. *American Psychologist*, 34(10), 932–937.

Boland, A. (2017). God of the hinge: treating LGBTQIA patients. *Journal of Analytical Psychology*, *62*(5), 688-700.

Bowlby, J. (1969). *Attachment and loss. Vol. I: Attachment.* New York: Basic Books. 62

Bowlby, J. (1973). *Attachment and loss. Vol. II: Separation, anxiety & anger.* New York: Basic Books.

Dolan, I. J., Strauss, P., Winter, S., & Lin, A. (2020). Misgendering and experiences of stigma in health care settings for transgender people. *Medical Journal of Australia, 212*(4), 150-151.

Fraser, L. (2009). Depth psychotherapy with transgender people. *Sexual and Relationship Therapy, 24 (2),* 126-142.

Gosling, J. (2018). Gender fluidity reflected in contemporary society. *Jung Journal, 12*(3), 75-79.

Guggenbühl-Craig, A. (1971). *Power in the helping professions.* Dallas, Texas: Spring Publications.

Hansbury, G. (2017). Unthinkable Anxieties: Reading Transphobic Countertransferences in a century of Psychoanalytic writing. *TSQ: Transgender Studies Quarterly*, 4(3-4), 384-404.

Hillman, J. (1985). *Anima: An Anatomy of a Personified Notion.* Dallas: Spring Publications. (trad. it. Anima: Anatomia di una nozione personificata, Adelphi, Milano, 2002).

Jenkins, D., & Johnston, L. B. (2004). Unethical treatment of gay and lesbian people with conversion therapy. *Families in Society*, 85(4), 557-561.

Jung, C. G. (1916). Individuazione e collettività. In *Opere vol. 7.* Torino: Bollati Boringhieri, 1993.

Jung, C. G. (1938/1940). Psicologia e religione. In *Opere vol. 11.* Torino: Bollati Boringhieri, 2007.

Jung, C. G. (1951). Aion. In *Opere vol. 9/II.* Torino: Bollati Boringhieri, 1997.

Kast, V. (2012). L'Anima/Animus. In R. K. Papadopoulos (Ed.), *Manuale di psicologia junghiana* (pp.181-204). Bergamo: Moretti&Vitali.

Literski, N. S. (2018). Dionysus reviled: Transgender visibility and the Pentheus Complex. *Immanence Journal, 2* (2), 54-66.

Marshall, E., Claes, L., Bouman, W. P., Witcomb, G. L., & Arcelus, J. (2016). Non-suicidal self-injury and suicidality in trans people: A systematic review of the literature. *International review of psychiatry, 28*(1), 58-69.

Marsman, M. A. (2017). Transgenderism and transformation: An attempt at a Jungian understanding. *Journal of Analytical Psychology, 62*(5), 678-687.

McKenzie, S. (2006). 'Queering gender: anima/animus and the paradigm of emergence'. *Journal of Analytical Psychology, 51,* 401–421.

McKenzie, S. (2010). Genders and sexualities in individuation: theoretical and clinical explorations. *Journal of Analytical Psychology, 55,* 91-111.

McKenzie, S. (2015). A response to Robert Withers. *Journal of Analytical Psychology*, 60(3), 413-418.

Porchat, P., & Santos, B. (2021). "Are We Safe Analysts?" Cisgender Countertransferential Fantasies in the Treatment of Transgender Patients. *The Psychoanalytic Review, 108*(4), 411-431.

Saketopoulou, A. (2014). Mourning the body as bedrock: Developmental considerations in treating transsexual patients analytically. *Journal of the American Psychoanalytic Association, 62*(5), 773-806.

Saketopoulou, A. (2020). Thinking psychoanalytically, thinking better: Reflections on transgender. *The International Journal of Psychoanalysis, 101*(5), 1019-1030.

Shamdasani, S. (2007). *Jung e la creazione della psicologia moderna: Il sogno di una scienza.* Roma: Magi.

Solem, D. (2017). Genders as Theater: The Dionysian dismemberment of the culturally normative narrative in service to the Self. *Psychological Perspectives, 60*, 333–344.

Toub, G. (2013). Jung and gender: Masculine and feminine revisited. C. G. Jung Institute of Colorado. Consultato da: http://jungpage.org/learn/articles/analytical-psychology/147-jung-and-gender-masculine-and-feminine-revisited

"Tell Me What Ails You and I Will Tell You Who You Are": Sufferings in individuation in Jungian clinical practice

Luciana Ximenez and Marcus Quintaes

Abstract

We live in a time of collapsing collective regulations, decling religious hope, disbelief in the discourses of the great Meta-narratives, and the withdrawal of the family centered on paternal authority. In times of absence of external references, anxiety imposes on us the need to quickly choose objects and depression marks the impossibility of connecting with the object. How can the analyst face these new challenges from a Jungian perspective? What tools does analytical psychology offer us, or invite us to reinvent, to function as compasses in the face of these new cultural, social and historical challenges that we are going through? Is there a way of thinking about these models of subjectivation based on Jungian categories such as archetypes, images, collective unconscious, cultural complexes, objective psyche, Soul and many others? How do we find a unique way of functioning within society when as individuals we have to go through the homogeneous discourses of culture? This article does not intend to answer such questions, but rather to bring some theoretical reflections in the light of Jungian and archetypal psychology, which can contribute to the practice of a contemporary clinic.

It is impossible to read Jung's works without considering the influence of culture on his body of work. His definition of archetypes as structures, empty at first, that only take form when in contact with culture, validates that statement. This contact constellates what we call archetypal images. Thus, archetypes can be considered mutable, because they are only accessed when they are formed and actualized by the interaction of the individual with the cultural images that permeate a specific time.

By translating the archetypes within a mythopoetic language— a language that characterizes Jungian thought— we understand gods as psychic powers and strengths that pass through us and direct us. In this sense, Jung draws attention to how, in his time, society disregarded its relationship with the soul, the psyche and the unconscious content. He states that "the gods have become diseases" (1931/2002, para. 54). This statement remains as true as ever because the excess of clarity, information, and demands of Western culture has been bringing more and more of a narrowed consciousness, which can be translated as the *hybris* or ego inflation, propelling us further and further away from who we are, into mass thinking, sustained by cultural demands.

The gods have been disconnected from our daily lives, but Jung states that,

We have abandoned only the verbal spectra and not the psychic facts responsible for the birth of the gods. We remain just as much possessed by autonomous psychic contents, as if they were gods. They are currently called phobias, compulsions, and so forth; in a word, neurotic symptoms[70].

The gods have become diseases, and there is no better way to observe, converse with or even access the Olympic pantheon than through symptoms. Symptoms are the incarnation of the desire for individuation that ravages us beyond the want of egoic conscience.

Individuation, in Jung's work, can be briefly defined as a discovery of one's own singularity, a detachment of mass into the realization of oneself without, however, disregarding society around us. Jung[71] emphasizes that the process of individuation is in self-realizing and encompassing the world, since the individual is a unique being, but one who needs to relate collectively in order to exist.

Individuation means becoming an individual personality connected with the deepest layers of the unconscious, relating with and respecting that which is different, being respected and recognized in difference itself. Even though individuation is the differentiation of what is general and the formation of what is peculiar, the individual path cannot oppose collective norms. The Jungian proposal of individuation is the recognition and acceptance of each subject's singularity, which leads us to two important questions: what makes you absolutely different from other people? How can one learn to live with this difference in a world so saturated with standardized demands?

We live in the time of the collapse of collective regulations and traditional modes of socialization, with the decline of religious hope, disbelief in the discourse of great meta-narratives and the retraction of family as centered around paternal authority. Various denominations are applied to these new times, such as, for example, liquid modernity, by Zigmunt Bauman[72] and hypermodern times, by Giles Lipovetsky[73], and others.

---

[70] Jung, 1931/2002, para. 54.
[71] 1916/2000.
[72] 1998.
[73] 2004.

Philosopher Slavoj Zizek[74], faithful to his Lacanian roots, points towards a dominant figure of the super-self in our time, no longer linked to the repression of enjoyment from the satisfaction of drives, but to the despotic installation of enjoyment as an imperative: enjoyment turning into obligation. Our days are marked by the violent demand of incessantly pursuing immediate satisfaction. Our new processes of socialization are no longer linked to mechanisms of repression, as it was last century, but to mechanisms that demand, unrelentingly, boundless gratification.

It is no coincidence that anxiety and depression appear in psychology and psychiatry practices as the great symptoms of our time, resulting from the subject's inability to respond to the imperatives of the demand for satisfaction. We are facing a scenario where nothing placates the fury of enjoyment, because each and every object reveals itself to be precarious and inadequate to satisfy that request. A perfect scenario for a society of merchandise, of liberal capital parading before us its infinite and idyllic offers of objects that promise to fulfill our insatiable pursuits and requests. It is a vain illusion.

Anxiety imposes on us the need for a quick choice of objects, and depression marks the impossibility of bonding with the object. Psychic suffering ensues, generated by implicit and explicit components of culture: the pressure for similarity, the patriarchy— insistent on imposing rules on men and women— racism and prejudices in general. And here comes the greatest irony: the very society that generates suffering invalidates it. All while emphasizing that great imperative: Enjoy!

If every analyst must situate themself on the subjective horizon of one's time, how can we face these new challenges from the Jungian theoretical perspective? Which theoretical tools does analytical psychology offer us or invite us to reinvent in order to function as compasses in the face of these new cultural, social and historic challenges we have been going through? Will there be a specific way of thinking about these models of subjectivation in times of absolute enjoyment from Jungian categories, like archetypes, images, collective unconscious, cultural complexes, objective psyche, soul, and so many others?

Our desire is to take a stand against the idea of erasing the grain of madness – fantasies, dreams, reveries, symptoms – that exists in every human being, to adapt them to the demands of a society of consumption and production. Health, according to the WHO, was defined in the mid twentieth century as the greatest attainable state of happiness or well-being, both physical and mental. In these homogeneous discourses about culture, there comes the concept of happiness and a healthy life for all, crushing the singularities that do not subject themselves to these moral procedures. What was once an aspiration – being healthy – has become a duty.

---

[74] 2005.

The question to be asked in analyst practices is: what is unbending about the symptoms of individuation as it relates to the ideals of normalization? Here, what is revealed is our division and the peak of our multiplicity: on one hand, the neurotic egoic want of being part of the norm, of the whole, of being one of those who compose the "for all" in culture, and in the other, my subversive, resistant, unclassifiable sides, voices and desires of the soul rejecting the whole and objecting to it through symptoms. That is why we must believe the symptoms. They carry the truth of the unconscious and pave the way for the work of individuation. It is in symptoms that the truth of each person's unconscious hides because the norms, based on a standard of ideals, are always lying.

The Jungian clinical practice offers itself as a place of possibility for each person's particular symptom of individuation. There, we are erotically and generously invited to try to find a place for our particularity in the world in which we are confined. Among the possible paths for our singularities to meet, one concept stands out: pathologizing. This concept can help us reposition ethically and clinically facing an arbitrariness where all psychic pain is converted into pathological damage.

Pathologizing, as proposed by the archetypal psychology of James Hillman, is the mark of a new possibility of acceptance and warmth for these legitimate experiences of the soul: sadness, depression, melancholy, boredom, apathy, despondency, all the pains of existing. If clinical practice, supported by archetypal psychology, is not based on any ideal of a healthy life, creating spaces for the manifestation of pathologizing becomes a *sine qua non* condition for carrying out this psychological work. Unlike traditional medical practice and the biological psychiatry of today, which ended up reducing their practices to attempts at regulating the body's supposed biological dysfunctions, analysis intends to provide recovery and offer a place for the experience of suffering, through which the images of singularity and difference are made present in each person's individuation. This work is called "soul making."

In clinical practice, with images, and working on soul making, we have learned that making a pact with the healthy parts of the "I" is a useless task, because there are simply no healthy parts of the "I." After all, the "I" is a human symptom *par excellence*, their own mental illness. To present pathologizing as a specific and legitimate way for the soul to produce images implies that there are diverse and infinite ways to imagine the lived life. Going beyond egoic desires and restorative needs for stability and balance, the desires of the soul also claim their presence in the shape of images that are distressed, deformed, chaotic, strange, full of meaning that invites examination. What is revealed upon analysis is that there is often more life in crossing the storm than in the peace of calm seas.

Thus, we can understand that salvation does not come through an ideal of health for everyone, but through each person's individual madness. From Jungian or archetypal theoretical perspectives, there is no possibility of seeking a common norm. The more homogeneous, absolute, and globalized the ideals of contemporary culture are, and the greater the proposal of a common norm that applies for all, indiscriminately, boundlessly, the more we have to remember and sustain our individual madness. That is where the idiosyncrasy of Jungian clinical practice resides: to be able to bear what is excessive in the subject in order to individuate their pain, alchemically transforming them from the rags of *prima materia* to the riches of the philosopher's stone built along an analytical course.

In this context, each of us is and always will be an obstacle against the ideal of "for all" in civilization. With the strange traits that constitute our *opus* called individuation, each one will always be an obstacle against the norm of all. The archetypal psychology clinical practice sustained in the creation of a subject of exception is about soul making with that untreatable aspect of the symptom. It is the trait of difference— untreatable, undecipherable, impossible— that identifies someone, since they cannot help but be just that.

What remains for us is to affirm this very strangeness and forge a place in the world that supports it. The rest is silence. And neurosis. In times of watering down affections and homogenizing living, all that remains for us is taking a chance on the obscenity of the symptoms of the soul and affirming the scandalous aspect of every individuation.

References

Jung, C.G. (1931/2002). *Alchemical Studies*. O.C. vol.13. Vozes.

Jung, C. G. (1916/2000*). On the Nature of the Psyche*. O.C. 8/2. Vozes.

Zizek, S. (2005). *Zizek crítico: política e psicanálise na era do multiculturalismo (Critical Zizek: Politics and Psychoanalysis in the era of Multiculturalism)*. São Paulo: Hacker Editores.

Lipvetsky (2004). *Hypermodern Times*. Editora Barcarolla.

Bauman, Z. (1998). *Postmodernity and Its Discontents*. Jorge Zahar Ed.

Hillman, J. (2010). *Re-Visioning Psychology*. Vozes.

"Diga-me do que sofres e te direi quem és":
sofrimentos em individuação na clínica junguiana.

Luciana Ximenez e Marcus Quintaes

Abstract

Vivemos uma época do colapso das regulações coletivas e dos modos de socialização tradicionais tais como o declínio da esperança religiosa, a descrença nos discursos dos grandes Meta-narrativas e o retraimento da família centrada na autoridade paterna.

Em épocas de volatização dos afetos e de ausência de referências externas, a ansiedade nos impõe a necessidade da escolha rápida dos objetos e a depressão marca a impossibilidade da vinculação com o objeto.

Como o analista pode encarar estes novos desafios a partir da perspectiva teórica junguiana? Quais ferramentas a psicologia analítica nos oferece ou nos convida a reinventar, para funcionar como bússolas diante destes novos desafios culturais, sociais e históricos que atravessamos?

Haverá um modo próprio de pensar estes modelos de subjetivação a partir das categorias junguianas como arquétipos, imagens, inconsciente coletivo, complexos culturais, psique objetiva, Alma e tantos outros?

Como encontrar uma maneira própria e singular de funcionar dentro da sociedade quando as particularidades têm que passar pelos discursos homogêneos da cultura?

Esse artigo não tem a pretensão de responder tais perguntas, mas sim de trazer algumas reflexões teóricas à luz da psicologia junguiana e arquetípica, que possam contribuir na prática de uma clínica contemporânea.

Impossível ler a obra de Jung sem considerar a influência da cultura ao longo de toda sua obra. Sua definição de que os arquétipos são estruturas, à priori vazias, que só possuem forma no contato com a cultura, valida essa afirmação. Tal contato origina as chamadas imagens arquetípicas. Dessa forma, arquétipos podem ser considerados mutáveis, pois apenas são acessados quando formados e atualizados pela interação do indivíduo com as imagens culturais que preenchem uma determinada época.

Traduzindo os arquétipos dentro de uma linguagem mitopoética – linguagem esta que caracteriza o pensamento junguiano - entendemos deuses como potências e forças psíquicas que nos atravessam e nos direcionam. Neste sentido, Jung (1931/2002) chama a atenção para o descaso com que a sociedade de sua época se relacionava com a alma, com a psique e com os conteúdos inconscientes. Ele afirma que "os deuses tornaram-se doenças" (para 54). A afirmação permanece mais atual do que nunca, pois cada vez mais o excesso de clareza, informações e exigência da cultura ocidental traz uma estreiteza de consciência que pode ser traduzida como a *hybris* ou a inflação egóica, que nos lança cada vez mais para longe de quem somos e para uma massificação, apoiada pelas exigências culturais.

Os deuses foram desconectados do nosso cotidiano, porém Jung afirma que "abandonamos apenas os espectros verbais e não os fatos psíquicos responsáveis pelo nascimento dos deuses. Ainda estamos tão possuídos pelos conteúdos psíquicos autônomos, como se estes fossem deuses. Atualmente eles são chamados fobias, compulsões, e assim por diante; numa palavra, sintomas neuróticos". (1931/2002, para. 54) Os deuses viraram doenças e não há melhor forma de observar, dialogar ou mesmo acessar o panteão olímpico do que via sintoma. Os sintomas são a encarnação do desejo de individuação que nos assola para além do querer da consciência egóica.

A individuação, na obra de Jung, pode ser brevemente definida como uma descoberta da própria singularidade, um destacamento da massa para a realização de si mesmo sem, no entanto, desconsiderar a sociedade que nos cerca. Jung (1916/2000) ressalta que o processo de individuação está no realizar-se a si mesmo, englobando o mundo, uma vez que o indivíduo é um ser único, mas que necessita relacionar-se coletivamente para existir.

A individuação significa tornar-se uma personalidade individual conectada com as camadas mais profundas do inconsciente, relacionando-se e respeitando o diferente, sendo respeitado e reconhecido na própria diferença. Apesar da individuação ser a diferenciação do geral e formação do peculiar, o caminho individual não pode estar em oposição às normas coletivas. A proposta junguiana da individuação é o reconhecimento e aceitação da singularidade de cada sujeito, o que nos leva a duas importantes perguntas: qual a sua diferença absoluta em relação às outras pessoas? Como saber viver esta diferença neste mundo tão saturado de exigências *standards*?

Vivemos uma época do colapso das regulações coletivas e dos modos de socialização tradicionais tais como o declínio da esperança religiosa, a descrença nos discursos das grandes meta-narrativas e o retraimento da família centrada na autoridade paterna. Várias denominações são dadas a estes novos tempos, como por exemplo modernidade líquida por Z.Baumann (1998) e tempos hipermodernos por Gilles Lipovetsky (2004) entre tantos outros.

O filósofo Slavoj Zizek (2005), fiel à sua herança lacaniana, aponta para uma figura dominante do supereu na contemporaneidade que não está mais vinculada à repressão ao gozo das satisfações pulsionais, e sim à instalação despótica do gozo como imperativo: o gozo transformado em obrigação. Nossos dias são marcados pela exigência violenta de procura incessante de satisfação imediata. Nossos novos processos de socialização não estão mais vinculados aos mecanismos de repressão como no século passado, mas a mecanismos que nos cobram, implacavelmente, a gratificação irrestrita: Goza!

Não por acaso, a ansiedade e a depressão aparecem nos consultórios de psicologia e psiquiatria como os grandes sintomas da contemporaneidade, que resultam da incapacidade do sujeito em responder aos imperativos da exigência de satisfação. Estamos diante de um cenário onde nada aplaca a fúria do gozo, pois todo e qualquer objeto se revela precário e inadequado para satisfazer essa convocação. Cenário perfeito para uma sociedade de mercadorias, liberal-capital, que faz desfilar diante de nós suas ofertas infinitas e idílicas de objetos que prometem atender nossas insaciáveis buscas e solicitações. Vã ilusão.

A ansiedade nos impõe a necessidade da escolha rápida dos objetos e a depressão marca a impossibilidade da vinculação com o objeto. Surge um sofrimento psíquico gerado por componentes implícitos e explícitos da cultura: a pressão pela semelhança, o patriarcado que insiste em impor regras a homens e mulheres, os racismos e preconceitos em geral. E daqui surge a grande ironia, ou seja, a própria sociedade que gera o sofrimento, o invalida. E ressalta-se o grande imperativo: Goza!

Se todo analista deve situar-se no horizonte subjetivo de sua época, como podemos encarar estes novos desafios da perspectiva teórica junguiana? Quais ferramentas teóricas a psicologia analítica nos oferece ou nos convida a reinventar, para funcionar como bússolas diante destes novos desafios culturais, sociais e históricos que atravessamos? Haverá um modo próprio de pensar estes modelos de subjetivação em tempos de gozo absoluto a partir de categorias junguianas como arquétipos, imagens, inconsciente coletivo, complexos culturais, psique objetiva, alma e tantos outros?

Nosso desejo é de nos posicionarmos contra a ideia de se apagar o grão de loucura - fantasias, sonhos, devaneios, sintomas - que existe em cada ser humano para adaptá-lo às exigências da sociedade de consumo e produção. A saúde, segundo a OMS em meados do século XX, foi definida como um estado de felicidade ou de bem estar tanto corporal quanto mental, o maior que se possa atingir. Nestes discursos homogêneos da cultura, surge o conceito de felicidade e vida sadia para todos, que esmaga as singularidades que não se sujeitam a estes procedimentos morais. O que antes era uma aspiração – ser saudável – tornou-se um dever.

A pergunta a ser feita nos consultórios dos analistas é: o que há de irredutível nos sintomas da individuação em relação aos ideais de normalização? Aqui se explicita nossa divisão e o apogeu de nossa multiplicidade: de um lado, o neurótico querer egóico de fazer parte da norma, do todo, ser um dos que compõe o "para todos" da cultura, do outro, meus lados subversivos, resistentes, inclassificáveis, vozes e desejos da alma que recusam o todo e fazem objeção a isso pela via dos sintomas. Por isso, devemos acreditar nos sintomas. Eles carregam a verdade do inconsciente e pavimentam o percurso do trabalho da individuação. É nos sintomas que se esconde a verdade do inconsciente de cada um, pois as normas, calcadas num padrão de ideal, são sempre mentirosas.

A clínica junguiana se oferece como o lugar do possível para o sintoma de individuação particular de cada um. Lá encontramos o convite erótico e generoso de tentar encontrar um lugar para nossa particularidade no mundo em que estamos encerrados. Dentre as possibilidades de caminhos para o encontro de nossas singularidades, um conceito se destaca: o patologizar. Este conceito pode ajudar a nos reposicionarmos de modo ético e clínico frente a arbitrariedade na qual todo sofrimento psíquico é convertido em dano patológico.

Queremos discutir o patologizar, como proposto pela psicologia arquetípica de James Hillman, como sendo a marca de uma nova possibilidade de aceitação e acolhimento para estas legítimas experiências da alma: tristeza, depressão, melancolia, tédio, apatia, desânimo, todas as dores do existir. Se a clínica sustentada pela psicologia arquetípica não se baseia em nenhum ideal de vida saudável, criar espaços para a manifestação do patologizar torna-se condição *sine qua non* para o exercício deste trabalho psicológico. Diferente da prática médica tradicional e da atual psiquiatria biológica que acabaram por resumir suas práticas às tentativas de regulação das supostas disfunções biológicas do corpo, a análise deseja recuperar e oferecer um lugar para a experiência do sofrimento, via pela qual as imagens da singularidade e diferença se presentificam na individuação de cada um. A este trabalho, nomeia-se fazer alma.

Na clínica com as imagens e no trabalho de fazer alma, aprendemos que realizar um pacto com as partes sadias do Eu se faz tarefa inútil, pois simplesmente não há partes sadias do Eu. Afinal o Eu é o sintoma humano por excelência, sua própria enfermidade mental. Trazer o patologizar como forma específica e legítima da alma produzir imagens implica dizer que há formas diversas e infinitas de imaginação da viva vivida. Para além dos anseios egóicos e necessidades reparadoras de estabilidade e equilíbrio, os desejos anímicos também reivindicam sua presença sob a forma de imagens aflitas, deformadas, caóticas, estranhas, prenhes de sentidos a convidar ao aprofundamento. O que se revela numa análise é que, muitas vezes, há mais vida na travessia da tempestade do que na calmaria dos mares tranquilos.

Dessa forma, podemos entender que a salvação não é pela via do ideal da saúde para todos, mas pela via da loucura individual de cada um. A partir das perspectivas teóricas junguianas ou arquetípicas não há nenhuma possibilidade de se visar uma norma comum. Quanto mais forem homogêneos, absolutos e globalizados os ideais da cultura contemporânea, quanto maior for a proposta de uma norma que sirva indiscriminadamente para todos, sem limites, mais precisaremos lembrar e sustentar nossas loucuras individuais. É aí que reside a idiossincrasia da clínica junguiana: poder suportar o que há de excesso no sujeito a fim de poder individuar seu sofrimento, transformando-o alquimicamente, do lixo da *prima* matéria ao luxo da pedra filosofal construída ao longo de um percurso analítico.

Dentro deste contexto cada um de nós é e sempre será um obstáculo àquilo que serve ao ideal do "para todos" da civilização. Com os traços esquisitos que constituem nosso *opus* nomeado individuação, cada um será sempre um obstáculo à norma de todos. A clínica da psicologia arquetípica sustentada na criação de um sujeito da exceção diz respeito ao fazer alma com aquele aspecto intratável do sintoma. É o traço de diferença – intratável, indecifrável, impossível - que identifica alguém pelo fato de não poder deixar de sê-lo.

Resta-nos afirmar a sua própria estranheza e forjar um lugar no mundo que o suporte. O resto é silêncio. E neurose. Em tempos de pasteurização dos afetos e homogeneização do viver, só nos resta apostar na obscenidade dos sintomas da alma e afirmar o traço escandaloso de toda individuação.

Bibliografia

Jung, C.G. (1931/2002). *Estudos Alquímicos*. O.C. vol13. Petrópolis: Vozes.

Jung, C. G. (1916/2000*). A Natureza da psique*. O.C. 8/2. Petrópolis: Vozes.

Zizek, S. (2005). *Zizek crítico: política e psicanálise na era do multiculturalismo*. São Paulo: Hacher Editores.

Lipovetsky (2004). *Os tempos hipermodernos*. São Paulo: Editora Barcarolla.

Bauman, Z. (1998). *O mal-estar da pós modernidade*. Rio de Janeiro: Jorge Zahar Ed.

Hillman, J. (2010). *Re-vendo a psicologia*. Petrópolis: Vozes.

The Plane's Wreckages, the Broken Dream
A personal story about the trauma of the Yom Kippur War, its symbolism and coping with it

Moshe Alon

Abstract

Moshe Alon served during the Yom Kippur War as a drone commander. In this paper he remembers the moments when a Syrian plane dived at his drone and crashed a few meters away. Alon recounts his personal testimony, recalling the prayer before the storm, the atmosphere of helplessness, and the moments of terror between life and death. The young officer, who has become an educational psychologist and Jungian analyst, seeks to sketch, through the story of his personal trauma, the outlines of national trauma, as well as the way to 'experiential treatment' on a joint trip with him and his son to the area where everything happened.

PART 1

My Yom Kippur War started in the summer of 1973. During the summer vacation, between the second and third year of university, I studied psychology, and I worked as an instructor at the Egged drivers' children's camp on the beach in Ashdod City. After two graceful training cycles, with a team of young guides, it was decided to give us, as a gesture, a two-day trip to the north of the country. On the Egged bus we went north in August for a weekend. In the evening we stayed in Tiberias, the next day the bus climbed to the Golan Heights from south to north. A peaceful, quiet Shabbat, the air as if standing from exhaustion and heat, quiet that does not give away anything. We walked past sites that are well known to me in the plateau: Kibbutz Mevo-Hama, which my army unit established in 1968, Kibbutz Ramat Magshimim, Gamla Waterfall, the Druze settlements, Birkat Ram, a lake in a crater of vulcan. Magical, beautiful places, a sense of security, a feeling that this is ours forever, nothing testified to what will happen here in less than two months.

In my home, meanwhile, a permanent assignment was waiting for me as a reserve officer in an armored battalion. The battalion's seat is located at the Soreq base near Ramla City. Itzik, Zvika and I, three young officers, who served together regularly as instructors in the officers' school, were assigned to the same battalion, to the same company. The division commander, Musa Peled, summoned us for an introductory interview, said a few words about the division-brigade-battalion, and here I am a platoon commander in an armored battalion. And yes, I am invited back in August to a divisional-skeleton exercise in the Tze'elim Base at the south of the country, at the Negev Desert. Tze'elim base was one of my unloved bases: difficult conditions, hard training, sleepless nights. And here, in August 1973, I was stationed at the Tze'elim base for a three-day skeletal exercise. I, with an officer older than me, get on a drone and represent a company or battalion in the exercise. We start driving, and within half an hour I find myself lying on the floor of the drone and sleeping deeply. It lasted for three days: from time to time I woke up, inquired about what was going on. The officer who was with me informed me that we had captured a number of targets: "We swept them," and we continued to the next targets. From all the divisional exercise, I remember the fatigue, the sleep, the conquests in the flight, and most importantly the armored personnel carrier moved behind, after the tanks: the tanks do most of the work, we come in the second wave just to make sure, to ensure, to complete small things...

Yom Kippur Eve in 1973, for 24 hours there were no vehicles on the streets, it is considered the most important Holy day of the year. There are still no clear signs that anything is going to happen the next day. The plans are as usual: from my parents' house in Bat Yam City I will walk in the evening to the synagogue in Jaffa, a southern neighborhood of Tel-Aviv, from there after the prayer I will continue to the center of Jaffa to the house of a friend, where friends from Jaffa and the "Scouts" liked to meet. Towards eight o'clock, the members gathered by foot, except for one. The same one was the focus of a conversation for a few minutes after the gathering: the sucker who was assigned a permanent position in the army, who "ate it" now and did not receive a vacation. There is talk of some kind of alert in the IDF, but in its non-combat role possibly. After a few minutes of ridicule, we turned to other matters to pass the time, including hot backgammon games. Close to midnight, we parted ways and the march back to Bat Yam City began. The streets are quiet, no vehicles on the roads, even the era of bicycles has not yet begun.

Saturday morning, Yom Kippur. I am still at an age when the day and prayer are significant to me: on a personal level, it is my birthday on the Hebrew date, from a family point of view, I lived with my parents who are traditionally religious and the day is very significant to them. I still believed and identified with the day on a religious level (a day of fasting, torture, and soul-searching.).

It's ten in the morning, the sound of vehicles driving on the road reaching my ears as I sit in the depths of the synagogue, my ears straightened: "What is this?" At eleven, the sounds of the engines of the cars driving on the road near the synagogue increased. Restlessness begins to intensify within me, and I notice that I am no longer attentive to prayer. I decide to go outside. I am amazed to see a lot of traffic of vehicles on the road, and especially of military vehicles. It is clear that something is happening: military and civilian vehicles of this magnitude are never moving on Yom Kippur. It is not a joke. I feel the intensification of anxiety inside me. Outside, I meet a friend from high school, who also came from another synagogue, nearby. We exchange words between us, and we agree that it is clear that something military is happening. It is noon. I decide I cannot stay in the synagogue anymore, and decide to leave for my house and to figure out what is going on. I go back into the synagogue to say goodbye to my father. I remember the way home well, mainly because two thoughts ran through my head. One is that I really like the "closing prayer" in the synagogue of the Jewish Moroccan community where I prayed for years with my father. The prayer was characterized by the fact that all the worshippers cover their heads with prayer shawls and pray-sing loudly, powerfully, enthusiastically, with a naïve belief that, indeed, as promised, it is possible in the closing minutes of the holy day to change the evil of the decree. I loved this prayer and its melody: "Oh god almighty and full of plot..." And here I am going to miss this prayer today. A second thought crossed my mind, that here I am going towards war, and I turn to God and ask that if I am doomed to fight, I seek to fight in a "fair" battle, and if I get hurt then in such a "manly" fair battle, not to be hit by an obscure shell, or a hidden mine, but to fight and feel potent and not be hurt by something that cannot be so defended against.

I arrive at my house and make a phone call to Itzik. The situation is clear to us: a war is about to break out. We conclude that there is no point in waiting for them to recruit us. We decided to meet at his home in Tel Aviv at three o'clock and leave for Soreq base. I decide to go to my brother to say goodbye. I take my scooter and drive to his apartment. My brother lives in another neighborhood in Bat Yam City and had been recently discharged from the army as a captain. He had not yet been assigned to a reserve unit. It was clear to me that he would be recruited as well. I got to him. My brother, his wife, and their little boy were at home. It's two o'clock. Suddenly, an alarm pierces the airspace. *What should I do? Where are we going? We have a small child with us, how do we take care of him?* We decide to go downstairs towards the shelter of the building. I change my mind and decide not to go down to the shelter but to continue back to my parents' house, pack up, and say goodbye. The road is packed with cars. I pack my belongings and towards three o'clock say goodbye to my mother and younger sister and head to Tel Aviv. (My mother told me after the war that the draft order came to me in the evening at eight o'clock when I was already deep in the preparations at Soreq base). I arrive with the scooter to the house of Itzik, who was living with his wife's parents at that time. I left the scooter near the entrance of the building. The scooter stayed there until my first holiday after the war. (Itzik's mother-in-law later shared with me her anxieties: every time she saw the scooter parked near her house; she was afraid that it would be abandoned if I never returned).

We reached the Soreq base, Itzik and I, hitchhiking. We found our company commander and staff sergeant, whom we first met. Itzik, Zvika and I were immediately placed as platoon command-ers in the armored corps company, and we began to get to know our soldiers little by little. I was given a platoon, about 20 fighters on two drones. The soldiers knew each other for several years. They are all veterans of the Six-Day War. The jokes flew from all sides. They were invited for another trip like in the Six Days, what did they do then? They sat down on the drones and drove around Sinai Desert, just like we practiced in the divisional exercise: clean-sweep after the tanks to collect booty and captives. It seems that the difference for them this time is only the direction: then they were intended for the south and this time we are destined for the north of the country,

119

for The Golan Heights. We still do not know the magnitude of the disaster. During our preparations I passed by a television set: Golda Meir, the Prime Minister, looked out of it in black and white and announced the attacks on us in Sinai Desert and The Golan Heights. It is clear that this is not a known war, something else is happening, we were surprised in a big way!

The next day, Sunday, we moved on chains to the north. The division was intended for containment in the southern of The Golan Heights. The soldiers of my department joked all the way to the north, that they were going to collect booty, a name was chosen for the operation: "Golan's Diamonds."

The first 24 hours with my platoon gave me an initial idea of who my platoon soldiers were: One introduced himself as a soldier who was in charge of the 0.3 machine gun in the drone, because he had a leg problem and could not run. His friends, who knew him, whispered into my ear that I would agree and that I should be careful with him because he is nervous and already has a number of files with the police. The other, looking so unsmiling, not belonging, covered in a coat in the heat that prevailed, I watched him as he loaded his cartridges with bullets and insisted on putting them in the opposite direction. And the other, the older one, who coined the name of the operation we are going to, and who conveyed a lot of confidence, and the other that the whole platoon knew the size of his "tool" and laughed at him with jealousy and he participated in their laughter, and the other who constantly insisted on talking to me about sex issues: "Moshe, are you going down? Moshe are you licking? Moshe, do you like to be sucked?" "Come on, leave me alone, where am I supposed to go down and what to lick besides popsicle, and what to suck, I haven't been that age for a long time?" What is the big difference between my new soldiers and the cadets of the officers' course that I taught at the officers' school for almost two years in the regular service? Or maybe I was so naïve.

In the early evening, we approached the night parking lot, passing by a small town, Kfar Tavor. Itzik announces over the radio that he has a mechanical problem with his drone and needs assistance. Due to lack of time, they decide to drag it and I volunteer my drone to tow. Approaching Poriah, another small town where the battalion parking lot is for the night. The battalion commander gathers the battalion officers for a briefing: "Tomorrow we enter the line of fire, the front, the situation in the Golan Heights is very bad, there are no forces to stop the enemy!"

What? With the rehabilitated drones from World War II we planned to enter the first line of fire in front of Syrian tanks? And with these soldiers of my new platoon, whom I'm getting to know? What are you talking about? The situation is that bad? Apparently, yes. I come back from the briefing in a depressed mood, the situation is really desperate.

The next morning, Monday, we get organized and start circling the Sea of Galilee from the south and ascending to the plateau from the direction of Zemach junction. Near the Zemach junction, I notice a gathering from the drone and identify my friends who remained in Kibbutz Mevo-

Hama after we were discharged from the IDF. I call them and ask what the situation looks like, they say that they were evacuated from Mevo-Hama. Less than two months ago I was traveling here, the soul expanded then from the expanses, from the landscape, from the tranquility, from the security, from the pride. What do you mean you were evacuated from home? What is not sure there? We go up to the Golan Heights via Korsi junction, approaching Kibbutz Ramat Magshimim. The kibbutz is surrounded by abandoned Syrian tanks, some still burning, some with camouflage branches. The Syrian tanks were found exactly on the route of the trip from the summer, on and inside the fences of the kibbutz. What is going on here over the last couple of days? Ambulances with wounded soldiers passing us towards Tiberias' City hospital, it's not a joke, it's a war! An order is heard in the radio telling to get off the central road. We drive in a column parallel to the main road of the plateau. Suddenly, another order sound to return to the road because mines have been placed in the section we are driving on.

In the early evening, we reach the Tel a-Saki hill. The remnants of the battles that have taken place since Yom Kippur are evident here: war vehicles of the Syrians and ours are mixing with each other. Burnt and crushed IDF drones, next to scorched, damaged, and abandoned Syrian tanks. In each of our tools and theirs were human beings, and most of them have been killed or injured physically and/or mentally.

We prepare for an overnight stay and sleep on the ground. We settled ourselves closer to the east-north side of the hill before going to sleep. Sleeping in a row, organizing a guard. I am among the guards for the first half of the night. I wake up early in the morning, a number of my soldiers laughing mockingly at the guard that was not there at night. After I guarded apparently no one filled his mission of guarding, anyone who was required to get up to guard woke up immediately the next one after him, supposedly it was time to guard, and so at an early hour the guard stopped. Again I am struck with amazement at the level of my soldiers' morale.

We get up early in the morning, and in the daylight we could see where we were at night: in the center of a whole sooty field of thorns, all around are the burned bodies of Syrian fighters who were hit the day before by napalm bombs that burned them in their vehicles. Our awe is in the indifference in their faces: neither joy nor shock, bodies are lying that only yesterday were living human beings, and again I have thoughts of the terrible waste of souls in war.

Wednesday—today— is the eve of Sukkot Holy day. The Syrians are shooting at us in the area of Tel Saki Hill. Mortar shells are falling all around us. Shrinking in the drone, in the distance we can see Tel Fares Mountain. The situation is ambiguous; it is not clear who controls this strategic ridge: us, or the Syrians? Bombs fall on the mountain: who fires at whom? Are we on them? They are on us?

We lack so much information. The company commander is equipped with a photocopy of a map, but we have no maps, no binoculars. In my hands is an Uzi submachine gun, which turns out to be not at all suitable for today's type of combat due to its short range. I notice a soldier who, from day one, seemed incomprehensible to me, the one who was curled up in a coat when it was so hot. His "friends" constantly laughed at him, mocked him (one could also say abused him), he was chosen as the scapegoat to throw their anxieties upon. He also did not do the right practices while we were bombed and seemed overwhelmed. I decided to take him under my wing, to attach him to me, and thus the injuries to him by the others diminished. I ordered him to take off his coat, drink water, do everything I do, and go with me wherever I went. Only later, when I specialized more in the subject of trauma, did I realize that he was in shock and thus paralyzed. As well, the older fighter who coined the name of the operation was evacuated the night before because he was not feeling well and my platoon sergeant had an ulcer attack and was also evacuated.

Wednesday afternoon there is some calm in the shelling. Soon the Sukkot Holiday will begin, and yet we are so far from the holiday. We are in an open area, to the east of us Tel Saki Hill, about 500 meters north of Tel Fares Mountain, and several kilometers south of us is Kibbutz Ramat Magshimim. The area is full of terraces and small hills. Several eucalyptus trees are close to us, a water tower farther off between the trees and Tel Saki. I am attached with the caterpillar to the terrace which gives me a sense of security and protection, at least on one side.

The silence is disturbed by a sound and the sight of a lone plane passing over us. It is immediately identified as a Syrian MiG-17 that identifies targets below as if he is a bird of prey. We are laid exposed and visible to him, and all that is left for him is to choose one of the many targets that were scattered on the ground. I acted like an automaton: as soon as I noticed the plane, according to the practice, I ordered everyone to get off the two drones and move away from them, because for the plane, the drone is the target and not the lone soldier in the field. I also ordered two fighters to be left in each drone to operate the 0.5 machine gun and to fire at the plane. In my drone, I remained as the machine gun operator along with another fighter and opened fire on the MiG. He was also a convenient target: he flew slowly through the sky at a relatively low altitude. Flying in a circle, he completed one turn. I thought that he was choosing his target and now he would dive towards it and shoot it with his machine guns and rockets. Meanwhile one crate of ammunition has run out, already 100 bullets have been fired at the plane. The fighter next to me has placed a new crate and the plane begins its second round. Suddenly out of nowhere, a Mirage plane appears and sits on the tail of the MiG, no firing is seen from the direction of the Mirage on the MiG, but the Israeli plane has clear superiority. I keep shooting at the MiG, it looks close and a relatively easy target. I see the bullets hitting the plane and suddenly the MiG makes a turn and starts lowering. It flies in a direction straight to my drone, to me. I keep shooting at it with a machine gun, the MiG is very low, it gets close to the ground. I shoot, but then I stop, because the MiG has lowered so much that the side of the drone does not allow me to lower the machine gun anymore. The MiG went down so low, it is clearly flying towards me, about to collide with the drone. I shout: "Immaaaaa, No!" (Mother, no!). I lower my head and body into the caterpillar and wait for the boom. After a huge explosive sound, parts of an airplane were flying, burning, next to mine and the other drone. The plane went down so low, either the pilot was hit and did not control the plane, or the plane was hit and out of control, and in it fell towards the ground, only by chance towards my drone, encountering a ground fold about 25-30 meters from the drone and crashed on its pilot. It turns out my new platoon sergeant was a photographer by profession, and the camera was with him in a retrieval position, so as soon as the plane fell, while its parts were burning, he pulled out the camera and took pictures of the plane. A few minutes after the fall of the aircraft, and another few minutes of recovery, soldiers began to appear from distant places to observe the spectacle: A MiG-17 plane smashed to the ground, the pilot killed, beheaded, and laid among the fragments. The tail stood out, the engine, the wings, and many other parts scattered on the ground. Everyone who arrived was interested to know whether the pilot's gun had already been taken. I am again amazed at my indifference in the face of the body of the pilot killed next to me. I still cannot digest the full experience.

I prefer to end the story of my Yom Kippur War here. Although I was recruited for 153 days, most of them I served in the Sinai Desert on both sides of the Suez Canal. There were other events that were significant to me in the war, but the fall of the plane was, for me, a peak experience that symbolized the whole war: unskilled fighters that find themselves in front of an airplane, exposed, vulnerable—a tremendous advantage for the enemy's plane—and miraculously, it falls. The feeling that I was so close to death and yet survived. This is how the state of Israel is in the Yom Kippur War: uneven power relations, weapons incompatible with those of the enemy, unskilled, unprepared, exposed and wanton soldiers on all fronts. Stuck between the fall of the state in the face of the concentrated attacks in the Golan Heights and the Sinai Desert. In general, we were prepared for one war, as in the Six Days, and here we entered another war unprepared, and not equipped properly. It is clear that trust in the army, in politicians, and in the state, has cracked, and cannot be reunited as in the past, and perhaps it is better that way.

Sometimes other thoughts occurred to me: The Syrian plane represents the State of Israel in the Yom Kippur War: a lone plane in the sky, exposed, moving slowly as a convenient target for interception, not aware of its situation, flying with excessive confidence, easily shot down by fighters from the ground, falling to the ground and crashing. Yes, this is the Israeli experience (and mine) before Yom Kippur 1973 and after it: The Israeli's reality and the image, which was in the sky and not anchored in reality, are not aware of the changed reality. We dove abruptly to the ground and crashed. From these pieces we had to be rehabilitated.

The experience of the plane has gone with me throughout my life. It seems to me that more than any soldier who was in the area, I am one of the few who was affected by this. I returned to this place ritually— compulsively at times. Something called me to return again and again to this place and to relive what happened to me on the eve of Sukkot 1973, and in general, to that difficult war. I did not experience a rebirth experience necessarily, not really trauma either, but the place with the wreckage of the plane was a place of pilgrimage for me.

PART 2

Later, when my children grew up, I wanted to be there with them as well. For the first time I visited there with my son Gilad on a trip to the north of the country and The Golan Heights when he was seven years old. Navigating the plane was easy, the map of the area is so clear in my head. Gilad was passionate about the sight of the wreckage of the plane. It is clear that most of its parts were removed: the tail and wings were taken, but there remained enough parts scattered in the territory: the engine, a wheel, the pilot's seat, the machine gun, a rocket hive and hundreds of other small unidentified parts. I chose a few pieces, mostly from the plane's canopy, and brought them home. I placed them on the library shelf. Whoever asked what it was, got the truth.

Tuesday is the day between the New Year and Yom Kippur. I do not work typically on this day. Gilad my son, now in the eighth grade, went with his class on a trip to northern Israel and The Golan Heights for three days. It is lunchtime, I have showered, I am resting in my bed, and the phone rings. The principal from Gilad's school informs me that during the trip, Gilad was hit in the head as a result of a fall in the Gilabun Waterfall in The Golan Heights. He was taken to Ziv Hospital in Safed City and I have to go to him. I called my wife Shuli, get organized, and go to the north. All the way I have anxious thoughts in my head: What happened? What damage was caused? Will he recover completely? Arriving at the hospital, after X-rays and stitches in the head, Gilad is conscious. The doctor announces that a miracle has occurred and the injury is external only. Three days later, Gilad was transferred to a hospital in the center of the country and after two months he fully recovered from the head injury. But what about the injury to the soul?

Today, I am skilled in traumatic injuries, and understand the significance of the danger of such injuries. I come up with an idea and I bring it to Gilad: "I bought a new car, let's just go on journey with it. We will not just drive, but we will travel to the Golan Heights and connect the two events that you and I went through. We will drive to the place where the plane fell and reconstruct everything that happened there in the story and in the photograph, then we will drive to the place where you fell in the Gilabun Waterfall and we will reconstruct it again in the story and in the picture." And so on a cloudy and rainy day, during the Hanukkah holiday, we got up early in the morning and drove north. The navigation is easy for the plane: after Kibbutz Ramat Magshimim near Tel Saki Hill, break on a dirt road to the west, walk about 500 meters. After the water tower, near the eucalyptus trees, we reach the wreckage of the plane. I reconstruct what happened, find the exact place where my drone stood. We dig in the ground and find a crate of ammunition of a crushed 0.5 machine gun and casings of the bullets. We took pictures and parts of the plane as souvenirs, including the ammunition box and bullet pods, and say goodbye to the place.

Then we drove to the Gilabun Waterfall.

It is raining. We leave the car in the parking lot, get organized, and get going. We reach the waterfall from above and descend to its foot. I ask Gilad to reconstruct exactly what happened. Gilad stands on a rock close to the water's edge. While standing there, the instructor joked that whoever wanted could get in and jump into the water. Gilad did not linger and jumped. I asked him to make a jumping motion and immortalize everything on camera. We got to the moment after the jump into the water. Gilad described that within seconds he was covered in blood. Everyone around him was frightened, his fellow students, the accompanying teachers, the instructors. We look together at the place of the jump. We cannot clearly see that the water is shallow and at the bottom of it are rocks because of the turbidity of the water and the dark rocks. It is clear that Gilad was hit by rocks that were close to the surface of the water and got a strong blow. Then the evacuation journey begins. Gilad and I began to reconstruct the evacuation: Gilad remembered everything in detail, the way they went, how he felt. We started walking, a drizzle accompanying us all the time. I cannot believe Gilad had walked such a long way to the point where a vehicle could have reached him for evacuation. We walked along the Gilabun river and then the road separated from the route of the stream and continued through a field. In this season of December everything is green and red-fleshy anemones are already blooming, but then it was a hot summer.

"How did you go all this way on foot, injured, frightened?" We reached a place called the Officers' Pool, where a military vehicle was waiting for him, which evacuated him to an ambulance, which with sirens rushed to Ziv Hospital at the city of Safed City. From the Officers' Pool, we walked back to the Gilabun Waterfall and from there back to the car.

The main part of building and restoring our self-confidence was completed. There is one more point left for rehabilitation, just in case. During the Passover vacation, I suggested to Gilad that we take another trip to The Golan Heights: this time to the Hexagonal Pool. On a spring day we went there. We walked down the stream. This time we bathed in the waters of the stream and made friends with the place and the entrance to the water, that is, to remove the part that may have remained of fear of the water and a controlled and safe entry into the waters of the stream in The Golan Heights.

The story of the connection between my rescue from the plane during the Yom Kippur War and Gilad's rescue from an uncommitted jump is over. I keep visiting the place where the plane crashed from time to time, sometimes alone and sometimes with other friends, tell the story, take pictures. I don't think all of them were so impressed, or at least do not give any real expression to it. Even when we were there, Itzik, Zvika, and I (the three platoon commanders and the wives), they were more amused by my attitude towards the event than by the experience, even though it was theirs too.

And Gilad? Gilad enlisted in the IDF to the Unit 669 whose main mission is to retrieve soldiers and civilians who need rescue and evacuation, including those who jump/fall in the Golan Heights' streams, including a rescue at the Gilabun waterfall. Sometimes we participate in extraction and rescue operations, he as a fighter in the Air Force Rescue Unit, and I as an educational psychologist who helps residents who have been harmed in acts of terrorism or other traumas. We have already participated in operations where he brings those he rescues to the hospital, and I am continuing in the mental health treatment of the victims and their relatives.

סיפור אישי על טראומת מלחמת יום הכיפורים, סמליותה וההתמודדות עמה.

המטוס ושברו

> *משה אלון שירת כמפקד מחלקת נגמ"ש ם במלחמת יום הכיפורים. במאמר זה הוא נזכר ברגעים בהם מטוס סורי צלל*
> *לקראת הנגמ"ש בו היה והתרסק מספר מטרים ממנו. אלון משחזר את התנסותו האישית ונזכר בתפילה שלפני הסערה,*
> *אווירת חוסר האונים ורגעים של חרדה שבין חיים ומוות. הקצין הצעיר אשר לימים נעשה לפסיכולוג חינוכי ואנליטיקאי*
> *יונגיאני מנסה לשרטט דרך סיפור הטראומה האישית את המתאר של הטראומה הלאומית וכן את האופן של 'טיפול*
> *התנסותי-חווייתי' בטיול משותף עם בנו, שעבר גם כן אירוע טראומטי באזור כנער, מסע לאזור שהכול התרחש בו.*

מלחמת יום הכיפורים שלי התחילה בקיץ 1973. בחופשת הקיץ, בין שנת הלימודים השנייה לשלישית באוניברסיטה,
בלימודי הפסיכולוגיה, אז עבדתי כמדריך בקייטנה של ילדי נהגי "אגד" בחוף באשדוד. לאחר שני מחזורי הדרכה חיניים,
עם צוות מדריכים צעירים, הוחלט להעניק לנו כמצווה טיול דו-יומי לצפון הארץ. באוטובוס של "אגד" נסענו צפונה בחודש
אוגוסט לסוף שבוע. בערב לנו בטבריה, למחרת טיפס האוטובוס לרמת-הגולן מדרומה לצפונה. שבת שלווה, שקטה, האוויר
כאילו עומד מרוב עייפות וחום. שקט שלא מסגיר כלום. עברנו על פני אתרים המוכרים לי היטב ברמה: הישוב מבוא-חמה,
שגרעין הנח"ל שלי הקים ב – 1968, קיבוץ רמת מגשימים, מפל גמלא, יישובי הדרוזים, ברכת רם. מקומות קסומים, יפים,
תחושת ביטחון, תחושה שזה שלנו לעד, שום דבר לא העיד מה יתחולל כאן בעוד פחות מחודשיים ימים.
בינתיים חיכתה לי הצבה קבועה כקצין מילואים-מ"מ חרמ"ש בגדוד שריון. מקום מושב הגדוד בבסיס שורק ליד
רמלה. איציק, צביקה ואני, שלושה קצינים צעירים, שרתנו יחד כמדריכים בבית-הספר לקצינים, הוצבנו לאותו
גדוד, לאותה פלוגה. מפקד האוגדה, מוסה פלד, זימן אותנו לריאיון היכרות, אמר מספר מילים על האוגדה-חטיבה-גדוד
והנה אני מפקד מחלקה חרמ"ש בפלוגת חרמ"ש בגדוד שריון. וכן, אני מוזמן עוד בחודש אוגוסט לתרגיל אוגדתי-שלדי במרחבי
צאלים. בסיס צאלים היה אחד הבסיסים הלא אהובים עלי: תנאים קשים, אימונים קשים, לילות ללא שינה. והנה באוגוסט
1973 אני מתייצב בבסיס צאלים לתרגיל שלדי, תלת-יומי. אני עם קצין ותיק ממני עולים על זחל"ם ומייצגים בתרגיל
פלוגה או גדוד. אנחנו מתחילים בנסיעה, תוך חצי שעה אני מוצא עצמי שרוע על רצפת הזחל"ם וישן עמוקות. זה נמשך
שלושה ימים: מפעם לפעם התעוררתי, בירררתי מה נשמע. הקצין שהיה איתי בישר לי שכבשנו ביעף מספר יעדים,
"טאטאנו" אותם ואנחנו ממשיכים ליעדים הבאים. מכל התרגיל האוגדתי זכורה לי העייפות, השינה, הכיבושים ביעף, והכי
חשוב שהחרמ"ש נע מאחור, אחרי הטנקים: הטנקים עושים את עיקר העבודה, אנחנו באים בגל השני רק לוודא, להבטיח,
להשלים דברים קטנים...
ערב יום הכיפורים 1973. עדיין אין סימנים ברורים שמשהו עתיד להתרחש למחרת. התוכניות כרגיל: מבית הורי בבת-
ים אלך רגלית בערב לבית הכנסת ביפו, משם לאחר התפילה אמשיך ללב של יפו לביתו של חבר, שם נדברנו החברים מיפו
ו"הצופים" להיפגש. ואכן לקראת השעה שמונה בערב התכנסנו החברים פרט לאחד. אותו אחד היווה מוקד שיחה למספר
דקות לאחר ההתכנסות: הפרחייר שחתם קבע בצבא, ש"אכל אותה" עכשיו ולא קיבל חופשה. כן, מדברים על איזו שהיא
כוננות בצה"ל, אבל בתפקידו הלא קרבי? ולאחר מספר דקות של לעג, פנינו לעיסוקים אחרים להעברת הזמן ובינתיים

127

משחקי שש-בש לוהטים. קרוב לחצות נפרדנו והחלה הצעדה חזרה לבת-ים. הרחובות שקטים, אף רכב לא נוסע על הכביש, עידן האופניים טרם החל.

שבת בבוקר, יום הכיפורים. אני עדיין בתקופה שהיום והתפילה משמעותיים לי: ברמה אישית זהו יום ההולדת שלי בתאריך העברי, מבחינה משפחתית גרתי עם הורי שהם דתיים-מסורתיים והיום מאד משמעותי להם. עדיין האמנתי והזדהיתי עם היום ברמה דתית (יום צום, עינוי, ושל חשבון נפש...). השעה 10 בוקר, קולות כלי רכב הנוסעים על הכביש מגיעים לאוזני ביושבי במעמקי בית הכנסת, האוזניים הזדקרו: "מה זה?". בשעה 11.00 גברו קולות המנועים של המכוניות שנשעו על הכביש סמוך לבית הכנסת. חוסר שקט מתחיל להתעצם בתוכי, ואני שם לב שכבר אינני קשוב לתפילה. אני מחליט לצאת החוצה. אני נדהם לראות תנועה רבה של כלי רכב בכביש, ובעיקר של כלי רכב צבאיים. ברור שמשהו מתרחש: אף פעם לא נעים ביום הכיפורים כלי רכב צבאיים ואזרחיים בהיקף כזה. זה לא צחוק! אני מרגיש בתוכי את התעצמות החרדה. אני פוגש בחוץ חבר מבית הספר התיכון, שיצא גם הוא מבית כנסת אחר, סמוך. אנחנו מחליפים מילים מספר בינינו, שברור שמשהו צבאי מתרחש. השעה 12 בצהריים, אני מחליט שאינני יכול להישאר יותר בבית הכנסת, ומחליט לעזוב לביתי ולהתחיל לברר מה קורה. אני חוזר לתוך בית הכנסת נפרד מאבי. הדרך הביתה זכורה לי היטב, בעיקר משום שתי מחשבות שחלפו-התרוצצו בראשי. האחת, שאני מאד אוהב את "תפילת הנעילה" בבית הכנסת של העדה המרוקאית בו התפללתי שנים עם אבי. התפילה אופיינה בכך שכל המתפללים מכסים את ראשם בטליתות ומתפללים-שרים בקול רם, בעוצמה, בהתלהבות, באמונה נאיבית, שאכן כפי שמובטח, ניתן בדקות הנעילה לשנות את רוע הגזרה...אהבתי את התפילה הזו והמנגינה שלה: "אל נורא עלילה..." והנה אני הולך להחמיץ תפילה זו היום, אני הולך לרשום לעצמי חיסור של תפילה זו. מחשבה שנייה שחלפה בראשי, שהנה אני הולך לקראת מלחמה, ואני פונה לאלוהים ומבקש שאם נגזר עלי להילחם אני מבקש להילחם בקרב "הוגן", ואם להיפגע אז בקרב הוגן "גברי" כזה, לא להיפגע מפגז עלום, או מוקש נסתר, אלא להילחם ולהרגיש אונים ולא להיפגע ממשהו שאי אפשר להתגונן כ"כ מפניו.

אני מגיע לביתי, טלפון לאיציק, תמונת המצב ברורה לנו, מלחמה עומדת לפרוץ. אנחנו מסכמים שאין טעם להמתין עד שיגייסו אותנו. החלטנו להיפגש בביתו בת"א בשעה שלוש אחה"צ ונצא משם לבסיס שורק. החלטתי לנסוע לאחי להיפרד ממנו. לקחתי את הקטנוע שלי ונסעתי אליו. אחי גר בשכונה אחרת בבת-ים, אחי השתחרר לא מזמן מצבא קבע, וטרם שוב ליחידת מילואים. ברור היה לי שהוא יגויס גם. הגעתי אליו. אחי, אשתו וילדם הקטן היו בבית. השעה 14.00. לפתע אזעקה מפלחת את חלל האוויר. מה עושים? לאן הולכים? יש אתנו ילד קטן, איך נשמור עליו? אנחנו מחליטים לרדת למטה לכוון המקלט. אני משנה דעתי ומחליט לא לרדת למקלט אלא להמשיך חזרה לבית הורי, לארוז ולהיפרד. הכביש הומה מכוניות.

אני אורז חפצים ולקראת השעה 15.00 נפרד מאימי ואחותי הצעירה ויוצא לכוון ת"א. (אימי ספרה לי לאחר המלחמה שצו הגיוס הגיע אלי בערב בשעה שמונה כשכבר הייתי עמוק בשלבי ההיערכות בבסיס שורק). אני מגיע עם הקטנוע לביתו של איציק, שגר אז עם הורי אשתו. השארתי את הקטנוע ליד הכניסה לבניין. הקטנוע נשאר שם עד לחופשתי הראשונה לאחר המלחמה. (חמתו של איציק שתפה אותי לאחר מכן בחרדותיה: בכל פעם שראתה את הקטנוע חונה ליד ביתה, חששה שמא יישאר מיותם).

הגענו לבסיס שורק, איציק ואני, בטרמפים. מצאנו את המ"פ והסמ"פ שלנו, שהכירנו אותם לראשונה. איציק, צביקה ואני הושמנו מיד כמפקדי מחלקות בפלוגת החרמ"ש. התחלנו להכיר את חיילינו לאט, לאט. אני קיבלתי מחלקה, כעשרים לוחמים ועליה על שני זחל"מים. החיילים הכירו זה את זה מספר שנים. כולם בוגרי מלחמת ששת הימים. הבדיחות עפו מכל עבר. הזעיקו אותם לעוד טיול כמו בששת הימים, מה הם עשו אז? התיישבו על הזחל"מים ונסעו במרחבי סיני, בדיוק כמו שתרגלנו בתרגיל האוגדתי: ניקו-טאטאו אחרי הטנקים, ואספו שלל ושבויים. נראה שההבדל עבורם הפעם הוא רק הכיוון: אז הם יועדו לדרום והפעם אנחנו מיועדים לצפון, לגולן. עדיין אינם יודעים את גודל האסון. בתוך ההתארגנות המחלקתית-פלוגתית חלפתי ליד מכשיר טלוויזיה: גולדה מאיר, ראש הממשלה, ניבטה ממנו בצבעים שחור-לבן ובישרה על המתקפות עלינו בסיני ובגולן. ברור שאין זו מלחמה מוכרת, משהו אחר מתרחש, הפתיעו אותנו בגדול!

למחרת, יום א', נענו על שרשראות לצפון. האגודה יועדה לבלימה בדרום רמת-הגולן. אנשי מחלקתי התלוצצו כל הדרך לצפון, שהם הולכים לאסוף שלל, נבחר שם למבצע: "דיאמונד (יהלומי) הגולן". 24 שעות ראשונות עם המחלקה שלי נתנו לי מושג ראשוני מי הם חיילי המחלקה שלי: הציג עצמו בפני חייל שאמר שהוא האחראי על מקלע 0.3 בזחל"ם המ"מ,

זאת משום שיש לו בעיה ברגל ואיננו יכול לרוץ. חבריו, המכירים אותו, לחשו לאוזני שאסכים ויש להיזהר ממנו כי הוא עצבני וכבר יש לו מספר תיקים במשטרה. האחר, נראה כזה לא משתלב, לא שייך, מכוסה במעיל בחום ששרר, התבוננתי בו כאשר הטעין את מחסניותיו בכדורים והתעקש להכניסם בכיוון ההפוך... והאחר, המבוגר, שטבע את המבצע אליו אנו הולכים, ושידר המון ביטחון, והאחר שכל המחלקה הכירה את גודל "הכלי" שלו וצחקה עליו מקנאה והוא השתתף בצחקם, והאחר שכל הזמן התעקש לדבר איתי על נושאי מין: " משה אתה יורד? משה אתה מלקק? משה אתה אוהב שמוצצים לך?", "בחייך עזוב אותי, לאיפה אני אמור לרדת ומה ללקק חוץ מארטיק, ומה למצוץ, כבר מזמן אני לא בגיל זה?". מה גדול ההבדל בין חיילי החדשים לצוערי קורס הקצינים שהדרכתי בבית-הספר לקצינים כמעט במשך שנתיים בשרות הסדיר.

לפנות ערב מתקרבים לחניון לחניון הלילה, עוברים ליד כפר תבור. איציק מודיע בקשר שיש לו בעיה מכאנית בזחל"ם שלו והוא זקוק לסיוע. מפאת חוסר זמן מחליטים לגרור אותו ואני מנדב הזחל"ם שלי לגרירה. מתקרבים לפורייה, שם החניון הגדודי לילה. המג"ד אוסף את קציני הגדוד לתדריך: "מחר אנחנו נכנסים לקו האש, לחזית, המצב ברמת-הגולן בכי רע, אין כוחות לבלימה!" רק רגע, אני אומר לעצמי, מה עם התרגיל האוגדתי, תרגלנו שאנחנו בקו השני, מה פתאום לחזית? מה, הזחל"מים "המשוקמקים" ממלחמת העולם השנייה מתוכננים להיכנס לקו האש הראשון מול טנקים מול טנקים סורים? ועם החיילים האלו של המחלקה החדשה שלי, שאני לומד להכירם? על מה אתה מדבר? מה, המצב כ"כ גרוע? מסתבר שכן. אני חוזר מהתדריך במצב רוח מדוכדך, המצב באמת נואש.

למחרת בבוקר, יום ב', התארגנות ומתחילים להקיף הכנרת מדרום ועולים לרמה מכיוון צמח. ליד צומת צמח אני מבחין מהזחל"ם בהתקהלות ומזהה חברי גרעין שלי שנשארו בקיבוץ מבוא-חמה לאחר שחרורנו מצה"ל. אני קורא להם ושואל מה נשמע, הם מספרים שפינו אותם ממבוא-חמה. רגע, לפני פחות מחודשיים טיילתי כאן, הנפש התרחבה אז מהמרחבים, מהנוף, מהשלווה, מהביטחון, מהגאווה, מה זאת אומרת פינו מהבית? מה לא בטוח שם? עולים לרמת הגולן דרך צומת קורסי. מתקרבים לקיבוץ רמת מגשימים. הקיבוץ מוקף בטנקים סורים נטושים, חלקם בוערים עדיין, חלקם עם ענפי הסוואה. הטנקים הסורים נמצאו בדיוק על ציר הטיול מהקיץ, על ובתוך גדרות הקיבוץ. מה מתרחש והתרחש כאן ביומיים האחרונים? אמבולנסים עם פצועים חולפים על פנינו לכיוון טבריה, זה לא צחוק, זו מלחמה! פקודה נשמעת בקשר לרדת מהציר המרכזי. נוסעים בטור מקביל לכביש הראשי של הרמה. לפתע פקודה אחרת לחזור לכביש כי מוקשים בקטע שאנו נוסעים עליו...

לפנות ערב מגיעים לאזור תל א-סאקי. שרידי הקרבות שהתחוללו מאז יום כיפורים ניכרים כאן: כלי רכב מלחמתיים של הסורים ושלנו מתערבבים זה בזה. זחל"מים צה"ליים שרופים, מעוכים, לצד וליד טנקים סורים חרוכים, פגועים, נטושים. בכל אחד מהכלים שלנו ושלהם היו בני אדם, היו חיים ועכשיו רובם כולם נהרגו, נפצעו בגופם ובנפשם. לילה, נערכים ללינה בשטח. מקרבים אותנו לצד המזרחי–צפוני של התל לקראת השינה. ישנים בשורה, מארגנים שמירה. אני בין השומרים במחצית הראשונה של הלילה. אני מתעורר בבוקר מוקדם, מספר מחיילי צוחקים בלעג על השמירה שלא הייתה בלילה. לאחר שאני שמרתי נראה כנראה אף אחד לא שמר, כל מי שנדרש לקום לשמור העיר מיד את הבא אחריו, כביכול הגיע זמנו לשמור, וכך בשעה מוקדמת נפסקה השמירה...ושוב אני מוכה בתדהמה מרמת החיילות והמוסריות של חיילי. קמים בבוקר מוקדם, ובאור יום אפשר לראות היכן היכן לנו בלילה: במרכזו של שדה קוצים מפויח כולו, מסביב גופות שרופות של לוחמים סורים שכנראה נפגעו יום קודם מפצצות נפלם שריפו אותם על רכבם. המדהים הוא האדישות שלנוכח המראה: לא שמחה ולא הזדעזעות, כך שרועות להן גופות שרק אתמול היו בני אדם חיים, ושוב מחשבות על הביזוי הנורא במלחמה ברכוש, בנפש.

יום רביעי, היום ערב חג הסוכות. הסורים מטווחים אותנו באזור תל סאקי. פגזי מרגמה נופלים סביבנו. מתכווצים בזחל"ם. מרחוק רואים את תל פארס. המצב כל כך מעורפל שלא כך ברור מי שולט על רכס אסטרטגי זה: אנחנו או הסורים? פצצות נופלות על התל: מי יורה על מי? אנחנו עליהם? הם עלינו?

המצב כל כך לא ברור, כל כך חסר לנו מידע. המ"פ מצויד בצילומים של מפה ולנו המ"מים אין בכלל מפות, אין משקפות. בידי תת-מקלע עוזי, שמסתבר שבכלל אינו מתאים לסוג לחימה של היום מפאת הטווח הקצר שלו. אני שם לב לחייל שכבר מהיום הראשון נראה לי לא משתלב, ההוא המכורבל במעיל כאשר חם כ"כ. "חבריו" כל הזמן צחקו עליו, לגלגו עליו,

אפשר גם לומר התעללו בו, נבחר כשעיר לעזאזל להשליך עליו את חרדותיהם. הוא גם לא ביצע התרגולות הנכונות בזמן שטווחנו, נראה המום. החלטתי לקחת אותו תחת חסותי, להצמיד אותו אלי וכך פחתו הפגיעות בו על ידי האחרים. פקדתי עליו להוריד המעיל, לשתות מים, לעשות אחרי כל מה שאני עושה וללכת איתי לכל מקום שאלך. רק אחר כך, כאשר התמחיתי יותר בנושא הטראומה, הבנתי שהוא לקה בהלם והיה משותק. וכן, גם הלוחם המבוגר שטבע את שם המבצע, שפונה לילה קודם, לא הרגיש טוב, כי לא הרגיש טוב, וסמל המחלקה שלי שקיבל התקף אולקוס ופונה גם הוא.

יום רביעי אחה"צ. רגיעת מה בהפגזות, מעט ניניחים, עוד מעט חג סוכות יחל ואנחנו רחוקים מאד מהחג. נמצאים באזור פתוח, ממזרח לנו תל סאקי מהלך כ- 500 מ', מצפון תל פארס, מהלך מספר קילומטרים, מדרום לנו קיבוץ רמת מגשימים. האזור הוא של טרסות, גבעי קל. מספר עצי איקליפטוס קרובים אלינו, מגדל מים בין העצים לתל סאקי. אני צמוד עם הזחל"ם לטרסה שנותנת לי תחושת ביטחון, מוגנות, לפחות בצד אחד. את השקט מפר קול ומראה מטוס בודד שחולף מעלינו. הוא מיד מזוהה כמיג 17 סורי שמבצע מעין טיסת יעף מעלינו, כביכול מזהה המטרות מתחת, כציפור טרף מעל.

אנחנו מונחים חשופים וגלויים בפניו, וכל אשר נותר לו זה לבחור מטרה אחת מני רבות שהיו מפזורות בשטח. פעלתי כמו אוטומט: ברגע שהבחנתי במטוס, לפי התרגולת, נתתי לכולם הוראה לרדת משני הזחל"מים ולהתרחק מהם, משום שעבור המטוס, הזחל"ם הוא המטרה ולא החייל הבודד בשטח. כמו כן הוריתי להשאיר בכל זחל"ם שני לוחמים להפעיל המקלע 0.5 ולירות על המטוס. בזחל"ם שלי נשארתי אני כמפעיל המקלע יחד עם לוחם נוסף, פתחתי באש על המיג. גם הוא היה מטרה נוחה: הוא טס לאיטו בשמים בגובה נמוך יחסית, הוא טס במעגל, השלים סיבוב אחד, חשבתי שהשנה הוא בחר במטרה ועכשיו הוא יצלול לעברה ויטווח אותה במקלעיו ובברקטות שלו. בינתיים ארגז תחמושת אחד נגמר, כבר 100 כדורים יריתי על המטוס, הלוחם שלידי הניח ארגז פעולה חדש, המטוס מתחיל את סיבובו השני. לפתע משום מקום מופיע מטוס מיראז' ויושב על זנב המיג, לא נראה ירי מכיוון המיראז' על המיג, אבל למטוס הישראלי עליונות ברורה. אני ממשיך לירות על המיג, הוא נראה קרוב, מטרה קלה יחסית, אני רואה את הכדורים פוגעים במטוס, לפתע ביצע המיג פנייה והחל להנמיך, הוא טס בכיוון ישר אל הזחל"ם שלי, אלי, אני ממשיך לירות עליו במקלע, המיג מנמיך מאד, הוא מתקרב לקרקע, אני יורה, אבל יותר אינני יכול לירות, משום שהמיג הנמיך כל כך שדופן הזחל"ם לא מאפשרת לי להנמיך המקלע יותר, המיג ירד כ"כ נמוך, הוא נראה בבירור טס לכיוון הזחל"ם, הוא עומד להתנגש בזחל"ם, אני צועק: "א י מ א, לאאאא!!!" מוריד את ראשי וגופי לתוך הזחל"ם ומחכה לבום, והוא בא...נשמע קול נפץ אדיר, חלקי מטוס עפו בוערים ליד הזחל"ם שלי והשני של מחלקתי. המטוס ירד כ"כ נמוך, כנראה הטייס נפגע ולא שלט במטוס, או שהמטוס נפגע ויצא מכלל שליטה, ובמרוצתו לקראת האדמה, במקרה לקראת הזחל"ם שלי, נתקל בקפל קרקע כ- 25-30 מ' מהזחל"ם והתרסק על טייסו. הסתבר שסמל המחלקה החדש שלי, היה צלם במקצועו, והמצלמה היתה עימו בעמדת שליפה, כך שמיד עם נפילת המטוס, בעוד הוא וחלקיו בוערים, הוא שלף את המצלמה וצילם תמונות המטוס בעודו בוער (מעניין שלאחר המלחמה כל הלוחמים הצטיידו בתמונות אלו והיו גם אחרים שהחזיקו תמונות אלו, שלאו דווקא היו באזור אז...). מספר דקות לאחר הנפילה של המטוס, לאחר דקות של התאוששות, החלו להופיע ממקומות מרוחקים חיילים שבאו להתבונן במחזה: מטוס מיג 17 מרוסק על הקרקע, הטייס הרוג, ערוף ראש, מונח בין השברים, הזנב בלט, המנוע, הכנפיים וחלקים רבים אחרים פזורים על הקרקע. כל מי שהגיע התעניין לדעת האם כבר נלקח האקדח של הטייס... ושוב אני מתפלא על האדישות שלי לנוכח גופת הטייס הרוג לידי. עדיין אינני מעכל את מלוא החוויה.

אני מעדיף לסיים פה את סיפור מלחמת יום הכיפורים שלי. אומנם הייתי מגויס במשך 153 ימים, מרביתם שרתי דווקא בסיני משני צדי התעלה. היו עוד אירועים משמעותיים לי במלחמה, אך נפילת המטוס היתה עבורי חווית שיא שסימלה את כל המלחמה: לוחמים לא מיומנים מוצאים עצמם מול מטוס, חשופים, פגיעים, יתרון אדיר למטוס האויב, ובכ"ז באורח נס, הוא נופל, והתחושה שהייתי קרוב כ"כ למוות והינצלות...כך המדינה במלחמת יום הכיפורים: יחסי כוחות לא שקולים, נשקים לא תואמים את אלו של האויב, חיילים לא מיומנים, לא מוכנים, חשופים מופקרים בכל החזיתות, כפסע בין נפילת המדינה לנוכח המתקפות המרוכזות ברמה ובסיני. בכלל, הכינו אותנו למלחמה אחת, כמו בששת הימים, והנה נכנסנו למלחמה אחרת לא מוכנים, לא מצויידים. ברור שהאמון בצבא, בפוליטיקאים, במדינה, נסדק ולא יכול להתאחות מחדש כבעבר, ואולי מוטב כך... לעיתים עלו בי מחשבות אחרות: המטוס הסורי מייצג את מדינת ישראל במלחמת יום כיפור: מטוס בודד בשמים, חשוף, נע לאיטו כמטרה נוחה לירות, לא ער לביטחון מופרז, טס בביטחון מופרז, מופל בקלות על ידי לוחמים

מהקרקע, צונח לאדמה ומתרסק. כן, זו החוויה הישראלית ושלי בין לפני יום כיפור 1973 ולאחריו: המציאות הישראלית עד אז והדימוי, שהיו בשמים ולא מעוגנים במציאות, לא ערים למציאות שהשתנתה. צללנו בבת אחת לקרקע והתרסקנו. משברים אלו צריך היה להשתקם.

החוויה של המטוס הלכה והולכת איתי לאורך כל חיי. נדמה לי שיותר מכל חייל שהיה באזור אני בין היחידים שהושפעה מזה. חזרתי למקום זה באופן ריטואלי - כפייתי מספר פעמים: משהו קרא לי לחזור שוב ושוב למקום זה ולחוות מחדש את אשר קרה לי ערב חג הסוכות 1973, ובכלל במלחמה הקשה ההיא. לא ממש חוויה של לידה חדש שם, גם לא ממש טראומה, אבל המקום עם שברי המטוס היו מקום עלייה לרגל עבורי ולא לבד.

לימים כאשר ילדי גדלו רציתי להיות שם איתם גם. לראשונה ביקרתי שם עם גילעד בני בטיול בצפון הארץ וברמה. הניווט למטוס היה קל, מפת האזור מצויה בראשי באופן כל כך ברור. גילעד נלהב ממראה שברי המטוס. ברור שמרבית חלקיו נלקחו משם: הזנב והכנפיים נלקחו, אבל נשארו מספיק חלקים מפוזרים בשטח: המנוע, גלגל, מושב הטייס, המקלע, כוורת רקטות ועוד מאות חלקים קטנים לא מזוהים. בחרתי כמה חלקים, בעיקר מחופת המטוס, והבאתי הביתה. הנחתי אותם על מדף הספרייה. מי ששאל מה זה, קיבל תשובה.

•••

יום שלישי בשבוע, הימים הם הימים שבין כסה לעשור. גילעד בכיתה ח', יצא עם כיתתו לטיול בצפון הארץ והרמה לשלושה ימים. שעת צהריים, התקלחתי, אני נח במיטתי, ולפתע טלפון מצלצל. המנהלת מבית-הספר של גילעד מודיעה לי שבמהלך הטיול גילעד נחבט בראשו כתוצאה מנפילה בנחל הג'ילבון, הוא פונה לבית חולים "זיו" בצפת ועלי להגיע לשם. אני מזעיק את שולי אשתי, מתארגנים ונוסעים לצפון. כל הדרך מחשבות מעוררות חרדה בראש: מה קרה? איזה נזק נגרם? האם יחלים לחלוטין או לא? מגיעים לבית החולים, גילעד לאחר צילומים ותפרים בראש, בהכרה, הרופא מרגיע ומודיע שהתחולל נס והפגיעה היא חיצונית בלבד. לאחר שלושה ימים גילעד עבר לבית חולים במרכז הארץ ולאחר כחודשיים החלים לגמרי מהפגיעה בראשו, אבל מה עם הפגיעה בנפש?

כיום, אני כבר מיומן בפגיעות טראומטיות, ומבין את משמעות הסכנה של פגיעות כאלו. עולה בי רעיון ואני מביאו בפני גילעד: "קניתי רכב חדש, בוא נצא שנינו בלבד למסע היכרות אתו. לא סתם ניסע, אלא ניסע לרמת-הגולן ונחבר את שני האירועים שעברנו אתה ואני. ניסע למקום נפילת המטוס ונשחזר את כל אשר קרה שם בסיפור ובצילום, אח"כ ניסע למקום שאתה נפלת במפל הג'ילבון ונשחזר זאת שוב בסיפור ובתמונה". וכך ביום מעונן וגשום, בחופשת חנוכה, קמנו בבוקר מוקדם ונסענו צפונה. הניווט קל למטוס: לאחר קיבוץ רמת מגשימים, בסמוך לתל סאקי שוברים בדרך עפר מערבה, הולכים כ- 500 מ', לאחר מגדל המים, ליד עצי האקליפטוס, אנחנו מגיעים לשברי המטוס. אני משחזר את שהיה, מוצא את המקום המדויק שעמד שעמד הזחל"ם שלי. אנחנו חופרים באדמה ומוצאים שם ארגז תחמושת של מקלע 5.0 מעוך ותרמילים של הכדורים. אנחנו מצלמים ומצטלמים, לוקחים חלקי מזכרת, כולל ארגז התחמושת והתרמילים, ונפרדים מהמקום. נוסעים למפל הג'ילבון.

גשם יורד, אנחנו משאירים האוטו בחניון, מתארגנים ויוצאים לדרך. מגיעים למפל מלמעלה, יורדים למרגלותיו. אני כאן מבקש מגילעד שישחזר בדיוק מה היה. גילעד ניצב על סלע קרוב לשפת המים. בעומדו שם התלוצצה המדריכה שמי שרוצה יכול להיכנס/לקפוץ למים, גילעד לא משתהה וקופץ. אני מבקש שיעשה תנועת קפיצה ומנציח הכל במצלמה. והגענו לשנייה שלאחר הקפיצה אז למים. גילעד מתאר שתוך שניות הוא היה מכוסה בדם. כולם מסביבו נבהלו, חבריו התלמידים, המורים המלווים, המדריכים. אנחנו מתבוננים יחד במקום הקפיצה, לא ניתן לראות בבירור שהמים רדודים ובתחתיתם סלעים משום עכירות המים והסלעים הכהים. ברור שגילעד נחבט מסלעים שהיו קרובים לפני המים וחטף מכה הגונה. ומכאן מתחיל מסע הפינוי. אני וגילעד מתחילים לשחזר את הפינוי: גילעד זכר הכל לפרטים, את הדרך בה הלכו, את הרגשתו. התחלנו לצעוד, טפטוף מלווה אותנו כל הזמן. אני לא מאמין שגילעד צעד כברת דרך ארוכה כזו עד לנקודה שכלי רכב יכול היה להגיע אליו לפינוי. צעדנו לאורך הג'ילבון ואחר כך נפרדה מתווי הנחל והמשיכה בתוך שדה. בעונה זו של דצמבר הכול ירוק וכלניות אדומות-בשרניות כבר פורחות, אבל אז בזמן הפינוי היה קיץ חם. "איך עשית את

131

כל הדרך הזו רגלית, פצוע, מבוהל?" אני ממש לא מאמין וכל הדרך אני מציין זאת לגילעד. הגענו למקום הנקרא בריכת הקצינים, כאן המתין לו רכב צבאי שפינה אותו לקראת אמבולנס, שבצפירות דהר לבית החולים "זיו". מבריכת הקצינים צעדנו חזרה למפל הג'ילבון ומשם חזרה לרכב. הסתיים החלק העיקרי של בנייה ושיקום הביטחון שלי ושל גילעד. נותרה עוד נקודה אחת לשיקום, ליתר ביטחון. בחופשת הפסח הצעתי לגילעד שנצא לטיול נוסף לרמת- הגולן: הפעם לבריכת המשושים. ביום אביבי נסענו לשם. צעדנו רגלית למורד הנחל. הפעם התרחצנו במי הנחל, והתיידדנו עם המקום והכניסה למים, דהיינו להסיר את החלק שאולי נותר של פחד מהמים וכניסה מבוקרת-בטוחה למי נחל ברמת-הגולן.

תם ונשלם סיפור החיבור בין הינצלותי מהמטוס במלחמת יום הכיפורים והינצלותו של גילעד מקפיצה לא מחויבת. אני ממשיך לבקר במקום נפילת המטוס מפעם לפעם, כשכל פעם אני בא עם חברים אחרים, מספר הסיפור, מצטלם. לא נראה לי שהחברים כל כך מתרשמים, או לפחות לא נותנים ביטוי ממשי לכך. גם כאשר היינו במקום איציק, צביקה ואני, שלושת המ"מים במלחמה, והנשים, הם יותר השתעשעו מהההתייחסות שלי לאירוע מאשר לחוויה, שהם היו גם שותפים לה. וגילעד? גילעד התגייס לצה"ל ליחידת 669 ומציל חיילים ואזרחים שזקוקים לחילוץ ופינוי וביניהם כאלו שקופצים/נופלים ברמת הגולן לנחלים לנחלים שם....כולל חילוץ במפל ג'ילבון... וכן, לעיתים אנחנו משתתפים בפעולות חילוץ והצלה הוא כלוחם ביחידת החילוץ של חיל אוויר ואני כפסיכולוג-חינוכי המסייע לתושבים שנפגעו בפעולות טרור או טראומות אחרות. כבר השתתפנו בפעולות שהוא מחלץ לבית-החולים ואני ממשיך בטיפול הנפשי אצל הנפגעים וקרוביהם כתוצאה מהאירועים.

The Fascist Analyst & The New Myth of Analysis
Meeting and confrontation in the analytical room

Stefano Carpani

Abstract

This paper brings into focus the analyst's behavior towards the patient – to that it can retraumatize the person seeking help. In his considerations, Carpani broadens the term fascist beyond the political terminology, calling it a mind-set of the analyst who acts "one-sided, rigid and lacking the capacity for a rapport based on Eros." As much as fascist behavior should be condemned, the author also demands self-criticism to detect it in oneself, not only the opposite. The fictional vignette of the encounter between a training candidate and a training analyst serves as an example: here a casual but critical comment made by the analyst during the greeting-process leaves the patient with a set of negative feelings. In the further course the situation worsens as the analyst keeps making remarks that make his patient feel small. The two go separate ways. In an email half a year later, the analyst reveals his impression of the encounter with the training candidate. The sharing of analytical observations as well as the mix of psychodynamic impressions with moral value would show the unawareness of the email's sender of the possible impact on its recipient. It would become clear that the lack of integrity from the side of the analyst made him act this way. Carpani goes further: A fascist analyst would not even try to understand the patient and show no willingness to act with integrity. In the following, the author examines how the concepts of integrity and Eros serve as an antidote to the fascist by discussing works of John Beebe and James Hillman. He claims that in the 21st century there would be the need for a return to the search for Eros and love of the soul – a New Myth of Analysis

That was, when I thought about it, what I had against most analysts. They were such unquestioning acceptors of their social order. Their mildly leftist political views, their singing of peace petitions and decorating their offices with prints of Guernica were just camouflage. When it came to the critical issues: the family, the position of women, the flow of cash from patient to doctor, they were reactionaries. As rigidly self-serving as the Social Darwinists of the Victorian Era.

Erica Jong, *Fear of Flying*
(1973)

This paper examines *Eros*, *integrity* and *psychagogia*— instances when the analyst's attitude is problematic; that is, when the analyst's untamed complexes and countertransference infect the analysis (and re-traumatize the patient). This reflection has been inspired by works on fascism by Austrian writer and dramatist Thomas Bernhard, Italian poet Giovanni Raboni and (Czech-born) former US Secretary of State Madeleine Albright.

In an interview about her book titled *Fascism: A Warning*[1], Madeleine Albright underlines that "There is no consensus definition, which may explain why the term is so indiscriminately tossed about. In my book, fascism is not an ideology of left, right or center, but rather an approach to seizing and consolidating power by an individual or party that claims to be acting in the name of a nation or group."[2]

In his piece titled *Heldenplatz*, Thomas Bernhard (1988, p.62) wrote: "There are more Nazis in Vienna now / than in thirty-eight." More than thirty years after its premiere, we know that Bernhard was right, although his vision cannot be limited to Vienna. In fact, if we swap the word "Nazi" with "fascist," we have a picture of 2020's apocalyptic political scenario (Trump/USA, Putin/Russia, Orban/Hungary, Bolsonaro/Brazil, LePen/France, Salvini/Italy, Farage and Johnson/UK, AfD/Germany, and of course Austria). The list is still longer if other continents are taken into consideration.

Raboni, in his poem entitled *Politica estera* (2006/1966, p.53), wrote that: "The speaker has to say / the things he says and maybe not / or maybe others. But it is a fact that those who keep silent / let everything happen to them and what is worse / let what has been done to them / be done to someone else."

Both authors propose that remaining silent is not an option. Both insist that it is an ethical duty to speak up, so that what might have happened to one will not happen to anyone else. Both Bernhard and Raboni wrote a *j'accuse* against the collective shadow of their own countries.
I propose that, today, fascism is not a party, it is a *forma mentis*. It is trans-national, trans-cultural,

trans-religious, trans-gender, and trans-personal. Moreover, if we are unconscious and unable to tame our own complexes, we all— at some point— become fascist. Therefore, a fascist can be a person of whatever sex and gender, of any color, religion, ethnicity, age, nationality, or place of birth.

With this reflection, I wish to propose a *j´accuse* against the fascist analyst (among us and within us) and hence the fascist in the analytical room: when the fascist is the analyst (not the fascist de jure, or the other or the patient).

---

[1] 2018.
[2] https://www.economist.com/open-future/2018/07/30/on-tyranny-populism-and-how-best-to-respond-today

I wish to ask: Are you a fascist? Have you ever been a fascist? Asking myself the same question, I will propose that the answer is, unfortunately, yes. Where the answer is yes lies the basis for self-criticism, transformation, and, following Watkins[3], liberation. Because it is too easy (and vile) to see a fascist in the other (the "true" fascist), but it is very difficult (and courageous) to see the fascist in us and among us.

This *j´accuse* is against the fascist analyst who becomes a fascist *de facto* (therefore unconsciously in the encounter with the other/patient). Perhaps only for a moment, but sufficient to repeat and reinforce trauma.

Because both Bernhard and Raboni insisted on the need to speak up, I will share a fictional case in line with James Hillman's and Susie Orbach's fictional work as an example. My fictional vignette builds on John Beebe's[4] courageous statements at the "Jung and Activism" conference in Prague 2017 on how the concept of the anima was sometimes used by analysts as a bias against the individuation of people who were not projecting and sexualizing a contrasexual archetype, because instead they were living their homosexuality in that way. This led me to imagine a hypothetical encounter between a training candidate and training analyst that could still occur today. This vignette is about a meeting and confrontation in the analytical room and looks specifically at the problematic behavior of the analyst.

The patient is a 35-year-old man who began training analysis in 2015. Patient and analyst met twice in June 2015. The first probatory session was positive and they both agreed to meet again the following week. When they met again for the second probatory session, the patient (when entering the door and shaking the analyst's hand) greeted him and said: "Yesterday I met Mrs. Valencia at a sand-play seminar in Zürich. I told her I was meeting you today and she asked me to send you her greetings. She also added 'Dr Behala is so nice. Do start training analysis with him!'" The patient then added: "She must be a very good sand-play therapist. The Institute invited her although her English is not good, and she was there with a translator." In that very moment, the face of the analyst changed, and he said: "You are very critical!" The patient was puzzled; he felt small and wrong. He didn't know what to say. He felt guilty.

The mood experienced by the dyad during the first session was gone and although the patient did not feel good, he decided to open up and share a fantasy he had had many years previously when at university: *If I could spend the rest of my life reading, writing and thinking, I would consider myself lucky.* He then added: *If now, as a consequence of the training in Zürich, I could do so and work as a psychoanalyst, I would consider myself very lucky.*

The analyst, listening to this, claimed that to work as psychoanalyst is a serious thing because it means to "heal people" and added that to be a writer is not the same. The patient was puzzled again and felt even smaller and more wronged than before. Therefore, he felt guilty again. But

---

[3] 2003.
[4] 2020.

guilty of what? He didn't know! He felt he had opened up but had not been understood. He felt scolded.

The analyst proposed that, before he could start a training analysis, they should have four sessions to understand and clarify if the patient wanted to become an analyst or a writer. The patient left the session feeling angry and sad and felt the urge to contact another training analyst. That same night he had a very long and articulated *big dream*.

After a few days, he decided to share this dream with the analyst via email and to accept the therapist's proposal of "four trial sessions to understand if you want to heal people or become a writer!" He never received a response to his email.

The two met again – almost six months later – at a book presentation in December 2015. They greeted each other cordially and the patient asked the analyst if he had ever received his email and agreement to have four sessions. The analyst said he had answered the patient. The patient stated that he had never received the email.

After a few days, the patient decided to email the analyst again:

From: I. Kupper-Meynen
Sent: Wednesday, December 30, 2015 6:54 PM
To: Dr. Behala W.
Subject: Re: Meeting and dream

Dear Dr. Behala,

I'm taking the liberty to write to you to wish you a serene 2016 and also to tell you that it was nice to meet again and chat at the beginning of December.

I felt we both wondered what happened and now we know: "I never received your email." Can we consider it a synchronicity or just a technological failure?

I would also be delighted to read what you wrote me last July about my dream. And hopefully we can look at it together in the future. Or maybe even to meet to look at it together (although not very orthodox since I am in analysis with a colleague of yours).

Best regards,
I. Kupper-Meynen
        The analyst wrote the following:

From: Dr. Behala W.
Sent: Thursday, December 31, 2015 2:41 PM
To: I. Kupper-Meynen
Subject: Re: Meeting and dream

Dear Mr. Kupper-Meynen,

First, I wish you all the best for the New Year.

I am sorry, but I don't have the mail any more[5] which I sent you last year. I remember the feeling tone of my response: Your dreams provoked some negative feelings, because the aggressivity of the symbolism (a big snake beating an old man, and you are silently watching this, and so on[6]). It was also because you obviously did not tell me all about your activities to find a training-analyst[7]. I felt abused, there was no apparent positive feeling, and my countertransference told me that I will not do analysis with you. Without a basic positive feeling one should not start an analytical relationship.

I thought and wrote to you that you should undergo a therapeutic analysis. I don't want to get much into details of where I see your problem. I think you projected on me (and not only on me) energies of your strong negative father complex and an overcompensation by grandiosity. Nobody is sufficient for you. In our meetings this complex was constellated by the fact, that the health assurances don't pay for education[8] and not for a training analysis. You may say that each analysis has also therapeutic aspects, but in Germany with our generous health system we need and we have strict laws and requirements. This is very important, and you must know that no analytical training institute in Germany will accept a therapeutic analysis as part of the training. If the Swiss institute handles this different it is because they don't have this assurance system. It is tricky if you want to slip into the gap between two different social systems. But I

---

[5] Could it be that the analyst had such a negative feeling and counter-transference that he didn't bother to reply to the patient's email? Among certain colleagues it seems common practice not to answer undesired patient requests nowadays! This is also part of the fascist's attitude.

[6] This is incorrect because in the dream there is not "a big snake beating an old man, and you are silently watching this." Here is the relevant part of the dream (which reverses the analyst's perspective):

> I felt like a spectator. In a spielplatz or a garden there are different people (all males). I know nobody. I hear somebody saying "watch out there is a snake!" And suddenly all the people stand up and look for the snake. Somebody moves the water pumps hiding under the flowerbeds and there is the snake. Although not a scary one. A fat one. Anaconda like. I think: this snake has a strange skin. It look like the skin of the belly of an old fat man that has recently lost weight (shrivelled). Then I see the snake jumping like a dog trying to bite the left hand of a man in his thirties. Here the snake looks clearly like an old anaconda with a bellyful of food. As if it had just eaten. To bite the left hand of the young man the snake has to get fully erect but not like a cobra. It also looks like he has to jump a little bit. I want to shout and tell the young man to watch out "the snake is about to bite you." But I keep silent. I see this scene from behind.
> Then the scene develops, and the same snake has his head fully inside the mouth of another young man. This man is on the left side of the garden. I think I should get closer and pull the tail but I don't move. I am petrified. Then calm is restored and somebody says something like "there were 3 young men bitten by an old snake" and another man who is sitting exactly where the snake was found says "no! There were not 3 men bitten. There were only 2!"

[7] This also seems incorrect. The patient, when telling me the story, told me that he explained to the analyst that he was looking for a training-analyst and that he was also in contact with other colleagues. Therefore, which complex got activated in the analyst? Inferiority? Abuse? Abandonment?

[8] The patient was unaware of this.

don´t recommend this, not only because it is unethical, but also because it may be an expression of the same negative father complex and – as I suppose – will not be helpful to work through it. It is the son, who will find a positive father, and not the trickster. I wish you a good and successful way!

With my best wishes
Dr. Behala

This email from the analyst is problematic because his comments (in an email to the candidate months after their first and only meeting) are offered with veiled hostility, and because he seems to be unaware of, or not interested in, the impact on, and context of, his statements to the candidate (especially because the analyst has no way of evaluating the impact of his statements). Particularly problematic is the way in which the analyst shared highly charged analytic observations in an email to the candidate; to do so is both un-analytic in nature as well as un-ethical (although the analyst accused the patient of being unethical!).

Secondly, the analyst mixes psychodynamic impressions with moral evaluation, implying that there is something immoral in the trainee's approach. While this may not be unethical, per se, again, it is not analytic in nature.

I propose that the problematic and hostile behavior of the analyst (who is well-known and respected internationally, and who is considered to be a "leftist" and an activist) helps me uncover the theme of the fascist in us and among us and ask: Why did the analyst decide to write such an email to the candidate, with such veiled hostility? Why did he become a fascist *de facto*? A fascist, I propose, is a person of whatever sex and gender, nationality, class and status who is one-sided, rigid and lacking the capacity for a rapport based on Eros. Therefore, it is a one-sided state of being that prevents relatedness.

I propose that the theory of complexes and countertransference is not sufficient to explain his attitude. I echo Beebe[9], that it is a matter of integrity which the analyst lost in his actions. Perhaps he lost his integrity because he became trapped in a complex (of course!), but this does not excuse his attitude. Such an attitude can re-traumatize the candidate. Another problem adding insult to injury is the fact that reparation never occurred (because reparation outside of the analytical context is not possible).

Following Kalsched (2020, (p. 144)), I propose that the analyst dissociated when hearing that a colleague had been invited to teach in Zürich. This dissociation, as a "primitive defence," helped him to "hold feeling at a distance" and "sever head from heart so that conscious feeling is not possible."

---

[9] 2005.

I propose the patient opened a scar that the therapist had forgotten about. A scar that started bleeding (transforming into a wound) and that with such bleeding, unconscious material stepped between the two.

This is why the patient felt puzzled, small, and wrong. Because the therapist (being unable to tame his own complexes) made it impossible for the patient— again following Kalsched (2020, p. 145), to feel safe so that "that vulnerable 'child' in you can join us." This is why the patient felt so full of anger when leaving the session and wanted to find a different therapist. This is okay since the patient eventually found the right therapist for him— a man who accompanied him in his professional and personal development.

The New Myth of Analysis: *Integrity, Eros and Psychagogia*

The clinical vignette discussed in the previous section obliges us to examine the concept of *integrity*, as antidote to the fascist, – and *Eros* – which according to Jung[10] means *relatedness*.

In so doing, I will employ Hillman and Beebe and introduce the concept of *psychagogia* (as further enhancement of the work of psychoanalysis, analytical psychology and archetypical psychology; or even – perhaps – a unifying factor after one-hundred years of separation).

Integrity

David H. Rosen[11] in the preface to Beebe's *Integrity in Depth* (2005), wrote that "both integrity and the Self are spiritual concepts that unify and facilitate transcendence and transformation" (p. xi). Beebe underlines that "integrity must be pursued as a desideratum in itself" (p. 15) and adds that "the implication is that the real pleasure in exercising integrity in dealings with others is the discovery of integrity in itself" (2005, p. 15).

Let us examine integrity in the analytical room (as per the previous vignette). Beebe underlines that integrity "means, literally, the stage of being untouched" (2005, p. 6) and he agrees with Robert Grudin (1999, pp. 73-75) that "integrity may be defined as psychological and ethical wholeness, sustained in time…integrity…is not a painfully upheld standard so much as a prolonged and focused delight" (2005, p. 17).

From this, he examines integrity versus violation and proposes that:

> "when an individual's own integrity flourishes in relationship, both patient and therapist share the discovery of the integrity of interpersonal process as well. This

---

[10] In Beebe, 1993, p. 47.
[11] 2005.

shared field of integrity is the ground of any depth psychotherapy, and it is impossible to understand the burgeoning of psychotherapy in our century if one does not recognize the profound pleasure that the discovery of integrity brings." (p. 19)

Beebe then adds that "our search for the psychological definition of integrity cannot be confined to the experience of its pleasure, self-validating though that pleasure is. Just as frequently (and some might argue, more frequently) integrity is located through the experience of violation. We may not even know we have a self until it becomes anxious, or angry - or until it has been raped" (p. 19). He therefore proposes that "psychotherapy has been forced to realise [...] that its principal subject matter has always been, not, as Freud thought, pleasure and unpleasure but rather integrity and violation" (p. 19).

Let us stick to the concept of violation, because this is the topic of the above vignette. Not "a fantasy of violation, fertile for exploration and best handled by a meta psychology like Freud's or an archetypal psychology like Hillman's, but, as their earlier Freud recognised and then abandoned, a literal violation that demands concrete response" (p. 19). On this, Beebe underlines that "therapists have to do something to acknowledge when they transgress those boundaries, and to atone for the violation of them" (p. 19). The vignette is such a case of non-acknowledgment; of omitted response by the therapist. Beebe underlines that:

> like the real body, the subtle body of the psyche demands respect for its limits - and all hell breaks out when they are not respected. [...] the bodily sensations and the associations point to the reality of inner psychic boundaries, which require respectful handling. They are a sign of outrage, another indication that there is a pre-existing integrity." (pp. 19-20)

Beebe also claims that "patients expect a therapist to uphold integrity in the analytic relationship. The therapist is supposed to stand for something. It may be just as hard on a patient to witness a lapse of integrity by the therapist as to be violated by the therapist in other ways" (p. 20). Beebe continues, claiming that the therapist has two obligations:

1. "To protect the self-esteem of the client at all costs, even when the client is actively provoking the therapist to injure that self-esteem."

2. "To protect the setting or the institution of psychotherapy itself as a place where healing can occur."

3. "This would mean, for instance, that a therapist might terminate" or not begin a therapy – as in the case of this vignette, "but in doing so, rather than blaming the patient, the therapist will make it clear that what has transpired demonstrates only the therapist's present limits, leaving open the possibility that the patient may be able to work effectively with another therapist whose skill and holding capacity are greater or different." (p. 20)

Therefore, Beebe proposes that "if pleasure is the thesis, and violation the antithesis of the psychological experience of integrity, recovery is the synthesis" (p. 21). But what happens when recovery is not possible (as in the above vignette)?

Recovery, I propose, can only happen through *repair*. I say so because "integrity presupposes a connection with ourselves that permits an ethical connection to everything else in the universe" (p. 32). Therefore, I propose that in the above-mentioned vignette, the analyst – when dissociating – had no connection with himself, and therefore lost his ethical connection with the universe and with the patient.

I propose that the fascist analyst is not connected to him/herself and even less connected with everything else in the universe. The fascist (analyst or human) is one sided and trapped by Wotan's (and Lilith's) thirst for destruction.

Beebe is correct in claiming that "when we face a problem of integrity, we are caught by an archetypal drive to restore order to a troubled state" (p. 36). Here the work of Bernhard and Raboni comes in again. Ultimately, "in the effort to restore integrity, facing the shadow is essential" because "psychotherapy is a moral ritual, propelled by the archetypal drive to restore order" where the "experience with patients in psychotherapy teaches that in the effort to restore integrity, facing the shadow is essential" (p.37).

In conclusion, "when psychotherapy is conducted with integrity, the miracle [of Tuccia's sieve] occurs. The unconscious libido is free to flow yet stays contained" (pp. 52-53). When integrity is lacking, stagnation and death reign supreme.

Eros

The attentive reader will already have noticed my lightly veiled reference to James Hillman's *The Myth of Analysis* (1998). With a bit of bravado (and even perhaps inflation!), I have taken possession of Hillman's title with the precise intention of paying tribute to that author. Therefore, I shall propose my own 21st-century view regarding *The Myth of Analysis*, specifically examining the concepts of *Eros, integrity* and *psychagogia*.

In *The Myth of Analysis*, Hillman (p. 297) underlines that "we can see the psyche going into therapy in search of eros" and that "we have been looking for love of the soul." He therefore claims that "this is the myth of analysis." In the fictional vignette above, the patient— going into analysis— was exactly doing so (although unconsciously) in search of Eros and in search of love of the soul.

I propose that Hillman's "myth of analysis" must turn into "the new myth of analysis"—a return to the search for Eros and to go anew in search of love of the soul. However, this will only be possible after recovery; thus, "if pleasure is the thesis, and violation the antithesis of the psychological experience of integrity, recovery is the synthesis" (Beebe, 2005, p. 21). I propose that in a 21st-century affluent and individualized society, there is a need for a *new myth of analysis*, and that this is the job of my generation! There is a need for Eros (relatedness and rapport in Jung´s view) versus linear thinking.

When this occurs, *psychagogia*[12] (which translates as "guidance of the soul" or "soul-leading") will be possible. *Psychagogia* is accompaniment of the patient´s soul by the therapist, thanks to the art of rhetoric. Therefore, the *new* myth of analysis is when the psyche enters therapy in search of eros and psychagogia – in search of love of the soul through relatedness and accompaniment.

Donald Kalsched (2020) gave an excellent example of this in his keynote paper at the 2019 IAAP Congress in Vienna when presenting the case of a patient who dissociated because of the injury to her capacity to feel:

> Sensing that Beth was still struggling, I moved my chair closer to her and said, ´Beth please, just look at me!´ Slowly her gaze met mine. `Listen`, I said, ´this is no longer just your problem… or just your lonely struggle´… ´because my eyes have seen it too. I´m in this with you now, and I´m invested in what happens. It´s our story now, and we´re in it together. If we´re going to get that child in you some help we´ll have to do this together – so come back to me.´ I extended my hand and slowly, she reached over and took it."

This is not only an amazing example of rhetoric leading to *psychagogia* (accompaniment of the soul), but it is also an example of *Eros* between two human beings, who happen to be a patient and therapist. Two human beings who can wish to learn dancing together, mutually, smoothly and with the utmost respect for one another. In contrast, the fascist analyst does not move the chair closer to the patient: s/he moves the chair away (to protect him/herself).

Beyond the Damage: The Mockery

In the course of analysis— as a therapeutic tool— the patient wrote down his story in the form of a letter. After concluding his training (somehow following Raboni´s poem), the patient decided to send that letter to Dr. Behala. He, the fascist, replied as follows:

From: Dr. M Behala
Sent: Monday, March 21, 2021 12:18 PM
To: I. Kupper-Meynen
Subject: Re: Meeting and dream

---

[12] Socrates (in Plato's Phaedrus, 261a): claims that "Is not rhetoric in its entire nature an art which leads the soul by means of words, not only in law courts and the various other public assemblages."

Dear Mr Kupper-Meynen,

You are writing about "patient and analyst." I don´t recognize me and our meeting in these terms. You were not my patient, and I was not your analyst. We had only two probatoric meetings because of your wish to find a training analyst. You found somebody else, this was o.k. for me. I remember only that I wondered why you didn´t answer to my responding email.
That's all I have to say. You made a successful training, congratulations!
Best wishes on your way.
Dr. Behala

This email— adding damage to the mockery— is again problematic, because it is anti-analytic and opens to clear ethical questions when the analyst claims that— although within the context of two probatory sessions— there is no "patient & analyst" relation.

To conclude, the fascist analyst, contradicting Beebe´s (1988/2018, p. 99) suggestion, does not "try to understand its impact on the patient" and has no "willingness to act with integrity from within the selfobject role. This starts with the recognition that one´s own idiosyncratic reality as a person plays a part even in the patient´s unconscious decision to let one be a selfobject" (1988/2018, p.102). Beebe continues: "yet the person chosen for the role will usually be someone the patient can feel close to, who has demonstrated a capacity for empathic participation in the patient´s world, and whom the patient can respect" (1988/2018, p.102). The fascist, being unable to build a psychagogic relationship fed by eros, is none of this.

Hence, reparation is not possible when integrity is not there and, unfortunately, the analyst did not want to see or understand the pain and suffering he had provoked in the patient. He did not realize how important his behavior was for the patient and he did not understand how dependent the patient had become from the statements he made about him. All this helped the patient to understand that trained and experienced analysts are also vulnerable and in need of compassion.

References

Albright, M., (2018). *Fascism: A Warning*. HarperCollins.

Beebe, J., (2005). *Integrity in Depth*. Texas A&M University Press.

Beebe J., (2020). *C.G. Jung, Anima/Animus, Homosexuality, and Integrity* in Carpani, S. *Breakfast at Küsnacht: Conversations on C.G. Jung and Beyond*. Chiron Publications.

Bernhard, T., (1995). *Heldenplatz*. Suhrkamp Verlag.

Carpani, S., (2020a). *The Consequences of Freedom* in Brodersen E. & Amenazaga P. (ed.) (2020). *Jungian Perspectives on Indeterminate States: Betwixt and Between Borders*. Routledge.

Carpani, S. (2020b). *Breakfast at Küsnacht: Conversations on C.G. Jung and Beyond*. Chiron Publications.

Grudin, R., (1999). *The Grace of Great Things*. Ticknor & Fields.

Jung, C. G. (1966) Two Essays on Analytical Psychology, The Collected Works of C. G. Jung, Vol. 7. Fourth Printing 1977. Bollingen Series XX, Princeton University Press.

Kalsched, D., (2020). 'Opening the closed heart: affect-focused clinical work with the victims of early trauma.' In E. Kiehl (ed.), Vienna 2019. *Encountering the Other: Within us, between us and in the world. Proceedings of the Twenty-First Congress of the International Association for Analytical psychology*. Einsiedeln: Diamon Verlag.

Plato's Phaedrus, retrieved from the internet: https://www.perseus.tufts.edu/hopper/text?doc=Perseus%3Atext%3A1999.01.0174%3Atext%3DPhaedrus%3Asection%3D261a

Raboni, G., (2006(/1966). Raboni: L´Opera Poetica. Mondadori.

Rosen, D.H., (2005). Introduction to *Integrity in Depth*. Texas A&M University Press.

Watkins, M., (2003). 'Dialogue, development, and liberation.' In I. Josephs (ed.), *Dialogicality in development*. Greenwood.

PART 2

POETRY

Chun Yu

父親
—生命的故事

Father
—the story of life

沒有什麼能逃過
一個側耳聆聽的
孩子，睜大著眼睛
她聽見了你

Nothing escapes a child
in deep listening
head tilting
eyes widened
she hears you

你的故事
它從何而來
经你奔湧而出—
光之泉
如此耀眼
讓她的存在
充滿喜悅
悲之泉
如此憂傷
讓她的心靈
悄然啜泣
她的故事
剛剛開始

Where does it come from
your story
flowing out of you–
fountain of light
so dazzlingly bright
it fills her being with joy
fountain of sorrow
so profoundly sad
it makes her heart weep
as her own story
begins

你的故事
它從何而來
光明與悲傷—
深淵和
遠隔的岸—

Where does it come from
your story
of light and sorrow–
an abyss, with
two shores agape–

凝望中
她的故事
已然展開：
存在，夢想
和夢想之傷
心一般
跳動
自時間
之初

upon which
she gazes
as her own story
unfolds, of being
of dream, and
dream's wound
beating with a heart
of its own
since the beginning
of time…

沒有什麼能逃過
一個側耳聆聽
孩子，睜大著眼睛
她聽見了你
她輕述，輕述
她的故事—

光，夢之光
必須被恒持
傷，夢之傷
必須被承接—

直到光
幻耀出
暮光之金
直到傷口
愈合
朝向
時間的
盡頭

Nothing escapes a child
in deep listening
head tilting
eyes widened
she hears you
and whispers
her own story on
and on–

The light
of the dream
must be carried
the wound
of the dream
must be endured–

until the light
glows in
twilight's gold
until the wound
closes towards
time's end

母親
一生命的輪回

没有什麼能逃過
一個側耳聆聽的
孩子，睜大著眼睛
她聽見了你

你的勇氣
將勝利置於
危險之上

為時已晚—
你的孩子
她的眼睛已被點亮
注視著前方
千裏之外的光

「等等，回來！」
你向她轉身中
稚嫩的背影呼喚
她年輕的腳已邁向
漫長征途的第一步

為時已晚—
眼含星星的媽媽已成
眼含星星的孩子的
母親—

從現在開始
她的每一步
都是你的心
必須越過的
一道深淵—

從現在開始
你將帶著
新的勇氣
跟隨

Mother
– the cycle of life

Nothing escapes a child
in deep listening
head tilting
eyes widened
she hears you

Your courage
places victory above
danger

Too late—
your child
her eyes already lit
seeing the light
a thousand miles ahead

"Wait, come back!"
You call to her tender back
turning toward you
young feet reaching for the first step
on the long march of her own

Too late—
mother of starry eyes
becomes mother of
the starry-eyed child—

From now on, each step
an abyss, for your heart
to leap over—

From now on
you will follow
with newly found courage

直到有一天
疲憊中
你放慢了腳步
只能企足望向
她的背影

直到有一天
她停住了腳步
回身顧盼一
你卻已轉身
背影彎曲而虛弱

你的孩子
她向你呼喚一
「等等，回來……」

母亲
一生命的轮回

没有什么能逃过
一个侧耳聆听的
孩子，睁大著眼睛
她听见了你

你的勇气
将胜利置于
危险之上

为时已晚一
你的孩子
眼睛已被点亮
凝望前方
千里之外的光

"等等，回来！"
你向她转身中
稚嫩的背影呼唤
年轻的脚已然
迈出漫长征途的
第一步

Until one day
tired and worn
you slow down
tiptoeing
you just look at her back

Until one day
she pauses and
turns around
to look—
your back
already turned
hunched and frail

And your child
she calls—
"Wait, come back…"

为时已晚—
眼含星星的妈妈已成
眼含星星的孩子的
母亲—

从现在开始
她的每一步
都是你的心
必须越过的
一道深渊—

从现在开始
你将带着
新的勇气
跟随

直到有一天
疲惫中
你放慢了脚步
企足伫立
只能望向
她的背影

直到有一天
她停住了脚步
回身顾盼—
你却已转身
背影弯曲而虚弱

你的孩子
她向你呼唤—
"等等，回来……"

Byron Gaist

Truly Leave

You don't truly leave
Until you begin to notice
That the landscape
Has changed.

You don't truly leave
Until the birds
Sing a song
You haven't heard

You don't truly leave
Until you make new friends
And your new friends
Are not like the old friends

You don't truly leave
Until at night
The stories are different
And unexpected

You don't truly leave
Until the old stories
Become just stories

And you learn
To love your soul
In a quiet, curious
Objective way

For its own sake
Whatever it produces

You don't truly leave
Until you begin
To like your own company

You don't truly leave
Until your values
Are no longer the same

You don't truly leave
Until a new person
Gazes out
Through your eyes.

Η ΠΟΡΤΟΚΑΛΙΑ

Για καμιά πενηνταριά χρόνια
Βυζαίνεις το χώμα
Βαθύ πράσινο φύλλωμα
Κορμός σαν πόδι γερασμένο

Δεν ταξιδεύεις
Την μητέρα, δεν εγκαταλείπεις
Και όμως
Στο στόμα ξεχειλίζει
Ο ζουμερός σου καρπός
Γλυκός και οξύς
Σαν λόγος σοφίας

Εκεί όπου μια μέρα
Θα επιστρέψουμε
Θέλω να με γνωρίσεις
Από τα χέρια που σε τρυγήσαν
Όπως κι εγώ, το υπόσχομαι
Θα σε ξέρω από τους ρόζους
Και τους ανθούς
Ότι είσαι αυτή
Και όχι κάποια άλλη
Του είδους σου

The Orange Tree

You have been suckling the ground
For fifty years or so
Deep green foliage
Trunk like an ageing leg

You no longer travel
You never abandon mother
And yet
Your juicy fruit
Overflows in my mouth
Sweet and acid
Like a word of wisdom

There, where we will
One day return
I want you to know me
From the hands which harvested you
As I too, I promise
Will know from the gnarls
And the blossoms
That it is you
And not some other
Of your kind.

Cassie Fielding

The Perplexity of Naming

The purpose of my eyes is hidden in a sea of windows—
infinite (l)imitations of god
named
for a leaf,
  for a mountain,
    a lamppost,
      a snapdragon snap,
      a poppy seed
trapped between teeth for the assault of a cup of tea—
seeing by way of being
eyes, of being
named, fragmented
by the subjectivity of a life.

But for a moment, so inadequately named that it isn't …

Denamed and deframed,
each is each is none ongoing—
beauty beyond the aesthetic, devoid
of meaning, devoid
until it turns back in on itself as fullness—
a fleeting stretch of untime
sitting on the opening of a forehead—too empty
to be felt.
Or too full.

The Perplexity of Naming ii

Scarab in scaleskin suitcase cornered
    (*a cipher and a fact not known not questioned*—)
I will call you 'Moth' and carry you
                      swung
as incense ceremonial
    (*the unfinishing Mother?*—)
crystalline (of) octosyllabic
    (*why mystify a mystery?*—)
sentences in backward combinations
    (*useful is senseless and senselessness is used up*—)
you house simplicity within a house
    (*stretching does not mean reaching*—)
you sing prophecy with knock kneed rows
    (*the past cramped up from over-shoulder*—)
layers of brittlest silk cover the expectation of a mouth
    (*speaks in embellished silhouettes*—)
nowhere thoroughfare with appendages
    (*we are sameness incognito*—)
a secret too overt to be seen

All is Water

Punctuated delirious by tedium,
the fray of the mouth-well
persists in its insistence—shape-shift

is gospel
as the reflection that waves
the shallows of infinitude

Atomic, the ambit
rolling in the grasp of an open
palm's aperture—

dried up and hollow-set to shatter
a festoon fragmented
a scatter of skin-shod apparition

Ionic, this body
in the depths of undisturbed
disturbed—

alloyed both ways brimfully,
buoyancy submerged
and spillage in coaxial amniotica—

Gottfried Maria Heuer

All Souls
or: 'The Greatest of Blessings'

> 'No one knows whether death may not turn out to be the greatest
> of blessings for a human being; and yet people fear it as if they
> know for certain that it is the greatest of evils.'   Socrates

This bird will never fly again:
like snowflakes its white feathers
lie scattered on the grass at sunset.

This boat will never ride again
the wild and foam-crested waves:
its withered boards of silvery wood
barely rise above the bone-white sands
that have filled it to its very rim.

It's ready to set sail now
to take me to the starry clouds.
Will you, beloved bird,
be my spirit guide,
and carry me on soaring wings
to the very edge of time and space,
powered by my dreams,
to that vast, eternal place
of the ever-lasting Now,
right at the centre of the heart of light
where life is love — and love as life
is pouring forth — unending grace —
a waterfall of countless jewels,
blossoming in rainbow hues,
and glitterising all
in paradise regained?

Resurrection

Autumn Equinox (The 1st Anniversary)

'Resurrection Blues'[1] is almost
Arthur Miller's final play -
he worked on it
right up until his death.
It centers on a man
who has been taken prisoner,
and who may
or may not be
the Second Coming
of Our Lord.
(Oh, I am quite sure the Jewish writer
did not mean the Christ
of the Christian church –
and nor do I.)
The ruler of the un-named country,
is preparing
a second crucifixion –
no doubt, if asked,
'in order to protect the public'. . .

Almost exactly mirroring
the subject of the play
a review of its London run
concluded, 'nothing
was so disastrous
as the debacle
surrounding 'Resurrection Blues.'
Following 'horrendous reviews,
the play was forced to close'
one week earlier than planned.

I, then, in 2006,
had experienced the play

---

[1] Miller, A. (2006). *Resurrection Blues*. London: Methuen

as maybe the most deeply moving
I had ever seen on stage –
raising the question,
'What would *actually* happen,
if the Messiah came again,
today,
into this,
our world? –

Would I be able then
to *welcome* Him?
The almost presence of the Holy
sent shivers down my spine –
it was if an angel had
just outside of my conscious vision,
passed by –
and touched me with its wing . . .

II
Last Sunday in September,
2021:
Autumn Equinox,
as we almost can envision
Covid to relax its grip,
'a rare white stag appeared
in full daylight
in Bootle, Merseyside,'
near Liverpool –
remember, 'All you need is love, love, love?' –
'roaming the town's very centre'
for nearly one whole day.

Hearing of this
moved me close to tears,
put a lump into my throat –
and, again,
there was that angel,
touching me
with a feather of its wing . . .
The presence of the Holy.

In the end,
against advice
from the RSPCA[2],
'to leave the deer,
as it would make its own way home,'
the deer was killed by the police–
'to protect the public,'
a senior policeman said,
adding that he was proud
of the officers involved . . .

A further crucifixion,
'Murder of Crist,'[3] yet again.

III
One month earlier, I had a dream,
a particularly vivid one:
I am high up
on an indoor balcony
of a light and wide
serene hall,
white walls with golden ornaments.
Looking down with others,
I can see UK's Premier,
surrounded by the faithfuls,
standing
opposite a small crowd
open for questions
from the public.

He does not fare well in this –
I almost feel some pity:
He just cannot handle
the questions posed to him.
Then I see a friend of mine
calling to him from the back,
'It would be *so* good
if at least you'd listened

---

[2] Royal Society for the Prevention of Cruelty towards Animals
[3] The title of Wilhelm Reich's 1953 book, dedicated to 'The Children of the Future.'

to a Bach Cantata! –
'Rejoice, redeemed crowd!'[4] –
I've actually got one here with me!'
And from one person to the next,
he passes on a tiny music-player
until it reaches the PM.

And he -
refuses
the pure and holy music!
The people close to him
try to persuade him –
but to no avail:
he is *adamant,*
yet does become uncertain, shifty,
and retreats on shaky legs.
The crowd, restless,
first in low murmur,
then loud and ever louder
is shouting , 'Out.
Out! OUT!'
I, in the meantime,
go downstairs
to find my friend
so that we can embrace
and I congratulate him.

IV
What would it really do to me,
how would I react
if Christ, really,
were to come
a second time?
– And you???
Dare we, together,
hope
to give birth to the Christ,
another time –
resurrecting
the Divine ?

---

[4] Johann Sebastian Bach: Cantata No. 30

V

Or:
What if Arthur Miller's play
wants me – us – to realize
that there only, truly
is a single prison guard,
and that it's up to me
and all of us
to crucify Him
or to set Him free? –
Of course, today,
the Holy
just as likely
may be
a woman or a girl.

What if the White Stag
wanted me to know –
police or no police –
'I am here
all the time,
in fact,
I have never been away!

Is, what my dream is telling me,
as Bach, in his Cantatas
jubilates –
'Arise in joy:
I know where my Redeemer Lives![5] –
that we all shall know,
that darkness
shies away from light
and that in each and every Messianic moment
the longed-for Divine
is right *here,*
Now!

---

[5] Johann Sebastian Bach: Cantata No. 36.

"Remember the Yucatán"[6]

The whole world –
no, all of the universe,
known of as well as not,
unknowable –
is mirrored in
each grain of sand,
as William Blake might say,
in each and every atom –
also each of those
that we are made of –
you, yes, *you*, you, too –
and me, of course.

Correspondingly,
we might well imagine
that all of time,
aeon after aeon,
is mirrored,
thus contained,
in each and every moment
of the eternal
Now.

There is one moment
I can think of
which thus mirrors
and contains
so it seems to me,
all of history –
at least that part of it
that is about
the ruler and the ruled.

---

[6] A quote from Ryan, C., Jethà, C. (2010). *Sex at Dawn*. New York, NY: Harpercollins, p. 19. – Much further north, the name of the Alaskan city of Nome is said to have had a similar origin: 'The Eskimo expression *kn-no-me* means "I don't know" and is thought to have been the answer natives gave when foreign visitors landing on the shore asked the likely question, "What's the name of this place?"' Salsbury G., & L. Salsbury (2003). *The Cruellest Miles*. London: Bloomsbury, p. 14.

Just come with me,
back,
way back into the past:
1519, it is spring,
Cortés, conquistador-to-be,
and his men,
a mere handful of them, really,
have just reached
what became much later
mainland Mexico.
He, Cortés,
has ordered
some of his men
to bring aboard one of the natives,
so that he can ask him –
of course, what else?
In Spanish! –
'¿ Cómo llamas a esta área aqui?' –
'What
do you call this place 'round here?' –

Imagine, now,
just bear with me,
that native,
who,
has never ever seen before
men like these,
white,
as possibly,
only the dead can be,
yet these,

are obviously alive!
Think of his terror,
as he freezes,
his eyes filled
with tears of fear.
And they make sounds,
strange sounds,
through lots of facial hair!

Whereas Cortés,
already on the verge
of losing patience,
is repeating
with exasperation –
like talking to a child,
or an imbecile,
someone hard of hearing,
repeating every word,
with his voice raised a notch,
this time,
and very, *very* slowly,
'WHAT – DO – YOU
CALL – THIS – PLACE –
'ROUND – HERE?!'
Certain now,
that, of course,
this savage here, before him,
must have understood!

Now, at last,
he does respond,
thank Heavens!
'Ma c'ubah than,'
which Cortés hears
as 'Yucatán.'
'That must be it,'
he thinks,
'(why on earth
did you not tell me straight away?!)' –
And he proclaims,
now that at last he's got the *name*,
that this land *Yucatán* –
(weird name, indeed!) –
and all the *gold*, of course,
that it undoubtedly contains,
including, certainly,
the *whole* of its population,
not to mention women, children, dogs,
now belongs
to the Spanish crown.

Only *today* we know,
a mere 400 years,
almost to the day,
after that encounter
that 'Ma c'ubah than'
means, 'I
don't
understand you.'

Nadia Wardeh

نشأةٌ أُخرى (نص غير شعري)

هِيَ لَحْظَةٌ تَأْخُذُكَ مِنْ نَفْسِكَ الْقَدِيمَةِ الى نَفْسٍ أُخْرَى

تُحَاوِلُ التَّعَرُّفَ عَلَيْهَا وَلَا تَسْتَطِيع

تَقْتَرِبُ بِحَذَرٍ

تَنْظُرُ الى كَائِنٍ لا تَعرِفَهُ

تَدْنُو أَكْثَر، يَبْتَعِدُ وَيَتَوَارَى خَلْفَ نَجْمٍ بَعيد

حَدِّقْ ... لَا شَيءَ ... سَرَابٌ كَثِيفٌ

"أرجِع الْبَصَرَ كَرَّةً أخرى ... يَنْقَلِبُ الِيْكَ الْبَصَرُ خَاسِئًا وَهُوَ حَسِيرٌ"

•••

تَتَحَسَّسُ صُورَتَكَ وَتَتَفَقَّدُ وُجودَكَ

تُوَاسِي نَفْسَكَ وَتَقُول: أَنَا أُفِكِّر اذن انا مَوْجود

تُنَقِّبُ عَنْ بَقَايَا كَائِنٌ كَانَتْ قَبْلَ بِضْعَ ثَوَانٍ أنتَ

وَالآن مَلامِحٌ غَريبَةٌ، نَشْأَةٌ أُخْرَى وَرُوحٌ سَحِيق

•••

تَصْرُخُ بِلَا صَوْتٍ

تُنَادِيكَ أَصْوَاتٌ مُبَعْثَرَةٌ

تَنْزَلِقُ الى نَفَقٍ مُظْلِمٍ

لَا تَرَى مَا تَأْنَس به ... لَا ذَاتُك ولا رفيق

مَحْضَ عُزْلَةٍ، وَكُلُّ مَا حَوْلَكَ غَريب

•••

يَدْنُو منكَ كَائِنٌ مُبْهَم

تتساءلُ بِخَوْفٍ

أَهَذِه أنا " ي"؟

لِأُقْتَرِب أَكْثَر

لا... لَسْتُ هِي وَلَسْتُ أَنَا

شَبَحٌ مِنْ دُخَانٍ، من نارٍ وجَليد

•••

أين أنا؟

من أنا؟

سكتَ الوقتُ ...

•••

على أبقاع سِرّي تتسارعُ نَبضاتُ قلبي
تَعلو وتَخِفضُ
أهبِط في فراغٍ يُجرجرني الى ما لا أشتهي الان، الى ما لا أعرفُ وما لا أريد

•••

تعتقلني اللحظة
لا حولَ ولا قوةَ لي
لا موتَ ولا حياة
لا مُقام ولا رحيل

•••

لحظتي طويلة كمنارةٍ في أقاصي السماء
أُحَدِقُ الى سقفِ الكونِ
أراني هناك
ألوّحُ بيدي اليَّ
تُلَّوح لي
تبتسمُ .. أعبسُ
تقتَرَبُ مني .. أبتعدُ عني
أصحو...أنام .. ليلي طويل

•••

كونٌ آخرٌ أمامي
جوهرٌ واحد: حاضري ... أمسي ... وغد
أين امضي؟
إنفصم الوقت
زمني جِرمٌ هجين
مكاني بلا أبعاد ... خلاءٌ مُريع
أصبحت كلُّ ساكنٌ وجزءٍ لا يُرى
ريشةٌ بين الماضي والحاضر
لن أذهب مع الريح ... وأعرفُ ما اريد ...لا

•••

سأتخلصُ من قيودي ... سأفِرُ على جُنحِ غيمةٍ وأتعلقُ بأولِ نجمةٍ شاردة
سأبحثُ (عني) في الغدِ
سأجتَمِعُ بي (هناك) الآن ... ليس (أمس) ولا (بعدَ) حين

•••

وصلتُ
أستشرفُ من أعلى التل حقولاً بعيدة
بقايا حضورٍ لم يمر من هنا وحفنةٍ من ذكرياتٍ لم تولد بعد

ارى الفجرَ عند النافذة
أرى الشمسَ والقمرَ يتعانقان -ُولدَ نجمٌ جديد -

•••

أُغمِضُ عيني وافتحُ بابَ قلبي
لي حياةٌ هناك
لي بحرٌ وسماء
وَلي أحبةٌ ينتظرونَ في آخر الطريق

•••

اقتربي وقَرّي عينا
أتوثبُ للجري نحوحافةِ الحُلم
أدنو اكثر
أفتحُ عيوني
يبتسم قلبي
تأنسُ روحي
أتأهبُ لِنشأةٍ أخرى ولبعثٍ جديد.

Re-Creation

Translated from Arabic by Roula-Maria Dib

It is a moment that takes you away from your old Self to a new one.
You try to meet it. To get to know it. But you cannot.
You approach it, cautiously
looking at this unrecognizable creature.
You walk closer…it walks further, behind a distant star.
Gaze…nothing…a thick mirage
Then look again and again—your sight will return frustrated and weary.

•••

You feel for your image and check for your presence
You console yourself and say: I think therefore I am
You dig for relics that were *you* only a few seconds ago
and now—strange features, a re-creation and immemorial spirit

•••

You scream without a voice,
scattered voices call you.
Slipping into a dark tunnel,
You don't find any company…neither your own self nor a friend.
Downright isolation. Surrounded by bizarreness.

•••

An obscure creature draws near you.
You wonder, frighteningly,
is this Me, *my* Me?
Let me get closer
No…it's neither her nor Me.
A mere smoke ghost, from fire and ice

•••

Where am I?
Who am I?
Time lapses into silence…

•••

My heartbeat speeds according to a secret rhythm
rising, dropping.
I fall into a scathing emptiness that injures me with what I do not desire now,
with what I do not know and do not want

•••

The moment imprisons me
No strength for me
No death, no life
No locality, no departure

•••

My moment is long, like a lighthouse reaching out into the high depths of the sky
I stare at the Universe's ceiling
I see Me, there
I wave to Me
She waves back
She smiles
I frown
She walks nearer, I pull away from Me
I wake up…I sleep…my night is long

•••

Another Universe is in front of me
One essence: my present…my yesterday…and tomorrow
Where am I going?
Temporality is broken
My time is a hybrid crime
My place has no dimensions…a terrifying emptiness
I became a featureless whole, an invisible fragment
A feather between the past and the present
No… I will not go with the wind…and I know what I want

•••

I will get rid of my chains…I will flee on the wing of a cloud and hang onto the first stray star
I will search (for Me) in Tomorrowland
I will meet with Me (there) now…Neither (yesterday) nor (after) a while

•••

I have arrived
Viewing distant fields from a hilltop
Remnants of a presence that hadn't passed by here, and a handful of unborn memories

I see dawn at the window
I see the sun and moon embracing—a new star is born—

•••

I close my eye and open my heart's door
where I have a life
where I have an ocean and a sky
and where I also have loved ones waiting for me at the end of the road

•••

Come closer and put your heart at ease
I jump to run towards the edge of a dream
I go nearer
I open my eyes
My heart smiles
My soul leaps with joy
I marshal for a re-creation and a resurrection.

Roula-Maria Dib

The Wait

The hanged man in the tarot deck
told me to wait before I stuffed
a jellyfish with onions
I left hairbrushes in alley ways
closed every open window,
brought an upset sky-coloured phone
back to the grave I hated.
A Baloo bear walks into the garden
That died last year, shakes off
the sham rocked fur I weaved
the following week into silk
from there I cut out a house
to live in.

PART 3

RITE DE SORTIE

István Kupper-Meynen

The End of Certainties

"Suona il tuo violino se vuoi passare di qua",
grida il soldato israeliano al musicista
palestinese,
in coda al check point di Beir Iba.
"Suonalo ancora!" gli ordina,
prima di respingerlo negandogli il visto.

Gli USA, nel frattempo,
dopo la riforma Gross, rilanciano lo
spionaggio classico.
Tra breve l'arruolamento di 5000 nuove spie.
Il 50% in più di spie.

Ragioni contingenti?
Semplicemente impedire una nuova "Florida
2000":
Forse altro.

•••

L' uomo del potere
è stato ufficialmente proclamato vincitore.
Secondo la commissione elettorale
avrebbe 800 mila voti in più.
Il suo avversario, filo-occidentale,
certo di essere stato imbrogliato
si era già auto-proclamato vincitore
baciando la Bibbia, il 24 novembre.

Il presidente russo si congratula con
Yanukovich.

Gli Stati Uniti minacciano sanzioni,
e l'Europa chiede negoziati.
I soliti interessi divergenti.

"Play your violin if you want to pass,"
the Israeli soldier shouts to the Palestinian
musician,
queuing at the Beir Iba checkpoint.
"Play it again!" he orders him,
before pushing him back by denying him a visa.

The U.S., meanwhile,
after Gross' reform, revives classical
espionage.
Soon 5,000 new spies.
Soon 50% more spies.

Contingent reasons?
Simply to prevent a new
"Florida 2000."
Maybe more.

•••

The 'man in power' was
officially declared the winner.
According to the election commission
he would have 800,000 more votes.
His pro-Western opponent,
certain that he was cheated,
had already self-proclaimed himself the winner
by kissing the Bible, Nov. 24.

The Russian president congratulates
Yanukovich.

The U.S. threatens sanctions,
and Europe calls for negotiations.
The usual divergent interests.

•••

Nulla è accidentale.
Nulla di nulla.

•••

Secondo il parlamento ucraino
il voto del 21 novembre
è stato viziato
da brogli significativi
e non rispecchia la scelta popolare.
Gli Stati Uniti di George W. Bush
non riconoscono il verdetto
accusando il candidato filo-russo.

George W. Bush, 2000.
Victor Yanukovich, 2004.
Florida, Ucraina.
Dettagli coincidenti.

•••

L'opposizione sostiene
che sarebbero arrivati numerosi uomini delle
truppe speciali russe,
armati e con divise ucraine.
Mosca smentisce.
Propaganda d'ufficio,
oppure l'incubo di una prassi prettamente
sovietica?

Budapest 1956.
Praga 1968.

•••

La corte suprema
non ufficializza il risultato elettorale.
Il vecchio professor Polianskij si appella agli
studenti.

•••

Nothing is accidental.
Nothing at all.

•••

According to the Ukrainian parliament,
the November 21 vote
was marred
by significant fraud
and does not reflect the popular choice.
The United States of George W. Bush
does not recognize the verdict
blaming the pro-Russian candidate.

George W. Bush, 2000.
Victor Yanukovich, 2004.
Florida, Ukraine.
Coincidental details.

•••

The opposition claims
numerous Russian special troops would
arrive,
armed and in Ukrainian uniforms.
Moscow denies it.
Propaganda, or
the nightmare of a purely Soviet
practice?

Budapest 1956.
Prague 1968.

•••

The Supreme Court does
not make election result official.
Old Professor Poliansky appeals to
students:

177

"Your place is in the streets, not in the classrooms.
And we have to be there too,
otherwise we won't be able to look you in the
face anymore."
In Rome, a Ukrainian caregiver
rails against those who
would sell out her homeland to
the West,
defending, instead,
what remains of communism and the KGB.

Lech Walesa regrows his mustache
and shouts, "24 years ago
I was in the same situation as you.
We were fighting the USSR
and communism. We won with a peaceful
struggle."

Bogdan, just 11 years old, ran away from home
three days ago.
He had been told
he would lose his freedom.
He risked frostbite after
falling asleep under a tree,
ten degrees below zero.
Once in Kiev, he climbed
the government gate
waving his orange scarf.

•••

The two
call for a rejection
of violence,
the opening of political
negotiations, and
an implicit recognition of the Supreme Court's
power.
Yushchenko, however,
is only open to one understanding:
new elections.

Una commissione elettorale paritetica.
e pari accesso alle televisioni.

Per Yanukovich intanto,
sono arrivati a Kiev i minatori
del bacino carbonifero del Donets,
gli operai siderurgici di Zaporozhie,
che lavorano nelle fabbriche di motori per gli
aerei russi.
Sono arrivati in 25 mila. Ordinati
e secondo alcuni, pronti a menare le mani.
Tra gli arancioni si vedono
studenti, professionisti, preti cattolici e
ortodossi,
quelli ribellatisi al patriarcato
di Mosca, e signore in pelliccia.
Tra i bianco-blu
è tutt'altra cosa.
Giacconi in pelle,
denti d'oro
e fiato che sa di birra.
Sono pronti
alla secessione, dicono,
come il loro leader.

•••

Una certa Kiev sta
con Mosca, da sempre. Mentre Leopoli
assomiglia più a Praga, Cracovia.
o forse Milano.
Semplicistico è dire
che gli arancioni
vorrebbero svendere l'Ucraina
all'occidente, mentre gli altri,
la restaurazione comunista.
Forse sarà secessione,
forse no.
Forse sarà come tra Praga
e Bratislava nel 1993.
Forse
sarà una nuova Sarajevo.

A joint election commission.
Equal access to television stations.

Meanwhile for Yanukovich,
miners from the Donets coalfield,
steelworkers from Zaporozhie,
who work in engine factories for Russian
aircraft, have arrived in Kiev.
Twenty-five thousand of them arrived.
Orderly and according to some,
ready to beat hands.
Among the orange people you see
students, professionals, Catholic and
Orthodox priests,
those rebelling against the Moscow
Patriarchate, and ladies in fur coats.
Among the blue-whites
is a different story:
Leather jackets.
Gold teeth.
Breath that tastes like beer.
They are ready
for secession, they say,
like their leader.

•••

A certain Kiev has been
with Moscow forever. While L´viv
looks more like Prague, Krakow
and even Milan.
It is simplistic to say
that the orange
people would like to sell off Ukraine
to the West, while the others,
communist restoration.
Maybe it will be secession,
maybe not.
Maybe it will be between Prague
and Bratislava in 1993.
Maybe
a new Sarajevo.

179

...

Il Pope sta
con Mosca,
e così i suoi fedeli.
Gli altri
no.
I socialisti guardano
all'Europa, mentre Yanukovich,
con il pugno chiuso
saluta anacronisticamente il compagno
Putin.

...

Elezioni non valide.
Questo il verdetto della Rada.
L'Ucraina torna al voto.
Sergej Markov, da Mosca, accusa
la regia Europea nelle vicende
degli ultimi giorni.
Javier Solana e Aleksandr Kwasniewski,
da Bruxelles,
auspicano il dialogo, ma tacciono.
Nel frattempo, a Washington,
la famiglia Brzezinski preme
Bush affinché denunci l'incostituzionalità
delle elezioni ucraine, e la vittoria
del candidato filo-russo
Yanukovich.
Complotto polacco?
Esagerazione propagandistica?
Da Mosca risuona
l'eco di un'antica fobia russa.

...

Che ipocrita tiritera
questo anelito di guerra fredda.
Rimpiango
il 23 ottobre 1956,

...

The Pope stands
with Moscow,
and so do his faithful.
The others
do not.
The Socialists look
to Europe, while Yanukovich,
with clenched fist
anachronistically greets Comrade
Putin.

...

Invalid election.
This is the verdict of the Rada.
Ukraine returns to the ballot.
Sergei Markov, from Moscow, blames
European direction in the events
of the last few days.
Javier Solana and Aleksandr Kwasniewski,
from Brussels,
call for dialogue but remain silent.
Meanwhile, in Washington,
the Brzezinski family presses
Bush to denounce the unconstitutionality
of the Ukrainian elections, and the victory
of pro-Russian candidate
Yanukovich.
Polish conspiracy?
Propaganda?
Echoes of an ancient Russian phobia
resound from Moscow.

...

What a hypocritical spiel this
Cold War yearning is.
I have nostalgy of
October 23, 1956,

e il 5 gennaio 1968.
L'11 novembre 1989,
e il 5 ottobre 2000.
Rimpiango Nagy, e
i molti eroi senza nome.

•••

Le televisioni annunciano, ripetendosi,
l'imminente rivoluzione.
Cronaca oppure ingordo media planning?

•••

Il sospetto di molti è
che tra i pretoriani di Kuchma vi siano anche
agenti scelti
inviati da Mosca.
Così
al cambio della guardia
un manifestante gridava
ai soldati col volto coperto: "Tornatevene a
Mosca!".
Il soldato, togliendosi il passamontagna
rispondeva in ucraino stretto: "Ti sembra
una faccia da russo questa?"

•••

Penso a tutto.
Penso a niente.
E mi viene solo una gran
paura.

and January 5, 1968.
November 11, 1989,
and October 5, 2000.
I have nostalgy of Nagy, and
the many nameless heroes.

•••

Televisions announce, repeating themselves,
the coming revolution.
Chronicle or greedy media planning?

•••

The suspicion of many is
that Kuchma's praetorians include
elite agents
sent from Moscow.
Thus
at the changing of the guard
a protester shouted
to the masked soldiers, "Go back to
Moscow!"
The soldier, removing his balaclava
replied in tight Ukrainian: "Does this look
like a Russian face to you?"

•••

I think of everything.
I think of nothing.
And I just get really
scared.

CONTRIBUTORS

PART 1

Ludmilla Osterman M.A. is a journalist and editor. She currently works for different German media outlets on political, social and economic topics. Among other publications she recently contributed to a series of interviews initiated by the University of Bielefeld about the war in Ukraine. As an online editor, she is creating content for Futurium, a museum in Berlin dedicated to future topics since 2019, she is in charge of digital content. As a member of the founding team, her focus there is on scientific journalistic contributions on research and socio-political topics. She completed a traineeship at the daily newspaper Westfalen-Blatt (Bielefeld) and devoted herself to political and social issues in the East Westphalian province from 2009 to 2019. Since 2022 she is back at the Westfalen-Blatt (Bielefeld) as freelance journalist, news manager, and digital consultant. Her first edited book is titled *War as Reset* (co-authored with Stefano Carpani, Routledge, forthcoming 2024).

Professor Julia Herzberg has held the professorship of History of East Central Europe/Russia in the Pre-Modern Period since October 2016. She is based at both Ludwig-Maximilians-Universität (LMU) Munich and the University of Regensburg (UR). Her research and teaching focus includes the history of science, technology, and the environment in East Central and Eastern Europe, as well as religious practices. Julia Herzberg studied German, history, and Russian in Cologne, Volgograd and Moscow. She received her doctorate from Bielefeld University with a study of peasant autobiography between the tsarist empire and the Soviet Union.

Elana Lakh, PhD is an art therapist-supervisor and Jungian Analyst, a member of the Israeli Institute of Jungian Psychology in honor of Erich Neumann. She holds a doctorate in cultural studies and is the author of *The Origins of Evil in the Human Psyche: A Jungian reading of creation mythologies* (Carmel, 2017, in Hebrew) based on her doctoral dissertation. She teaches and practices in Jerusalem and internationally, specializing in treatment of sexually abused individuals. She researches archetypal aspects of creation mythologies and of paintings and other artworks. She writes about the Israeli-Palestinian conflict from a Jungian perspective, drawing on 30 years of human rights activism in this context.

Caterina Vezzoli is a Jungian psychoanalyst, member of IAAP (International Association of Analytical Psychology), a training analyst and supervisor at the C. G. Jung Institute in Zurich and CIPA (Italian Center for Analytical Psychology for the Southern Institute and Sicily). She is a fellow Analyst of the Association of Group Psychoanalytic Psychotherapy (APG), on the standing committee of Art & Psyche and member of the Executive Committee of IAAP. She is President of the Philemon Foundation and part of the Board of Directors of the same association since 2012. She lives and works in Milan, Italy.

Livia Di Stefano is a psychologist, Jungian psychoanalyst member of the International Association of Analytical Psychology. She is treasurer of C.I.P.A. (Italian Center of Analytical Psychology) Southern Institute; Teacher and supervisor at C.I.P.A. - Southern Institute and IAAP (International Association for Analytical psychology). She is a member of the Editorial Board of Enkelados-Rivista Mediterranea di Psicologia Analitica. She lives and works in Catania, Italy.

Paul Attinello, Ph.D., is a Jungian Analyst in private practice who has taught at Newcastle University, the University of Hong Kong, and UCLA. He received his PhD in musicology from UCLA and diploma as an analyst from the Jung Institute in Zürich. He has lived and worked on four continents, been involved in creative and academic events and projects, HIV groups and programs, and is co-founder of Psychosocial Wednesdays. He is published in numerous collections, journals, and reference works, including the groundbreaking *Queering the Pitch: The New Lesbian & Gay Musicology* (1994). He has written on contemporary music, the culture of AIDS, and psychological and philosophical topics.

Giulia Pepe graduated from the University of Palermo, she is currently a psychologist and a trainee analyst at the CIPA Southern Institute (Italian Center for Analytical Psychology). Her research interests include LGBTQI+ themed studies, queer theory, gender studies and their relationship to analytic psychology. She is in private practice in Palermo, focusing on adults and adolescents and she is involved in psychology in the third sector.

Luciana Ximenez is a clinical psychologist, holds a Masters in Jungian Studies at PUC-SP, Analyst in training at IJUSP, AJB and IAAP. She is a member of Lapa, Archetypal Psychology Laboratory, founding member of Coletivo Aisthesis and coordinator of Thiasos: Shared Imagination Workshop.

Marcus Quintaes is a psychotherapist, coordinator of seminars on James Hillman's Archetypal Psychology and Post-Jungian Thought. He is founder of Lapa: Archetypal Psychology Laboratory and Thiasos: Shared Imagination Workshop. He is the author of the book *Imaginative Letters: Brief Essays in Archetypal Psychology*.

Moshe Alon is a Jungian Analyst-trainer, member of the New Israeli Jungian Association (NIJA), educational psychology supervisor, group leader, organizational consultant, and family therapist. For 31 years he directed the school psychology service in Tel-Aviv-Jaffa. He studied the Jewish-Arab conflict as it is manifest in Jaffa's education systems. For the last two years, he has been working in the city of Lod as a supervisor of Jewish and Arab school psychology interns at the local municipal service, where he also teaches an introduction to Jungian theory, systemic interventions, crisis interventions, and psychotherapy for children and adolescents. He works in private practice with children, adolescents, young people, and adults to old age. He sees himself as an activist psychologist, and recurrently asks himself what his role is in society and in the organization, he is involved with.

Stefano Carpani, Ph.D., curator of this volume and the creator of *Jungianeum: initiatives for contemporary analytical psychology and neo-Jungian studies*, is a psychoanalyst trained at the C.G. Jung Institute, Zürich (accredited analyst CGJI-Z/IAAP) and a sociologist (post-graduate at the University of Cambridge). He graduated in Literature and Philosophy from the Catholic University of Milan. He works in private practice in Berlin (DE) in English Italian and Spanish. He is the initiator of the YouTube interview series: *Breakfast at Küsnacht, Lockdown Therapy* and *War as Reset*. He is among the initiators of *Psychosocial Wednesdays,* "#TherapistforUkraine." He curates the "Chiron Publications" book series titled *JUNGIANEUM: Re-covered Classics in Analytical psychology.* Since 2021 he is a member of the *Analysis and Activism*´s steering group. His most recent edited books are: *Anthology of Contemporary Classics in Analytical Psychology: The new ancestors* (Routledge, 2022); *Individuation and Liberty in a Globalized World: Psychosocial perspectives on freedom after freedom* (Routledge, 2022); *Lockdown Therapy: Jungian Perspectives on how the pandemic changed psychoanalysis* (with Dr Monica Luci, Routledge, 2022).

PART 2 (Poetry)

Chun Yu, Ph.D., is an award-winning bilingual (English and Chinese) poet, graphic novelist, scientist, and translator. She is the author of an award winning memoir in verse "Little Green: Growing Up During the Chinese Cultural Revolution" (Simon & Schuster), and a historical graphic novel in progress (Macmillan), and more. Her poetry and stories have been published or are forthcoming in the Boston Herald, Orion, Poetry Northwest, Arion Press, MIT Tech Talk, Xinhua Daily, Poem of the Day (San Francisco Public Library), Heyday Books, and more. Her work is taught in world history and culture classes in the U.S. and internationally. Chun is an honoree of the 2020 YBCA 100 award for creative changemakers. She has been awarded grants from San Francisco Arts Commission, Zellerbach, Poets & Writers, Sankofa Fund, and more. Chun holds a B.S. and M.S. from Peking University and a Ph.D. from Rutgers University. She was a post-doctoral fellow in a Harvard-MIT joint program.

Byron Gaist is a registered counselling psychologist and licensed psychotherapist living and working in Cyprus with his family, his cat Zeus, and his disabled and happy dog Lucy. He has a PhD in Psychoanalytic Studies from the University of Essex in the UK, and works in a Jungian-oriented method with clients both locally in Cyprus and internationally online. He has been writing creatively since his teens and has had poetry published in journals in English and Greek. His study of the interface between Analytical Psychology and Eastern Orthodox Christianity was published with the title Creative Suffering and the Wounded Healer (Orthodox Research Institute, 2010).

Cassie Fielding is a poet from Merseyside, UK. Her work has appeared in various journals and her debut collection, 'The Arbitrary Fractals of an Oracle,' was published in 2021 by *Time is an Ocean Publications*. She is currently working towards an M.A. in Jungian Studies at the University of Essex.

Gottfried M. Heuer, Ph.D. is a Jungian Training psychoanalyst and Neo-Reichian body-psychotherapist who has practiced in London for over 45 years. He has worked in most European countries, in North, Central and South America, Australia, and Asia. He is an independent scholar with 70 papers published in 7 languages in therapeutic and analytic journals. His books include 10 Congress Proceedings (in Berlin, Dresden, Graz, Moscow, Munich, Vienna, Zurich, et al.) of the International Otto Gross Society (LiteraturWissenschaft.de), of which he was co-founder and president; *Sacral Revolution* (Routledge 2010); *Sexual Revolutions* (Routledge 2011; Russian edition 2017); and *Freud's 'Outstanding' Colleague/Jung's 'Twin Brother': The suppressed psychoanalytic and political significance of Otto Gross* (Routledge 2017). He is also a published graphic artist, photographer, sculptor, and poet.

Dr. Nadia Wardeh is an associate professor of Middle Eastern studies, distinguished scholar, passionate traveler, and a coffee lover. She holds a PhD in Islamic Studies-McGill University. She has 18+ years of multidisciplinary and international experience in higher education institutions at McGill University and the American University in Dubai (AUD). The variety of courses she teaches put emphasis on her multidisciplinary and international profession which is apparent in her distinguished scholarly achievements. Her passion, enthusiasm and professionalism qualified her to obtain various scholarly and teaching awards including the McGill "Faculty of Arts Teaching Award; the "AUD President's Award for Teaching Excellence;" the "AUD Outstanding Teaching & Service Award;" the "Social Sciences & Humanities Research Council of Canada Award;" and numerous certificates of recognition from different countries. She is the author of one book entitled *Problematic of Turath in Contemporary Arab Thought* & various book chapters, academic papers, and online artistic writings.

Roula-Maria Dib is the curator of part 2 of this issue and a holder of the UK Global Talent Visa as an award-winning literary scholar, poet, and editor. Her research interests are at the interstices of literature, modern poetry and poetics, creative writing, and Jungian psychology. She is the winner of the British Council's Alumni Awards 2021-2022 for the Culture and Creativity category in the UAE and is the recipient of the American University in Dubai's Provost's Award for Outstanding Literary Achievement 2020. Her book, *Jungian Metaphor in Modernist Literature* (Routledge, 2020) was shortlisted as a finalist for the international IAJS book awards, and some poems from her collection, *Simply Being* (Chiron Press, 2021) received Pushcart Prize nominations. She is the founding editor of the literary and arts journal, Indelible, and creative producer of literary event series, Indelible Evenings, as well as Psychreative, a virtual salon for researchers, artists, and writers with a background in Jungian psychology.

PART 3 (Rite de Sortie)

István Kupper-Meynen is a poet living in Budapest, Hungary. He writes in Italian, his mother tongue, and English. He is a political activist and open critic of the current Hungarian government. His work and writing are inspired by psychoanalysis at large; with a strong focus on analytical psychology. He teaches sociology at the University of Cambridge and graduated in Literature and Philosophy from the Catholic University of Milan. *The End of Certainties,* a collection of psychosocial poems he wrote between 2004 and 2006, published here for the first time.

www.ingramcontent.com/pod-product-compliance
Lightning Source LLC
Chambersburg PA
CBHW080239270326
41926CB00020B/4301